Quantitatives Controlling

Edited by
C. Homburg, Köln, Germany

The series serves as a panel for outstanding research in the field of accounting. The underlying concept of accounting goes beyond the scope of traditional corporate accounting including, for instance, aspects of behavior control. The series focuses on quantitative analyses of current topics in management and financial accounting and considers both analytical and empirical research designs.

Edited by
Carsten Homburg
Universität zu Köln

More information about this series at http://www.springer.com/series/12419

Dominik Nußmann

The Coinsurance Effect of Corporate Diversification

An Empirical Analysis of the Accounting and Economic Implications

With a foreword by Prof. Dr. Carsten Homburg

Springer Gabler

Dominik Nußmann
Cologne, Germany

Dissertation University of Cologne / 2017

Quantitatives Controlling
ISBN 978-3-658-19373-7 ISBN 978-3-658-19374-4 (eBook)
DOI 10.1007/978-3-658-19374-4

Library of Congress Control Number: 2017952377

Springer Gabler

Printed on acid-free paper

This Springer Gabler imprint is published by Springer Nature
The registered company is Springer Fachmedien Wiesbaden GmbH
The registered company address is: Abraham-Lincoln-Str. 46, 65189 Wiesbaden, Germany

Geleitwort

Die vorliegende Dissertationsschrift beschäftigt sich mit der Unternehmensdiversifikation und insbesondere dem Coinsurance-Effekt von diversifizierten Unternehmen. Dabei beschreibt Coinsurance (dt.: Mitversicherung) die nicht perfekte Korrelation der Gewinne oder der Cash Flows (d.h. die Wechselwirkungen zwischen den unterschiedlichen Geschäftstätigkeiten) der einzelnen Segmente eines diversifizierten Unternehmens. Als diversifiziert gelten grundsätzlich all jene Unternehmen, die in mindestens zwei unterschiedlichen Industrien operativ tätig sind. Neben einer Einleitung und einem Schlussteil besteht die Arbeit aus drei Hauptteilen.

Hauptteil 1 dient der Vorstellung der theoretischen Grundlagen und dem Überblick über den aktuellen Forschungsstand zur Unternehmensdiversifikation. In der wissenschaftlichen Literatur werden die Vorteile der Unternehmensdiversifikation aus Coinsurance als finanzielle Synergien beschrieben, z.B. durch ein geringeres Insolvenzrisiko diversifizierter Unternehmen mittels stabilerer Gewinn- und Cash Flow-Größen. Nachteile aus der Unternehmensdiversifikation entstehen hingegen im Wesentlichen durch Prinzipal-Agenten-Probleme, durch die Manager z.B. aus Eigeninteressen mehr investieren als für das Unternehmen bzw. die Anteilseigner optimal wäre (sog. „empire building"). Die Relevanz der Unternehmensdiversifikation als Forschungsobjekt zeigt sich dabei durch die seit den 1960er Jahren anhaltende kontroverse Diskussion, ob diversifizierte Unternehmen am Kapitalmarkt mit einer Prämie oder einem Abschlag auf den Unternehmenswert gehandelt werden.

In Hauptteil 2 wird das Paper „Corporate Diversification and Earnings Quality" behandelt. In diesem Teil steht die Frage im Blickpunkt, ob Coinsurance einen signifikanten Einfluss auf das Accounting – genauer gesagt die „Earnings Quality" (dt.: Ergebnisqualität) – von Unternehmen hat. Während die bisherige Literatur einen negativen Zusammenhang zwischen der Diversifikation und Earnings Quality aufgrund höherer Informationsasymmetrien (insb. Prinzipal-Agenten-Probleme) nachweisen konnte, zeigt diese Untersuchung, dass diversifizierte Unternehmen durch Coinsurance eine insgesamt bessere Earnings Quality als vergleichbare fokussierte Unternehmen aufweisen. Diesbezüglich wird auch gezeigt, dass die Earnings Quality bei diversifizierten Unternehmen mit weniger stark korrelierten Segmentgewinnen – gemäß dem Coinsurance-Effekt – überproportional steigt. Demnach bietet der Coinsurance-Effekt diversifizierten Unternehmen neben finanziellen Synergien (d.h. einem geringeren Insolvenzrisiko) auch Accounting-spezifische Synergien, da eine bessere Earnings Quality ein geringeres Informationsrisiko für sämtliche Interessensvertreter (engl. „Stakeholder“) darstellt. Diese Ergebnisse erweitern unser Verständnis, wie der Coinsurance-Effekt die Eigenschaften der Unternehmensgewinne (engl. „Earnings“) beeinflusst und somit zu einem insgesamt geringeren Informationsrisiko bei diversifizierten Unternehmen führt.

Hauptteil 3 konzentriert sich auf die Frage, ob das Accounting bzw. die Earnings Quality einen ökonomischen Einfluss in Bezug auf den Unternehmenswert von diversifizierten Unternehmen hat. Die Analyse zeigt, dass diversifizierte Unternehmen mit einer höheren Earnings Quality (d.h. einem geringeren Informationsrisiko) von einem höheren Unternehmenswert bzw. einem geringeren Abschlag (engl. „Discount“) profitieren. Folglich ermöglicht ein geringeres Informationsrisiko die Prinzipal-Agenten-Probleme zu reduzieren und somit einen positiven Einfluss auf die Bewertung von diversifizierten Unternehmen auszuüben. Dies gilt konsistent auch, sofern die „Earnings Volatility“ (dt.: Ergebnisvolatilität) statt der Earnings Quality als Maß für das idiosynkratische Risiko genutzt wird. Diese Ergebnisse verbessern sowohl unser Verständnis der Ursachen der Variation in der Bewertung von diversifizierten Unternehmen und verdeutlichen auch den Zusammenhang zwischen „agency costs“ (gemessen durch den „Diversification Discount“) und dem Informationsrisiko (gemessen durch die Earnings Quality bzw. die Earnings Volatility) diversifizierter Unternehmen. Insgesamt wird gezeigt, dass Investoren nicht nur den Informationsgehalt der aggregierten Earnings bewerten, sondern auch die unternehmensspezifischen Charakteristiken (z.B. Coinsurance) in ihren Investitions-entscheidungen berücksichtigen. Diese Erkenntnis bereichert die lang anhaltende und kontrovers geführte Diskussion in der wissenschaftlichen Literatur, ob und unter welchen Umständen diversifizierte Unternehmen mit einem Discount am Kapitalmarkt gehandelt werden.

Die Arbeit leistet zahlreiche neue Überlegungen und erzielt Ergebnisse, die für Praxis und Forschung gleichermaßen von Interesse sind. Insgesamt wird ein innovativer Beitrag zum Thema Unternehmensdiversifikation geboten, der eine gute Aufnahme in der Accounting-Community verdient.

Prof. Dr. Carsten Homburg

Vorwort

Die vorliegende Arbeit entstand im Rahmen meiner Tätigkeit als wissenschaftlicher Mitarbeiter am Seminar für Allgemeine Betriebswirtschaftslehre und Controlling der Universität zu Köln. Nach erfolgreichem Abschluss meiner Dissertation möchte ich die folgenden Zeilen dazu nutzen, den Personen herzlich zu danken, die zum Gelingen meiner Arbeit beigetragen haben.

Meinem Doktorvater und akademischen Lehrer, Herrn Prof. Dr. Carsten Homburg, danke ich für seine vielfältige Unterstützung. Er hat den Anstoß dieser Arbeit gegeben und in zahlreichen Diskussionen meine Ideen hinterfragt, unterstützt und vorangebracht. Insbesondere möchte ich mich bei ihm für das entgegengebrachte Vertrauen bedanken, indem er mir stets große Freiheiten bei der Erstellung meiner Arbeit eingeräumt hat. Weiterhin danke ich Herrn Prof. Dr. Michael Overesch für die Übernahme des Zweitgutachtens und Herrn Prof. Dr. Martin Fochmann für die Leitung meiner Disputation. Darüber hinaus danke ich dem Förderverein Controlling an der Universität zu Köln, dessen finanzielle Unterstützung die Präsentation meiner Forschungsergebnisse auf nationalen und internationalen Konferenzen und den Zugriff auf Unternehmensdaten für meine empirischen Analysen ermöglicht hat.

Meinen Lehrstuhlkollegen Daniel Baumgarten, Max Berens, Snjezana Deno, André Hoppe, Stefanie Liesenfeld, Tanja Lorenz, Christian Müller, Julia Nasev, Sabine Nentwig, Philipp Plank, Kristina Reimer, Lars Rothe, Roman Schick und Simon Zehnder danke ich für die hervorragende Zusammenarbeit und die schöne gemeinsame Zeit am Lehrstuhl. Besonders bedanken möchte ich mich bei Lars Rothe für die vielen fruchtbaren Diskussionen und natürlich seine Freundschaft, die ein wertvoller Gewinn aus meiner Promotionszeit ist. Weiterer Dank gilt den studentischen und wissenschaftlichen Hilfskräften des Lehrstuhls für ihre unermüdlichen Unterstützungsangebote. Hier möchte ich insbesondere Stefan Brinkmann danken, dessen hervorragende Unterstützung in der Endphase meiner Dissertation einen wichtigen Beitrag geleistet hat. Mein großer Dank gilt auch Elisabeth Tokarski-Eich, der guten Seele des Lehrstuhls. Sie hat stets für eine herzliche und aufmunternde Atmosphäre am Lehrstuhl gesorgt. Diesen Dank richte ich auch an Tanja Breuer, die eine wunderbare und ebenso herzliche Unterstützerin in der Endphase meiner Dissertation war.

Mein größter Dank gilt meiner Freundin Laura, die mein Leben mit ihrer unvergleichlich liebevollen, fröhlichen und zuversichtlichen Art unschätzbar bereichert. Für deine Liebe und

Unterstützung, und die vielen glücklichen Stunden fernab von der Welt der Universität kann ich dir gar nicht genug danken. Mein besonderer Dank gilt auch meiner Mutter Helga, die in unzähligen Gesprächen mir aufgezeigt hat, was wirklich wichtig ist. Weiterhin möchte ich mich ganz herzlich bei Karin, Gerhard und Leon von der Emde, meiner Schwester Patricia und allen meinen Freunden aus Köln und Osnabrück bedanken. Mit eurer verständnisvollen und vielfältigen Unterstützung habt ihr mir ein Umfeld geschenkt, das von Lebensfreude und Zuversicht erfüllt ist. Ohne Euch wäre meine Dissertation nicht möglich gewesen.

Dominik Nußmann

Table of Contents

List of Abbreviations

CAPM	Capital Asset Pricing Model
CEO	Chief Executive Officer
CRSP	Center for Research in Security Prices
Div	Diversified
e.g.	exempli gratia (for example)
EPS	Earnings Per Share
EQ	Earnings Quality
ERC	Earnings Response Coefficient
et al.	et alii (and others)
FASB	Financial Accounting Standards Board
Foc	Focused
i.e.	id est (that is)
I/B/E/S	Institutional Brokers' Estimate System
ln	natural logarithm
log	logarithm operator
M-form	Multi-divisional form
M&A	Mergers & Acquisitions
Med.	Median
NAICS	North American Industry Classification System
No.	Number
NPV	Net Present Value
NYSE	New York Stock Exchange
Obs.	Observations
p.	page
Pred.	Prediction
Q	Quintile
ROA	Return on Assets
SD	Standard Deviation
SEC	Securities and Exchange Commission
SFAC	Statement of Financial Accounting Concepts
SFAS	Statement of Financial Accounting Standards
SIC	Standard Industrial Classification

U-form	Unitary form
U.S.	United States
USA	United States of America
US GAAP	United States Generally Accepted Accounting Principles
VIF	Variance Inflation Factor
Vola.	Volatility
vs.	versus
WRDS	Wharton Research Data Services

List of Symbols

Latin Symbols

A_t	accruals in year *t*
$Abs(Acc)_{i,t}$	absolute value of total accruals of firm *i* in year *t*
$AC_{i,t}$, $Acc_{i,t}$	total accruals of firm *i* in year *t*
$AC\_vola_{i,t}$	accruals volatility of firm *i* in year *t*
$acc\_item_{i,t}$	accounting item (sales or assets) of firm *i* in year *t*
$Accfactor_{i,t}$	accounting factor of firm *i* in year *t*
$ACQ_{i,t}$	accruals quality (*ACQ1* or *ACQ2*) of firm *i* in year *t*
$ACQ1_{i,t}$	accruals quality following Dechow and Dichev (2002) of firm *i* in year *t*
$ACQ2_{i,t}$	accruals quality following Jones (1991) of firm *i* in year *t*
$actual\ EQ_{i,t}$	actual earnings quality of firm *i* in year *t*
$actual\ Vola_{i,t}$	actual volatility of firm *i* in year *t*
$ADV_{i,t}$	advertisitng expenses of firm *i* in year *t*
$ASSETS_{i,t}$	total assets of firm *i* in year *t*
$Auditors_{i,t}$	firm auditors (indicator) of firm *i* in year *t*
$Beta_{i,t}$	CAPM Beta (measure of market risk) of firm *i* in year *t*
C_t	cash flow in year *t*
$CA_{i,t}$	current assets of firm *i* in year *t*
$Capex_{i,t}$	capital expenditures of firm *i* in year *t*
$Cash_{i,t}$	cash of firm *i* in year *t*
$CF_{i,t}$, $CFO_{i,t}$	cash flow from operations of firm *i* in year *t*
$CF\_correlations_{i,t}$	cash flow correlations (measure of cash flow coinsurance) of firm *i* in year *t*
$CF\_vola_{i,t}$	cash flow volatility of firm *i* in year *t*
$CL_{i,t}$	current liabilities of firm *i* in year *t*
$COGS_{i,t}$	cost of goods sold of firm *i* in year *t*
$Corr_{i,t}$	correlations of firm *i* in year *t*
$Corr\_CF\_AC_{i,t}$	correlation between cash flow from operations and total accruals of firm *i* in year *t*
$Corr\_Rev\_Exp_{i,t}$	correlation between revenues and expenses of firm *i* in year *t*
$Correlations_{i,t}$	earnings (cash flow) correlations of firm *i* in year *t*

$CYCLE_{i,t}$	operating cycle of firm *i* in year *t*
$DACQ1_{i,t}$	discretionary component of *ACQ1* of firm *i* in year *t*
$DACQ2_{i,t}$	discretionary component of *ACQ2* of firm *i* in year *t*
$DEPN_{i,t}$	depreciation and amortization expenses of firm *i* in year *t*
$Disperse_{i,t}$	standard deviation of analysts' forecasts of firm *i* in year *t*
$Div\_Dummy_{i,t}$	diversification indicator of firm *i* in year *t*
$Div\_Measures_{i,t}$	diversification measures of firm *i* in year *t*
$EAR_{i,t}$, $Ear_{i,t}$	earnings of firm *i* in year *t*
$EAR\_Attributes_{i,t}$	earnings attributes (*PRED*, *ACQ1*, *ACQ2*) of firm *i* in year *t*
$EAR\_correlations_{i,t}$	earnings correlations (measure of earnings coinsurance) of firm *i* in year *t*
$EAR\_vola_{i,t}$	earnings volatility of firm *i* in year *t*
$Ebit_{i,t}$	earnings before interest and taxes of firm *i* in year *t*
$Ecofactor_{i,t}$	economic factor of firm *i* in year *t*
$EQ_{i,t}$	earnings quality of firm *i* in year *t*
$Error_{i,t}$	I/B/E/S consensus analyst forecast error of firm *i* in year *t*
$EX\_AC\_vola_{i,t}$	excess accruals volatility of firm *i* in year *t*
$EX\_CF\_vola_{i,t}$	excess cash flow volatility of firm *i* in year *t*
$EX\_Corr\_CF\_AC_{i,t}$	excess correlation between cash flow and accruals of firm *i* in year *t*
$EX\_Ear\_vola_{i,t}$	excess earnings volatility of firm *i* in year *t*
$EX\_value_{i,t}$	excess value of firm *i* in year *t*
$EX\_vola_{i,t}$	excess volatility of firm *i* in year *t*
excess $ACQ1_{i,t}$	excess accruals quality following Dechow and Dichev (2002) of firm *i* in year *t*
excess $ACQ2_{i,t}$	excess accruals quality following Jones (1991) of firm *i* in year *t*
excess $DACQ1_{i,t}$	discretionary component of *excess ACQ1* of firm *i* in year *t*
excess $DACQ2_{i,t}$	discretionary component of *excess ACQ2* of firm *i* in year *t*
excess $EQ_{i,t}$	excess earnings quality of firm *i* in year *t*
excess $IACQ1_{i,t}$	innate component of *excess ACQ1* of firm *i* in year *t*
excess $IACQ2_{i,t}$	innate component of *excess ACQ2* of firm *i* in year *t*
excess $PRED_{i,t}$	excess predictability following Dichev and Tang (2009) of firm *i* in year *t*
$EXVAL\_ASSET_{i,t}$	excess value computed with assets of firm *i* in year *t*
$EXVAL\_SALES_{i,t}$	excess value computed with sales of firm *i* in year *t*

$Follow_{i,t}$	average number of analysts following firm of firm *i* in year *t*
$Growth_{i,t}$	growth options of firm *i* in year *t*
h	index for the industry
$Herfindahl_{i,t}$	Herfindahl Index of firm *i* in year *t*
i	firm index
$IACQ1_{i,t}$	innate component of *ACQ1* of firm *i* in year *t*
$IACQ2_{i,t}$	innate component of *ACQ2* of firm *i* in year *t*
$impEQ_{i,t,k}$	imputed stand-alone earnings quality of segment *k* of firm *i* in year *t*
imputed $EQ_{i,t}$	sales-weighted average of imputed stand-alone earnings quality of firm *i* in year *t*
imputed $Vola_{i,t}$	sales-weighted average of imputed stand-alone volatility of firm *i* in year *t*
$impVola_{i,t,k}$	imputed stand-alone volatility of segment *k* of firm *i* in year *t*
$Ind_{i,t}$	multiple of focused firm *i* in year *t*
$INDUSTRY_t$	industry dummy in year *t*
$Interaction_{i,t}$	interaction term (for the respective variables) of firm *i* in year *t*
Inverse Mills $ratio_{i,t}$	inverse Mills ratio from a first-stage probit model of firm *i* in year *t*
j	index for the industry
k	index for the business unit (segment)
$Lagaccrual_{i,t}$	lagged total accruals of firm *i* in year *t*
$Leverage_{i,t}$	firm leverage of firm *i* in year *t*
$Litigation_{i,t}$	firm litigation risk (indicator) of firm *i* in year *t*
$LogAsset_{i,t}$	natural logarithm of total assets of firm *i* in year *t*
$LogCycle_{i,t}$	natural logarithm of operating cycle of firm *i* in year *t*
$MAR_{i,t}$	market adjusted stock return of firm *i* in year *t*
$Mergers_{i,t}$	firm merger (indicator) of firm *i* in year *t*
$MVE_{i,t}$	market value of equity of firm *i* in year *t*
n	number of business units (segments)
$NegEarn_{i,t}$	incidence of negative earnings (indicator) of firm *i* in year *t*
$Opcycle_{i,t}$	natural logarithm of operating cycle of firm *i* in year *t*
p	index for the business unit (segment)
$Performance_{i,t}$	firm performance of firm *i* in year *t*
$PNDIV_{i,t}$	fraction of diversified firms in the industry of firm *i* in year *t*
$PPE_{i,t}$	proprety, plant, and equipment of firm *i* in year *t*

$PRED_{i,t}$	predictability following Dichev and Tang (2009) of firm *i* in year *t*
$PSDIV_{i,t}$	fraction of sales of diversified firms in the industry of firm *i* in year *t*
q	index for the business unit (segment)
R-squared, R^2	coefficient of determination of a regression
$R\&D_{i,t}$	research and development of firm *i* in year *t*
$Rev_{i,t}$	total revenues of firm *i* in year *t*
$RMSE_{i,t}$	root-mean-squared-error (measure of idiosyncratic risk) of firm *i* in year *t*
$ROA_{i,t}$	return on assets of firm *i* in year *t*
S_t	revenues generated from sales in year *t*
$SALE(S)_{i,t}$, $Sales_{i,t}$	total sales of firm *i* in year *t*
$SalesGrowth_{i,t}$	firm sales growth of firm *i* in year *t*
$SalesVola_{i,t}$	firm sales volatility of firm *i* in year *t*
$Seg\_Count_{i,t}$	number of business segments of firm *i* in year *t*
$SFAS131_{i,t}$	adoption of SFAS 131 (indicator) of firm *i* in year *t*
$Size_{i,t}$	firm size of firm *i* in year *t*
$StdCFO_{i,t}$	standard deviation of cash flow from operations of firm *i* in year *t*
$STDEBT_{i,t}$	debt in current liabilities of firm *i* in year *t*
$StdRevise_{i,t}$	standard deviation of changes in the median analysts' forecasts of firm *i* in year *t*
$StdROE_{i,t}$	standard deviation of return on equity of firm *i* in year *t*
$StdSALES_{i,t}$	standard deviation of sales of firm *i* in year *t*
$Surprise_{i,t}$	difference between current year EPS and previous year EPS of firm *i* in year *t*
t	time index
$TA_{i,t}$	total accruals of firm *i* in year *t*
$TCA_{i,t}$	total current accruals of firm *i* in year *t*
$Vola_{i,t}$	Volatility of firm *i* in year *t*
$Vola\_Measures_{i,t}$	Volatility measures of firm *i* in year *t*
$w_{i,t,p\,(h)}$	sales share of the business unit (segment) *p* of firm *i* in year *t* operating in industry *h*
$w_{i,t,q\,(j)}$	sales share of the business unit (segment) *q* of firm *i* in year *t* operating in industry *j*
YEAR	year dummy

Greek Symbols

α_0		intercept in a regression
α_i	i =1,2,...,13	coefficients in a regression
β_0		intercept in a regression
β_i	i =1,2,...,13	coefficients in a regression
γ_0		intercept in a regression
γ_i	i =1,2,...,13	coefficients in a regression
Δ		delta (change)
δ_0		intercept in a regression
δ_i	i =1,2,...,13	coefficients in a regression
ε		residual of a regression (error term)
ρ		correlation coefficient
σ		standard deviation or covariance
σ^2		variance
$\sum_{k=1}^{n}(...)$		sum of (...) for k=1 to n
φ		constant proportion

Further Symbols

$	US Dollar
&	ampersand (and)
%	percent
*** (**,*)	significance at the 1%- (5%-, 10%-) level

List of Figures

List of Tables

1 Introduction

1.1 Motivation and Research Questions

The effects of corporate diversification on firms' market valuation have been subject of an extensive line of financial economics research for more than four decades. Core to this research has been the question whether corporate diversification creates or destroys firm value. The long-held belief that the potential costs of diversification outweigh the potential benefits is attributable to the empirical observation that diversified firms are, on average, valued less than comparable portfolios of focused firms (e.g., Lang and Stulz 1994; Berger and Ofek 1995). While this so-called "diversification discount" has been seen as evidence of value destruction arising from agency and behavioral problems, subsequent work calls into question this finding by showing that the mere existence of a discount can be attributed entirely to sample-selection bias (Campa and Kedia 2002) or data and measurement problems (Villalonga 2004). However, more recent studies emphasize the financial benefits of coinsurance, especially during financial constraints (e.g., market turmoil associated with the financial crisis between 2007 and 2009), which even indicate a diversification premium (e.g., Kuppuswamy and Villalonga 2010; Duchin 2010; Tong 2012; Hann et al. 2013).[1]

Because accounting information is supposed to reduce information asymmetries (e.g., agency problems) between corporate insiders and outsiders and thus facilitate decision-making, corporate diversification has also become a vital subject of accounting research. The reason is that asymmetric information is an important phenomenon underlying both the economic consequences of accounting information and the valuation implications of corporate diversification. For example, recent evidence shows that the complexity of diversified firms' business activities and resulting agency problems reduce the quality of accounting information for diversified firms (e.g., Bens and Monahan 2004; Bens et al. 2011; Demirkan et al. 2012). However, the benefits of coinsurance and the results of this effect on the quality of financial reporting have not been analyzed in the accounting literature. With this doctoral thesis, I aim to fill this research gap by examining the relation between a firm's organizational form and earnings quality.[2]

[1] The notion of coinsurance goes back to Lewellen (1971) and suggests that the combination of imperfectly correlated cash flows among a firm's business units can increase firm value through higher debt capacity (optimal leverage) and higher tax benefits for diversified firms.

[2] Earnings quality is a latent construct of desirable properties of earnings, which are viewed as the single most important measure of firm performance from financial reporting (see Section 3.2.1 for detailed informations).

Moreover, the focus of the ongoing controversial debate in the financial economics literature regarding the diversification discount has been on the average effect of corporate diversification on firm value. Researchers on both sides of the debate have found significant variation across diversified firms in the premiums and discounts at which they trade relative to their stand-alone peers. However, the sources of this variation have received much less attention (Stein 2003). Accordingly, I seek to fill a part of this research gap by investigating in this thesis whether accounting information quality (i.e., earnings quality) can explain cross-sectional variation in the value of corporate diversification.

This doctoral thesis provides two large-scale empirical analyses to advance our understanding of the accounting and economic implications of corporate diversification. In the first study, I examine whether coinsurance matters for a firm's earnings quality. I argue that coinsurance among a firm's business units changes the properties of reported earnings through less volatile operations (financial synergies) and less estimation errors in the accrual process (accounting synergies). Both of these coinsurance benefits are derived from the aggregate nature of reported earnings and its components (cash flows and accruals) for diversified firms. Regarding the cash flow component, standard portfolio theory suggests that less than perfectly correlated cash flows among a firm's business units likely reduce the volatility of firm-level cash flows. This is in the financial economics literature associated with an increase in firms' debt capacity, higher tax benefits, less financial constraints, and lower cost of capital. Regarding the accruals component, I argue that less than perfectly correlated estimation errors among segment-level accruals cancel out which may result in less estimation errors in firm-level accruals. In contrast, the complex nature of diversified firms' business activities may make managers' task of estimating accruals more difficult or even induce more agency problems, both of which lead to more estimation errors in accruals. Therefore, the net effect of diversification on earnings quality is an empirical question. I find that diversified firms have on average higher earnings quality compared to industry-matched portfolios of focused firms. Specifically, diversification leads to more predictable earnings, superior mapping of accruals to cash flows, and a lower absolute value of abnormal accruals. In addition, consistent with a coinsurance effect, I find higher earnings quality for diversified firms with less correlated segment earnings and I also find that the coinsurance effect is stronger for firms that operate in volatile and uncertain environments. This supports the important role of the coinsurance effect for firms facing higher operating volatility.

Overall, this study suggests that coinsurance is a unique firm characteristic affecting earnings quality that is not captured in previously identified determinants. This evidence complements prior findings on disadvantages of diversification for earnings quality (agency effect) by documenting a sizable advantage of diversification for earnings quality (coinsurance effect). My results are highly relevant for all users of accounting information (e.g., investors, managers, and standard-setters) because coinsurance creates a competitive advantage through affecting a firm's earnings quality and, in turn, its firm valuation attributes.

In the subsequent study, I analyze the valuation implications of corporate diversification for differences in firm's earnings quality. More specifically, I explore whether the association between earnings quality and firm value differs for diversified and focused firms. Because higher earnings quality (lower operating volatility) leads to less uncertainty about firms' financial performance, the coinsurance effect implies less asymmetric information and thus less accounting information risk. Prior evidence from accounting research suggests that accounting information of high-quality (low-risk) reduces agency costs, which arise from information asymmetries between managers and corporate outsiders (e.g., Lambert 2001; Leuz and Verrecchia 2000). In this respect, it is important to remember that the diversification discount is often explained by more agency and behavioral problems, ultimately resulting from asymmetric information. Accordingly, I argue that less accounting information risk (i.e., higher earnings quality or lower operating volatility) reduces agency costs of diversified firms and thus the diversification discount. I find that diversified firms benefit from higher earnings quality (lower operating volatility) by higher firm valuation. In particular, I find that for a given level of earnings quality (operating volatility), the firm excess value of diversified firms is higher compared with focused firms. Therefore, I reveal that accounting information of high-quality (low-risk) can explain differences in the value of corporate diversification. However, the discount in diversified firms' value is reduced but not eliminated by higher earnings quality (lower operating volatility).

Overall, my evidence suggests that diversified firms with less accounting information risk and thus less agency costs have a relatively lower discount in firm value. This finding may enrich the controversial debate on the valuation implications of corporate diversification. I reveal a new dimension on how coinsurance can affect firm value that thus far has received little attention, namely, accounting information quality (risk). Thereby, my analysis is of interest for researchers as well as for investors in terms of their capital allocation decisions.

My doctoral thesis comprehensively analyzes the coinsurance effect of diversification by discussing its theoretical background, its development in the financial economics literature and its application in the accounting literature. Furthermore, this thesis outlines important implications of coinsurance for earnings quality and its consequences for firms' market valuation by means of two comprehensive empirical analyses.

1.2 Structure of the Thesis

This doctoral thesis is structured as follows. In Chapter 2, I present the firm characteristic of corporate diversification in detail by discussing the development of the research field and providing a review of relevant studies of the broad financial economics literature. In anticipation of potential accounting implications of corporate diversification in Chapter 3, I also outline in Chapter 2 empirical studies which use diversification as a research setting for examining accounting-related research questions. Chapter 3 represents the centerpiece of this thesis. In this chapter, I empirically analyze the first research question, that is, whether diversification and, in particular, coinsurance – the imperfect correlation of business activities – matters for a firm's earnings quality. In Chapter 4, which is closely related to Chapter 3, I empirically investigate the second research question, that is, whether coinsurance benefits on earnings quality (operating volatility) affect firms' market valuation. I conduct several empirical tests that do not only explore the effects in total, but also examine whether investors differentiate between underlying sources that drive earnings quality (volatility), which allows for further insights. In Chapter 5, I summarize the main findings and results, present limitations, and indicate useful directions for future research. Figure 1 illustrates the structure of this thesis.

Figure 1: Structure of the Thesis

Chapter 1: Introduction	• What is the Motivation underlying this Thesis? • What is the Structure of this Thesis?
Chapter 2: The Firm Characteristic of Corporate Diversification	• What are the Basics about Corporate Diversification? • How do the Effects of Corporate Diversification relate to the Financial Economics and Accounting Literature?
Chapter 3: Corporate Diversification and Earnings Quality	• Empirical Study: Accounting Implications of Corporate Diversification • Does Coinsurance matter for a Firm's Earnings Quality?
Chapter 4: Implication for the Excess Value of Corporate Diversification	• Empirical Study: Economic Implications of Corporate Diversification • Does the association between Earnings Quality (Operating Volatility) and Firm Value differ for Diversified and Focused Firms?
Chapter 5: Concluding Remarks	• Summary of Main Findings • Implications for Future Research

Source: Own illustration.

2 The Firm Characteristic of Corporate Diversification

This chapter provides the basic knowledge for my subsequent examinations through a comprehensive discussion of the firm characteristic of corporate diversification. Section 2.1 presents the business strategy underlying the firms' diversification decisions as well as the empirical measurement of corporate diversification. Section 2.2 introduces and structures the existing research literature on the various effects (benefits and costs) of corporate diversification. Section 2.3 discusses studies that empirically examine the valuation implications (premium vs. discount) of corporate diversification. Section 2.4 presents research studies that apply the concept of corporate diversification to related accounting research fields. Therefore, Section 2.4 serves as a bridge to the following chapters, which yield various implications of corporate diversification for earnings quality and firm valuation.

2.1 Basics about Corporate Diversification

2.1.1 Diversification Strategy

The concept of diversification goes originally back to Markowitz (1952) and describes the notion of risk reduction by investing in a portfolio of securities. Depending on the correlations of those securities, such a diversified portfolio is either less risky (i.e., exhibits a lower variance of returns for a given level of expected returns) or more profitable (i.e., exhibits higher expected returns for a given level of variance of returns) than a weighted average of its individual securities. However, conceptual travelling has led to an adoption of this concept to many research areas other than finance (e.g., corporate development and corporate finance).

For example, from a strategic management perspective, corporate diversification describes the expansion of a firm into new business activities through internal business development, strategic partnerships or mergers and acquisitions (M&A).[3] As a result, the extent to which firms are operating in various industries (segments) is referred to as the degree of diversification or diversity.[4] In contrast, the concentration of business activities of a firm in its core competencies is referred to as focusing. In this context, Chandler (1962) coined the famous phrase "structure follows strategy" as guideline for strategic management decision making, which emphasizes that corporate structure is created to implement a predefined corporate strategy. While corporate strategy determines long-term goals and adopts courses of

3 See Ramanujam and Varadarajan (1989).

4 See Pitts and Hopkins (1982).

action for achieving these goals, corporate structure represents the organizational form through which corporate strategy is administered.[5]

Ansoff (1957) defines the decision for firms to diversify as a growth strategy by entering new markets with new products. Regarding the relationship between segments within a firm, Ansoff (1957, 1965) distinguishes between three different types of diversification. (1) Vertical diversification is explained by the integration of the production program (i.e., upstream or downstream of the value chain). (2) Horizontal diversification describes the introduction of new products for existing customers without contributing to the core product line. Both vertical and horizontal diversifications are also known as related diversification due to the defined field of interest (i.e., production program or costumers) and dependence on similar resources such as in technology. The contrary is described by (3) lateral or conglomerate diversification, in which the firm's intent is to launch itself into new but unrelated products or markets beyond current resources and capabilities. This is also known as unrelated diversification due to lack of common links between the firm's segments. In addition to growth as the main driver for diversification as business strategy, Ansoff (1957) also names risk reduction and excess productive capacity as other reasons for firms to diversify.

Similarly, Montgomery (1994) describes three comprehensive theories to explain the motives for firms to diversify. The market-power view suggests that firms diversify to gain advantages of reduced competition. Hence, diversification enables a reduction in the uncertainty of future earnings and the possibility of financial distress (i.e., bankruptcy risk). The resource-based view implies that excess capacity in resources and capabilities are transferable across different industries to generate synergies (e.g., economies of scope) within a firm. These two theories describe the general benefits inherent in corporate diversification. In contrast, the agency-theory view argues that managers (agent) are willing to diversify in order to enforce their own personal interests against the firm's shareholders (principal). Consequently, agency costs arise due to asymmetric information between managers and shareholders, which result in value-destroying actions from self-interested managers.[6]

---

[5] Chandler (1962) divides the organizational form into either the unitary form (U-form) or the multi-divisional form (M-form). While the U-form describes a company that groups similar activities together in one specialized unit, the M-form characterizes a company which is divided into self-contained units where complementary activities are grouped together. Accordingly, the U-form builds the basis for the M-form of an organization, which is created when the firm pursues a strategy of diversification.

[6] Those actions to invest in value-destroying projects that exceed the optimal level of diversification are caused by incentives of the management due to empire building (power and prestige), increasing managerial compensation, and entrenchment by investments related to manager-specific skills or the reduction of managerial employment risk. For a more detailed explanation see Montgomery (1994).

Finally, Teece (2010) explains that business strategies are essential facets in designing a competitively sustainable business model. He states that the notion of the business model refers to a more conceptual rather than a financial model of a business and that it essentially describes the way the firm *goes to market*.[7] This is in line with Penman (2013, p. 22) who describes the business model as "concept or strategy under which a firm operates to add value from selling products or services to customers". Therefore, a core component in designing a business model is explained by diversification strategy which represents the identification and decision about how market segments should be targeted. Teece (2010) argues that this includes segmenting the market, creating a value proposition for each segment, and setting up tools to deliver that value from each segment.

To illustrate the importance of the diversification strategy, I plot in Figure 2 the number of firm-year observations and return on assets (ROA) as measure of firm performance for diversified and focused firms for the time period of 1976 to 2015.[8] In terms of observations, the number of focused firm observations has increased substantially until 1997, while the number of diversified firm observations has slightly declined in the same time period. However, the adoption of the Statement of Financial Accounting Standards (SFAS) 131 marks a structural break in time because it requires new segment disclosures for fiscal years ending after December 15, 1997.[9] As a consequence, the number of focused firm observations has quickly decreased whereas the number of diversified firm observations significantly increased and has remained well above the number of focused firm observations. Therefore, SFAS 131 revealed the so-called "hidden diversified firms" which operated in more than just one business segment but reported to be focused under the old rule SFAS 14.

In terms of firm performance, two time series patterns are particularly noticeable. First, the ROA has declined more strongly and even becomes negative for focused firms compared to diversified firms during the stock market boom and bust (i.e., dotcom bubble) at the turn of the century. Second, the ROA has declined even more strongly for focused firms during the

7 The business model describes which benefit the firm delivers to customers, how it organizes to achieve this, and how it creates and captures value. Therefore, it contains implicit assumptions about customers' behavior, the forecast of revenues and costs, strategies to respond to changing nature of user needs, and analyses about likely competitor response (Teece 2010).

8 Diversified firms are defined as operating in at least two different industries (segments), whereas focused firms concentrate only on their core line of business. Concerning the assignment of firms to industries, I use the standard procedure in the literature by applying the Standard Industrial Classification (SIC) codes (see Section 2.1.2 for more information).

9 SFAS 131 requires that publicly traded diversified firms report financial and related information for their operating segments, if sales, profit or loss, or assets of those segments exceed 10 percent of all reported operating segments. In addition, this statement is based on the management approach which requires the management to report the segments, how they are organized within the firm (FASB 1997).

recent financial crisis between 2007 and 2009. Since then, diversified firms have outperformed focused firms, which can be explained by diversification strategy that helped to stabilize revenues and earnings during these turbulent times. I provide more useful numbers about the development of the degree of diversification and different trends in basic accounting items (i.e., total sales, total assets, earnings) for diversified and focused firms in Appendix A of this thesis.

Figure 2: Relevance of Corporate Diversification

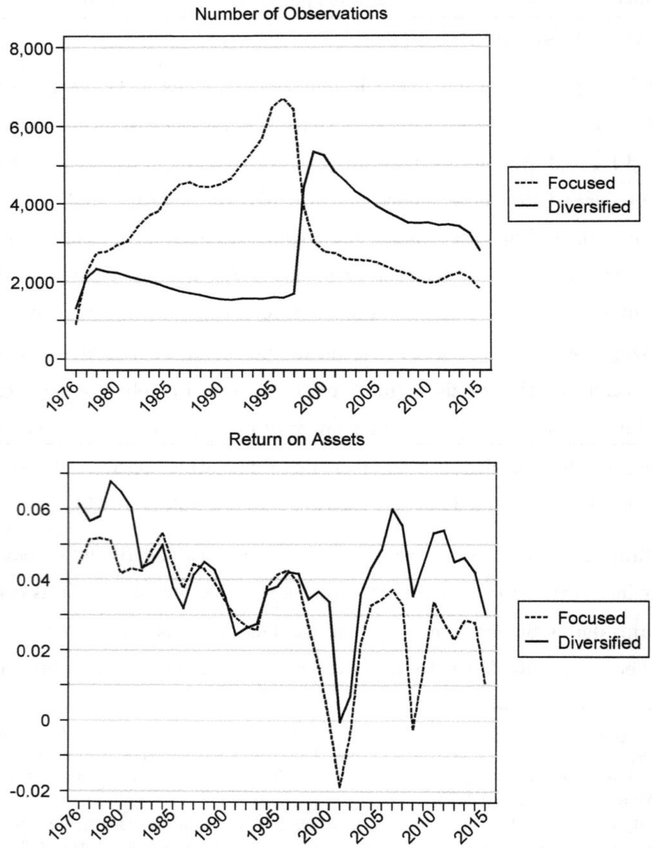

This figure presents the number of observations and the performance (measured by return on assets) of diversified and focused firms over time. The sample includes 246,718 firm-year observations (of which 110,625 are diversified). The data was retrieved from the intersection of the Compustat Annual Industrial and Compustat Industrial Segment files for the time period of 1976 to 2015 (for all firms with available accounting data on total sales, total assets and earnings – excluding financial firms in SIC code level 6000-6999).
Source: Own illustration.

2.1.2 Measurement

The industry affiliation in most empirical studies relating to corporate diversification is measured by the Standard Industrial Classification (SIC) codes. This industry classification scheme by the U.S. Census Bureau represents the standard procedure to assign firms to homogeneous groups.[10] Figure 3 illustrates the structure of the SIC allocation system for one (i.e., Division A) of the ten different divisions.[11]

Figure 3: Allocation of Firms into SIC Codes

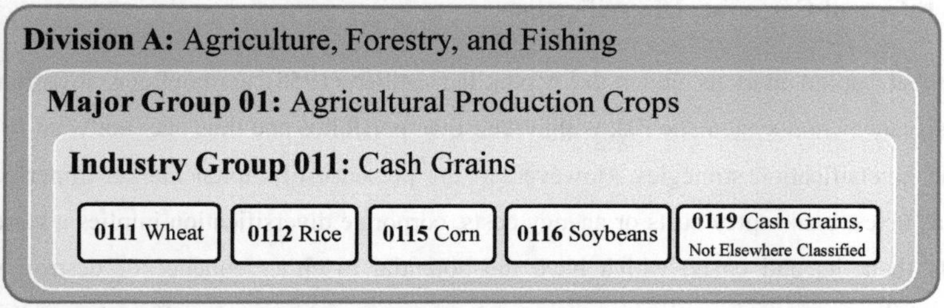

This figure presents an example of the system of classifying industries in the U.S. (established in 1937), which is used for the measurement of a firm's diversification status.
Source: Own illustration.

Most studies cited in this thesis avoid defining diversification in detail and rather consider firms as diversified (multi-segment) when their segments operate in at least two different industries (four-digit SIC codes).[12] Consequently, firms are treated as focused when they operate in only one single industry.[13] In addition, a distinction is made using SIC codes between related and unrelated diversification. Thus, related diversification is considered as a firm's segments operating in different industries (four-digit SIC codes) or industry groups (three-digit SIC code), whereas unrelated diversification is viewed as a firm's segments operating in different major groups (two-digit SIC codes) or divisions (letter SIC codes). Moreover, the status of diversity is measured by the number of industries (segments) in which

---

10 Bhojraj et al. (2003) report that industry definition with SIC codes has a long history in the academic literature. SIC codes have been available since 1937 and are used in more than 90 percent of studies that employ a general industry classification scheme.

11 The structure of the SIC codes is organized hierarchically, from divisions (letter SIC codes) to a finer separation named major groups (two-digit SIC codes), industry groups (three-digit SIC codes) and industries (four-digit SIC codes). For more information about the different SIC groupings see https://www.osha.gov/pls/imis/sic_manual.html.

12 See for example Berger and Ofek (1995) and Campa and Kedia (2002).

13 In this thesis, the expressions "focused", "single-segment", and "stand-alone" are used interchangeably for firms that operate in only one industry.

a firm operates (reported by different four-digit SIC codes). The SIC system is also used by Fama and French (1997) to reorganize firms by their four-digit SIC codes into 48 industry portfolios. While both systems are widely used in academic research and divide firms into homogeneous groups, the specific intent of Fama and French (1997) is to form groups of industries according to their common risk characteristics.[14] However, one weakness of the SIC system is that it was developed for traditional industries and thus is slow to recognize new and emerging industries.[15]

2.2 Effects of Corporate Diversification

In perfect capital markets under the Modigliani-Miller (1958) assumptions, investors can diversify away non-systematic risk within their own portfolios and thus may not want firms to pursue diversification strategies. However, in the presence of capital market imperfections such as taxes, bankruptcy costs or agency costs, corporate diversification implies a variety of effects (benefits and costs) which have the potential to either enhance or destroy value. Figure 4 illustrates the most important *ex ante* effects (i.e., coinsurance effect, internal capital market and agency problems), which will be discussed in the following two sections.

Figure 4: Effects of Corporate Diversification

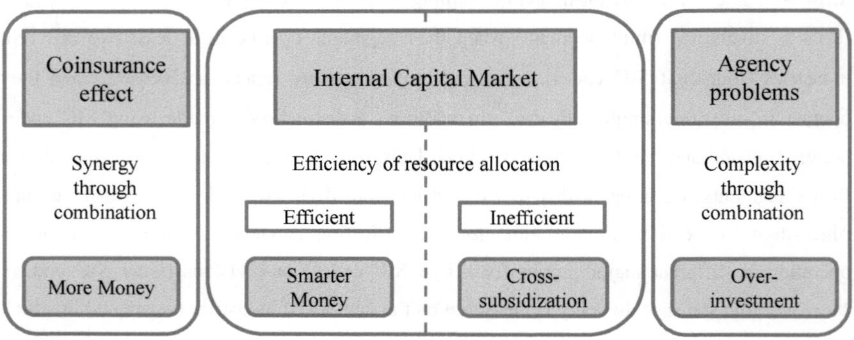

Source: Own illustration.

[14] For detailed information about Fama and French 48 industry classification, see the website of Kenneth R. French available at: http://mba.tuck.dartmouth.edu/pages/faculty/ken.french/.

[15] As an alternative, the North American Industry Classification System (NAICS) was developed and released in 1997 to replace the SIC system and to allow for a high level of comparability in business statistics among North American countries (i.e., USA, Canada, and Mexico). However, the U.S. Security and Exchange Commission (SEC) still uses SIC codes for industry classification as its standard.

2.2.1 Benefits of Corporate Diversification

Diversified firms are related to several benefits based on financial synergies and operating efficiencies. Lewellen (1971) explains that the combination of imperfectly correlated cash flows from different business segments enables firms to exploit additional leverage possibilities through improved satisfaction of their contractual debt criteria. This so-called "coinsurance effect" can create financial synergies through higher debt capacity (optimal leverage) for diversified firms, which implies a larger tax shield and higher firm value.[16] Leland (2007) confirms that diversified firms benefit from coinsurance by less risky firm-level cash flow realizations and thus less bankruptcy risk (costs). Moreover, diversification may further lower taxes by enabling the firm to offset immediately operating losses from a particular segment against the profits of other segments.

Williamson (1975) posits that each diversified firm creates an internal capital market which allows an efficient resource allocation because funding between the business segments is organized more efficiently (less costly) than through the external capital market. For example, Chandler (1977) suggests that diversification may lead to greater operating efficiency by enhancing economies of scope and increasing managerial coordination. Stulz (1990) documents that an efficient internal capital allocation in diversified firms mitigates the underinvestment problem by reallocating scarce resources to more profitable net present value (NPV) projects than their segments would make as stand-alone firms. In addition, Gertner et al. (1994) point out that control rights transferred to a firm's headquarter improve the monitoring of the diversified firm's segments and thus make the headquarter an efficient intermediary for the resource allocation process. Similarly, Stein (1997) notes that the benefit of internal capital markets lies in the reduction of costs of obtaining funds necessary for investments by transferring control rights and increasing monitoring of each business segment to engage in winner-picking.[17] Finally, Maksimovic and Philips (2002) explain that diversified firms can benefit from increased market power by cross-subsidized predatory pricing.

2.2.2 Costs of Corporate Diversification

Diversification is associated with creating several costs, which are finally due to information asymmetries. Jensen (1986) argues that managers have incentives to pursue their private

[16] This effect is also called the "more-money effect" because diversified firms are able to raise more money from the external capital market compared to focused firms (Stein 2003).

[17] Winner-picking (and loser-sticking) means the allocation of funds within a diversified firm to the most valuable segments (Stein 1997). This is also called the "smarter-money effect" of internal capital markets (Stein 2003).

benefits by reinvesting accessible free cash flows even when their companies have no profitable investment opportunities.[18] This overinvestment problem claims that diversification exacerbates managerial agency problems, which arise from higher organizational complexity and resulting monitoring problems between managers and corporate outsiders. Therefore, diversified firms are exposed to higher agency costs compared to their stand-alone peers.

Scharfstein and Stein (2000) find that less profitable segments are subsidized by more profitable segments through the internal capital market of diversified firms. They explain that inefficient internal investments (i.e., cross-subsidization) arise from behavioral problems between headquarters (CEO) and rent-seeking divisional managers inside diversified firms.[19] Shin and Stulz (1996) make a related argument that corporate bureaucracy causes an inefficient capital allocation within diversified firms resulting from a more complex intra-organizational coordination. Consequently, diversified firms incur costs associated with increased information asymmetries, which do not affect focused firms.

2.3 Relevance of Corporate Diversification for Financial Economics Research

Numerous studies in the financial economics literature examine the valuation effects of corporate diversification. These effects have led to an ongoing controversial debate whether diversified firms trade at a discount or premium relative to their stand-alone counterparts. For example, the conglomerate merger wave over the period from 1960 to 1970 was driven by the concept of economies of scope, whereas the refocusing wave in the 1980s and early 1990s was initiated by a trend towards more specialization and higher market valuations (Comment and Jarrell 1995; Servaes 1996). The prevailing view in the extensive literature is, however, that the potential costs of diversification outweigh the potential benefits.[20]

The empirical studies of Lang and Stulz (1994) and Berger and Ofek (1995) demonstrate that the typical diversified firm trades at a substantial discount compared to a benchmark portfolio of focused firms. They find that costs associated with overinvestment and cross-subsidization

[18] See Jensen and Murphy (1990) which point out that managers seek private benefits such as enhancement in power and prestige (i.e., empire building) as well as compensation. Shleifer and Vishny (1989) explain that managers spend enormous effort to make themselves valuable to the shareholders by investing in assets related to manager-specific skills (i.e., managerial entrenchment). Amihud and Lev (1981) note that managers tend to diversify in order to reduce firm-specific risk because this also lowers their individual employment risk.

[19] Scharfstein and Stein (2000) model a two-tiered agency conflict between (1) headquarters (CEO) and corporate outsiders and (2) between the CEO and divisional managers to explain cross-subsidization within a diversified firm.

[20] Table 1 presents a selection of some of the most influential studies about the *theoretical* effects of corporate diversification and their *empirical* valuation implications for diversified firms.

exceed the potential benefits and contribute to a significant diversification discount. Accordingly, Denis et al. (1997) emphasize the importance of agency costs in explaining misallocation of diversified firms and confirm that managers will reduce diversification only if forced to do so by market disciplinary forces (e.g., equity ownership or external corporate control threats).[21] Krishnaswami and Subramaniam (1999) document that misallocation of resources are caused by information asymmetry problems and misalignment of incentives between central and divisional managers.[22] More specifically, they find that firms which engage in a corporate spin-off (reduce diversity) show declining degrees of information asymmetries and raise more funds following the spin-off. Rajan et al. (2000) confirm that a "political battle" between different business segments leads to a misallocation of resources on internal capital markets. They explain rent-seeking divisional managers influence corporate headquarters by the use of distorted private information about the investment prospects of their segments and thereby drain resources from better performing segments which, overall, leads to an inefficient allocation of capital among segments.

However, several empirical studies argue that these value-destroying effects are attributable to factors other than diversification. For example, Campa and Kedia (2002) find that the diversification decision is endogenous and determined by the same firm-specific characteristics which cause the firms to be discounted. Graham et al. (2002) point out that the value reduction occurs because the firm acquires already discounted business units and not because diversification destroys value. In addition, Villalonga (2004) show that the discount of conglomerates is due to data and measurement problems and find that diversified firms even trade at a premium. More recent evidence emphasizes the value-enhancing effects of diversification. For example, Hann et al. (2013) find that coinsurance can reduce systematic risk by avoiding deadweight costs of financial distress and thereby reduce the cost of capital. Duchin (2010) shows that coinsurance enables diversified firms to hold less cash through more efficient fund transfers. In addition, Kuppuswamy and Villalonga (2010) detect that the independence from external capital markets increased the value of diversified firms during the 2007-2009 financial crises by reducing funding constraints through an efficient resource allocation. Similarly, Yan et al. (2010) emphasize the importance of less costly internal capital markets by avoiding transaction costs and the positive liquidity effects caused by these during recessions. Overall, there is still no clear consensus on the diversification discount.

---

[21] The agency cost hypothesis predicts that managers, when not monitored by corporate outsiders, deliberately make poor resource allocation decisions to enhance their private benefits from diversification.

[22] The information asymmetry hypothesis predicts that diversification creates an intra-organizational complexity which results in a greater level of asymmetric information within diversified firms.

Table 1: Corporate Diversification and Related Financial Economics Literature

Author(s)	Type	Value Effect	Main Finding
Lewellen (1971)	Theoretical	Benefit: Coinsurance	Financial benefits of mergers arise through the combination of imperfectly correlated activities that increase the firm's debt capacity (leverage).
Williamson (1975)	Theoretical	Benefit: Internal Capital Market	The internal capital market is seen as a competitive resource allocation process in which funding is organized more efficiently (lower transaction costs) than through the external capital market benchmark.
Jensen (1986)	Theoretical	Cost: Agency Problems	Managers have incentives to reinvest accessible free cash flows even when their companies have no profitable investment opportunities (over-investment problem).
Stulz (1990)	Theoretical	Benefit: Internal Capital Market	Efficient resource allocation in diversified firms mitigates the underinvestment problem by reallocating scarce resources to more profitable net present value (NPV) projects.
Berger and Ofek (1995)	Empirical	Discount: Over-investment & Cross-subsidization	Diversified firms are valued less than comparable portfolios of focused firms.
Denis et al. (1997)	Empirical	Discount: Agency Costs	Managers derive private benefits from corporate diversification and thus maintain value-reducing diversification strategies until market disciplinary forces interfere (e.g., acquisition attempts).
Krishnaswami and Subramaniam (1999)	Empirical	Discount: Information Asymmetry Costs	Firms which engage in corporate spin-offs show declining degrees of information asymmetry. For example, firms in need of external capital show a higher propensity to engage in spin-offs.
Scharfstein and Stein (2000)	Theoretical	Cost: Internal Capital Market	Higher level of information asymmetry between CEO and divisional managers leads to a subsidization of less profitable segments by more profitable segments (inefficient cross-subsidization or so-called "socialism").
Rajan et al. (2000)	Empirical	Discount: Information Asymmetry Costs	Information asymmetry between central managers (headquarters) and rent-seeking divisional managers leads to inefficient investment (i.e., cross-subsidization) and less valuable firms.
Campa and Kedia (2002)	Empirical	Premium: Correction for Selection-bias	After controlling for endogeneity of the firm's diversification decision, the calculated discount always drops and sometimes even turns into a premium.
Villalonga (2004)	Empirical	Premium: New Data Source	Diversification discount is an artifact of Compustat Segment data. Using an alternative data source, diversified firms trade at an average premium.
Leland (2007)	Theoretical	Benefit and Cost: Financial Synergies	Financial synergies can be positive (favoring mergers) or negative (favoring separation). More likely to be positive when correlations are low, volatilities are low and similar, and default costs are jointly high (i.e., risk-reduction of diversification).
Hann et al. (2013)	Empirical	Premium: Coinsurance	Coinsurance enables management to transfer resources from cash-rich to cash-poor segments and thereby reduces cost of capital through the avoidance of countercyclical deadweight costs (i.e., reduction of systematic risk).

This table presents some of the most influential studies of corporate diversification in the financial economics literature.

2.4 Application of Corporate Diversification to Related Accounting Research

The main purpose of financial reporting is to provide decision useful information about a firm's performance and thus reduce information asymmetries between corporate insiders and outsiders (see Section 3.2.1 for more details). Therefore, asymmetric information is an important phenomenon underlying both the economic consequences of accounting information and the valuation implications of diversification (see Sections 2.2 and 2.3).

Several studies examine accounting-related research questions in the context of corporate diversification because asymmetric information is likely more important for diversified firms than for focused firms (see Table 2 for an overview). Consequently, diversified firms deliver a powerful setting for evaluating potential effects attributable to more agency problems and higher organizational complexity. For example, Thomas (2002) and Duru and Reeb (2002) examine whether increased asymmetric information (e.g., through higher complexity) lead to less accurate analysts' earnings forecasts for diversified firms. Berger and Hann (2003) and Bens and Monahan (2004) investigate whether less agency problems through the monitoring role of higher disclosures quality result in higher firm excess value. Moreover, a recent study by Franco et al. (2016) is the first to find that higher segment disclosure quality aggravates the negative relation between diversification and the cost of debt because segment disclosures enable investors a better assessment of the coinsurance effect of diversification.

Table 2: Corporate Diversification and Related Accounting Literature

Author(s)	Research Field	Theoretical Link	Main Finding
Thomas (2002)	Analysts' Forecasts & Earnings Announcements	Information asymmetry	Greater industrial diversification is <u>not</u> associated with increased asymmetric information.
Duru and Reeb (2002)	Analysts' Forecasts	Information asymmetry: Increased complexity of the forecasting task	Corporate international diversification is associated with less accurate and more optimistic forecasts.
Berger and Hann (2003)	Disclosure Quality & Firm Value	Agency problems: Monitoring role of (mandatory) disclosures	Increased information environment through adoption of SFAS 131 (i.e., more disaggregated information), which affects firm valuation.
Bens and Monahan (2004)	Disclosure Quality & Firm Value	Agency problems: Monitoring role of (voluntary) disclosures	Positive association between voluntary disclosure and firm excess value because of less information problems.
Demirkan et al. (2012)	Earnings Quality & Cost of Capital	Internal agency problems	Diversified firms have lower discretionary accruals quality, which lead to higher cost of (equity and debt) capital.
Franco et al. (2016)	Disclosure Quality & Cost of Debt	Segment disclosure quality affects investors' assessment of the coinsurance effect of diversification	Negative relation between industrial diversification and bond yields becomes stronger for firms with high-quality segment disclosures (i.e., positive economic effect of coinsurance).

This table presents a selection of important corporate diversification studies dealing with accounting-related questions.

3 Corporate Diversification and Earnings Quality

The following chapter addresses the accounting implications of corporate diversification by examining the relationship between the coinsurance effect of diversification and earnings quality. In general, coinsurance arises through the combination of imperfectly correlated earnings (cash flows) within a diversified firm and can be beneficial through the reduction of bankruptcy risk (costs), financial constraints or even systematic risk (e.g., Lewellen 1971; Leland 2007; Duchin 2010; Hann et al. 2013). While prior studies find that more severe agency problems of diversified firms reduce the quality of accounting information, I provide an alternative approach to explain how coinsurance benefits affect a firm's earnings quality. The analysis in the following chapter is largely based on my research study, which I have presented at the 2015 *Workshop on Empirical Research in Financial Accounting* in Cordoba, Spain.[23]

3.1 Introduction

Prior research in accounting emphasizes the importance of controlling for differences in firm fundamentals when examining earnings quality, especially before inferring managerial opportunism (e.g., Dechow and Dichev 2002; Francis et al. 2005; Dechow et al. 2010). Such a difference in firm characteristics is addressed in the extensive financial economics literature about the role of corporate diversification on firm performance, because the organizational form creates both costs and benefits for diversified firms relative to their stand-alone peers (e.g., Williamson 1975; Jensen 1986; Stulz 1990; Gertner et al. 1994; Denis et al. 1997; Scharfstein and Stein 2000).[24] While agency and behavioral problems are popular explanations for an empirically observed diversification discount (e.g., Lang and Stulz 1994; Berger and Ofek 1995; Servaes 1996; Lins and Servaes 1999; Rajan et al. 2000), coinsurance can be value-enhancing through reduced bankruptcy risk (costs), increased debt capacity, and higher tax benefits (Lewellen 1971; Leland 2007), less financial constraints (Duchin 2010;

[23] See Homburg et al. (2016).

[24] The organizational form goes back to Chandler (1962) and is commonly divided into either the unitary form (U-form) or the multi-divisional form (M-form). While the U-form describes a company that groups similar activities together in one specialized unit, the M-form characterizes a company which is divided into self-contained units where complementary activities are grouped together. Accordingly, the U-form builds the basis for the M-form of an organization, which is created when the firm pursues a strategy of diversification. In this study, diversified (multi-segment) firms are defined as operating in at least two different lines of business segments (industries), whereas focused (single-segment) firms concentrate only on their core line of business.

Kuppuswamy and Villalonga 2010; Tong 2012), or even lower cost of capital (Hann et al. 2013; Franco et al. 2016).[25] Despite recent evidence that more severe agency problems of diversified firms reduce the information content of financial reporting (e.g., Bens and Monahan 2004; Berger and Hann 2007; Bens et al. 2011; Demirkan et al. 2012), whether coinsurance matters for a firm's earnings quality remains an open question. In this chapter, I aim to answer this question by examining the relation between a firm's organizational form and earnings quality.

I argue that organizational form affects earnings quality, and in particular, coinsurance – the imperfect correlation of business activities – among a firm's business units changes the properties of reported earnings through less volatile operations and less estimation errors in the accrual process.[26] Both of these coinsurance benefits are derived from the aggregate nature of reported earnings and its components (cash flows and accruals) for diversified firms. Regarding the cash flow component, standard portfolio theory suggests that less than perfectly correlated cash flows among a firm's business units (i.e., more cash flow coinsurance) likely reduces the volatility of firm-level cash flows, which lowers the level of operating risk for diversified firms. Consistently, Lewellen (1971) and Leland (2007) show that diversified firms can benefit from coinsurance by less bankruptcy risk (costs) and thus realize financial synergies.[27] Regarding the accruals component, I argue that less than perfectly correlated estimation errors among segment-level accruals (i.e., more accrual coinsurance) cancel out which may result in less estimation errors in firm-level accruals. Accordingly, diversified firms can benefit from coinsurance by less noise in accrual estimations and thus realize accounting synergies.[28] Because earnings quality is negatively related to the volatility of cash flows and the magnitude of accrual estimation errors (e.g.,

---

25 Value-destroying agency behavior is caused by empire building (prestige) and compensation (Jensen 1986; Jensen and Murphy 1990), managerial entrenchment (Shleifer and Vishny 1989), or the reduction of manager's personal employment risk (Amihud and Lev 1981).

26 The accrual process describes the managerial estimation and determination of accruals, which shift or adjust the recognition of cash flows over time. In general, accruals serve to mitigate timing and matching problems inherent in cash flows such that reported earnings better measure firm performance than realized cash flows (Dechow 1994; Dechow and Dichev 2002).

27 For example, Leland (2007) finds that imperfectly correlated cash flows among a firm's business units imply less risky firm-level cash flow realizations, which can create financial synergies through greater optimal leverage and higher tax benefits. In addition, Hann et al. (2013) argue that coinsurance enables a diversified firm to transfer resources from cash-rich to cash-poor units and thereby avoid deadweight costs that stand-alone firms cannot avoid on their own.

28 For example, I assume that imperfectly correlated accrual estimation errors among a firm's business units induce less noisy firm-level accrual estimations, which can create accounting synergies through less accounting information risk (e.g., Easley and O'Hara 2004; Francis et al. 2005; Hou 2015). In accordance to Hann et al. (2013), I argue that coinsurance enables internal transfers of resources which allow more accurate accrual estimations through offsetting estimation errors compared with stand-alone firms.

Jones 1991; Dechow 1994; Dechow and Dichev 2002; Francis et al. 2005; Dichev and Tang 2009; Dechow et al. 2010), I expect that earnings are of higher quality for diversified firms because of the coinsurance benefits.[29]

The complex nature of diversification, however, may deteriorate earnings (accruals) quality because the diversity of firms' business operations makes managers' accrual estimations more difficult (Palepu and Healy 2013) or even induces more agency problems (Demirkan et al. 2012), both of which lead to more estimation errors in accruals. Therefore, the net effect of diversification on earnings (accruals) quality is an empirical question.

I test my coinsurance hypothesis using a large sample of diversified and focused firms for the period from 1979 to 2011. I consider three measures of earnings quality that capture the volatility of a firm's business operations and estimation errors in accruals: the predictability of earnings (Dichev and Tang 2009), the extent to which accruals map into cash flows (Dechow and Dichev 2002), and the absolute value of abnormal accruals (Jones 1991).[30] In my empirical analyses, I use measures of *excess* earnings quality to benchmark the earnings quality of a diversified firm against that of a comparable portfolio of its stand-alone peers. In addition, I construct earnings and cash flow correlations among a firm's business units (i.e., cross-segment correlations) as inverse measures of coinsurance, which capture the imperfect correlation of a firm's business activities.

I find that diversified firms have on average higher earnings quality compared to industry-matched portfolios of their focused counterparts. In particular, diversified firms have more predictable earnings, superior mapping between accruals and cash flows, and a lower absolute value of abnormal accruals. More specifically, I find that high quality accruals and earnings are significantly related to the imperfect correlation of business activities (i.e., more coinsurance through less cross-segment correlations), consistent with a coinsurance effect. My results support the prediction that the diversification-specific advantage of coinsurance is

[29] I follow Dechow and Schrand (2004) and consider high quality earnings to be those that accurately reflect companies' current operating performance, truthfully indicate future operating performance, and provide a useful summary measure for evaluating firm value. I assume that the diversification-specific advantage of coinsurance jointly influences the volatility of cash flows and the magnitude of estimation errors in accruals and thus the properties of reported earnings (Dechow et al. 2010).

[30] The term "earnings quality" captures the general construct of high quality earnings, while the term "accruals quality" applies to the Dechow and Dichev (2002) and Jones (1991) based measures of earnings quality which focus on abnormal accruals. Abnormal accruals represent estimation errors in accruals induced by either innate (unintentional) sources arising from observable firm-specific fundamentals or discretionary (intentional) sources arising from unobservable managerial opportunism (Dechow and Dichev 2002; Francis et al. 2005). In my main analysis, I do not disentangle these accruals quality measures into innate and discretionary components because both components imply low quality accruals and earnings. However, I provide further analysis on this matter in my robustness section.

positively associated with the quality of earnings, even after controlling for previously identified determinants of earnings quality (e.g., firm size, growth, performance, leverage, and operating cycle).

However, because the volatility of a firm's business operations is systematically related to the propensity to make accrual estimation errors, firms with intrinsically low operating volatility and thus less uncertainty in their operating environment are likely to exhibit a lower magnitude of estimation errors in accruals (Dechow 1994; Dechow and Dichev 2002; Francis et al. 2005). Therefore, I further examine whether my findings can be explained by systematic differences in operating volatility between diversified and focused firms. I expect that the coinsurance effect is stronger for firms that operate in volatile and uncertain environments since such firms are more likely to exhibit more accrual estimation errors and thus benefit more from coinsurance on earnings quality. Consistent with my prediction, I find that the positive association between coinsurance and earnings quality increases with higher levels of operating volatility.

Moreover, I check the robustness of my main analysis for the subsample of diversified firms and for potential endogeneity concerns by (1) including firm-fixed effects to control for time-invariant unobserved heterogeneity and (2) estimating a Heckman (1979) two-stage model to control for self-selection. My inferences remain unchanged for all these alternative specifications. In addition, I decompose both of my accruals quality measures into innate and discretionary components to explain the source of the relation between coinsurance and earnings quality. I find a significant positive relation between coinsurance and innate accruals quality which highlights my main result that the organizational form is a fundamental firm characteristic affecting earnings (accruals) quality. In contrast, I find a negative but insignificant relation between coinsurance and discretionary accruals quality which indicates that the benefits of coinsurance do not explain more opportunistic accrual choices in diversified firms. Overall, my evidence suggests that coinsurance is a unique characteristic, not captured in previously identified determinants, that enables diversified firms to improve earnings quality relative to comparable portfolios of their stand-alone peers.

I contribute to both the earnings quality and the financial economics literature. First, I calculate a firm- and year-specific measure of *excess* earnings quality by adapting the procedure of Berger and Ofek (1995) for estimating segments' *imputed* values to compute *excess* values for diversified and focused firms.[31] *Excess* earnings quality allows me to benchmark the *actual* earnings quality of a diversified firm against the *imputed* earnings quality that its business units would have if operated as stand-alone firms in their respective industry. This approach yields a direct estimate of the advantage (disadvantage) in earnings quality for a diversified firm relative to a portfolio of comparable focused firms. Thus, I contribute by improving the comparison of earnings quality between diversified and focused firms.

Second, to the best of my knowledge I am the first to identify a strong relation between coinsurance benefits and earnings quality. I reveal that coinsurance is a unique firm characteristic that can create financial and accounting synergies and thus represents a competitive advantage associated with earnings quality for diversified firms. Therefore, I contribute to understand a fundamental factor that changes the properties of a diversified firm's earnings and its components (cash flows and accruals). In addition, I complement existing studies by providing empirical evidence that coinsurance is positively associated with earnings quality and thus extend prior findings that agency problems in diversified firms are not predominantly affecting earnings quality. My findings suggest that the diversification-specific advantage of coinsurance leads to overall less noise in accrual estimations, which emphasizes the importance of controlling for this fundamental firm characteristic when examining earnings quality.

Finally, I advance the discussion about the role of the business model in earnings quality. For example, evidence from a recent survey by Dichev et al. (2013) indicates that the business model is the most important fundamental factor influencing earnings quality, even more than accounting standards. While Demirkan et al. (2012) focus on more agency problems and resulting lower discretionary accruals quality for diversified firms, they note that innate accruals are of higher quality for diversified firms because of fundamental differences between the business models of diversified and focused firms. As one key element of the business model, the organizational form influences the way a firm creates value and converts revenue to cash and earnings (Teece 2010; Penman 2013).[32] Thus, I contribute to this

[31] This procedure is highly accepted in the financial economics literature and allows comparing a firm's *actual* market value to its *imputed* market value, which estimates the market value of a comparable portfolio of its stand-alone peers (e.g., Berger and Ofek 1996; Denis et al. 1997; Berger and Ofek 1999; Lins and Servaes 1999; Graham et al. 2002; Mansi and Reeb 2002; Bens and Monahan 2004, among others).

[32] Teece (2010) explains that the notion of the business model refers to a conceptual rather than a financial model of a business and that it basically describes the way a firm *goes to market*. He states that business strategies are essential facets in designing a competitively sustainable business model (e.g., how the firm organizes to deliver certain benefits of products or services to customers). This is in line with Penman (2013),

literature by providing empirical evidence and delivering new insights of how a firm's organizational form through the imperfect correlation of its business activities affects earnings quality. Overall, my results are important for all users of accounting information (e.g., investors, analysts, managers, regulators, and standard-setters) because the organizational form affects not only the firm's operations, but also its quality of earnings and, in turn, its firm valuation attributes.

The remainder of this chapter is structured as follows. Section 3.2 provides the theoretical background of earnings quality. Section 3.3 reviews the relevant corporate diversification and earnings quality literature and develops my hypotheses. Section 3.4 describes my empirical methodology and my sample. Section 3.5 presents the main empirical results and Section 3.6 reports robustness checks. Section 3.7 concludes this chapter.

3.2 Earnings Quality

3.2.1 Principles and Definition

The Financial Accounting Standards Board (FASB) evaluates the information quality of financial reporting from the perspective of its *usefulness* for decision making. In accordance to the Statement of Financial Accounting Concepts (SFAC) No. 2 and illustrated in Figure 5, decision usefulness of accounting information primarily depends on *relevance* and *reliability*. While the *understandability* of information enables users to perceive its significance and thus must be evaluated in relation to specific decision makers (e.g., investors, creditors, and analysts), *relevance* and *reliability* make information overall more desirable in terms of decision usefulness.[33] More specifically, *relevance* describes the capacity and timeliness of information to influence a decision "by helping users to form predictions about the outcomes of past, present and future events or to confirm or correct prior expectations." *Reliability*, on the other hand, represents "the quality of information that assures that information is reasonably free from error and bias and faithfully represents what it purports to represent." In addition, these two principles interact with *comparability* which enables users to identify similarities in and differences between companies (e.g., through benchmarking) and *consistency* which ensures the application of policies or procedures over time. Despite the

---

who describes the business model as "concept or strategy under which a firm operates to add value from selling products or services to customers".

33 *Relevance* and *reliability* are the two primary qualitative characteristics of accounting information in the US GAAP, see FASB (1980): SFAC No. 2.

potential trade-off between *relevance* and *reliability* (e.g., information is required to be timely which could reduce its reliability), the FASB does not assign a superior role to either of them because it is assumed that any kind of dominance threatens the *usefulness* of information.

Figure 5: Qualitative Characteristics of Accounting Information

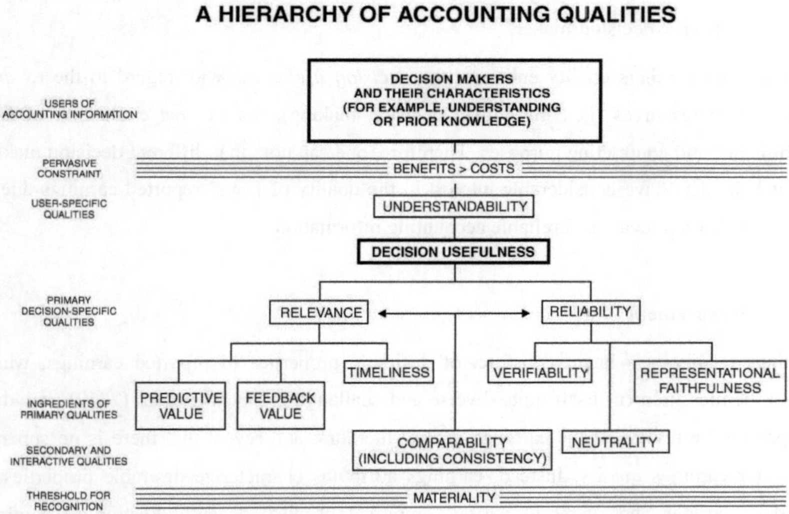

Source: FASB (1980): SFAC No. 2.

The SFAC No. 1 states that "the primary focus of financial reporting is information about an enterprise's performance provided by measures of earnings and its components."[34] Because Graham et al. (2005) confirm that earnings are the single most important measure of firm performance from financial reporting, the quality of earnings is viewed as a summary indicator for the *decision usefulness* of accounting information.[35] However, the accounting literature provides a variety of definitions for earnings quality. For example, from an equity valuation perspective, Francis et al. (2008a, p. 274) define high quality earnings as "precise with respect to an underlying construct that pertains to capital market participants." Dechow and Schrand (2004, p. 5) describe a high-quality earnings number as "one that accurately reflects the company's current operating performance, is a good indicator for future operating

[34] See FASB (1978): SFAC No.1, paragraph 43.

[35] For example, see survey studies of Healy and Wahlen (1999), Dechow and Skinner (2000), Schipper and Vincent (2003), Dechow and Schrand (2004), Francis et al. (2008b), Dechow et al. (2010), among others.

performance, and is a useful summary measure for assessing firm value." Schipper and Vincent (2003) consider earnings quality from the theoretical notion of (unobservable) "Hicksian income" as a context-free benchmark, which follows the idea that accounting earnings should faithfully represent changes in wealth.[36] Finally, Dechow et al. (2010, p. 344) derive a broad definition and state that "higher quality earnings provide more information about the features of a firm's financial performance that are relevant to a specific decision made by a specific decision-maker."

Overall, high earnings quality enhances the *decision usefulness* with regard to the *ex ante* allocation of resources (i.e., investment decision making), the *ex post* evaluation of firm performance and contracting purposes. Therefore, one can note that different decision makers and stakeholders have considerable interest in the quality of firms' reported earnings due to their reliance on relevant and reliable accounting information.

3.2.2 Measurement

Earnings quality is a latent construct of desirable properties of reported earnings, which makes the measurement itself quite diverse and challenging. Dechow et al. (2010) provide a comprehensive review of the earnings quality literature and reveal that there is no superior proxy for earnings quality. Instead, earnings attributes characterize desirable properties of reported earnings and represent various empirical proxies for an indication of earnings quality.[37] In general, the accounting research distinguishes between accounting-based and market-based measures of earnings quality. While accounting-based attributes only consider accounting information (e.g., cash flows and accruals), market-based attributes contain both accounting information and market data (e.g., information summarized in stock returns). Subsequently, I concisely discuss the most cited accounting-based and market-based earnings attributes, which are assumed to be correlated with the underlying theoretical construct.[38]

Accounting-based Attributes

Persistence captures the extent to which earnings currently persist or recur in the future. Highly persistent earnings are regarded as desirable because they indicate reduced variability

---

36 See Schipper and Vincent (2003).

37 In this thesis, I use the terms "earnings attributes" and "measures of earnings quality" interchangeably to describe desirable properties of reported earnings.

38 See the surveys in Schipper and Vincent (2003), Francis et al. (2008b), and Dechow et al. (2010), among others.

and thus are considered as sustainable and low-risk earnings. For example, based on persistent earnings, analysts can give more precise forecasts and investors receive more verifiable information. Hence, more persistent earnings lead to higher earnings quality.[39]

Predictability captures the ability of current earnings to predict future earnings.[40] Predictability of earnings is desirable because it is one component of relevance in the FASB's Conceptual Framework No. 2 as illustrated in Figure 5. High predictive earnings reduce the degree of uncertainty about a firm's performance and thus are associated with higher earnings quality.

Smoothness measures the volatility of earnings relative to the volatility of cash flows. A lower ratio indicates more smoothing of earnings compared to cash flows. Subramanyam (1996) explains that managers use their private information about the firm's future performance to smooth out transitory fluctuations in earnings by their reporting discretion using accrual accounting.[41] Therefore, smoothed (i.e., less volatile) earnings are desirable because they are persistent and predictable and indicate higher earnings quality. On the other hand, Leuz et al. (2003) show that smoothed earnings can be an indication of earnings management.[42] Because opportunistically manipulated earnings are less reliable, smoothed earnings are undesirable and lead to low-quality earnings.[43] Consequently, the dilemma of smoothness is that it is not clear whether it indicates a desirable or an undesirable effect on earnings quality.[44]

Accruals quality captures either the extent of how well accruals map into cash flows (Dechow and Dichev 2002) or the extent of estimation errors in the accrual process (Jones 1991). High-quality accruals are desirable because they either succeed in filtering the volatility of cash flows or lower the likelihood of estimation errors, both of which enhance decision usefulness. Therefore, accruals quality is positively related to earnings quality. In addition, accrual models are widely applied in the accounting research because abnormal

---

[39] See Sloan (1996) and Francis et al. (2004).

[40] See Lipe (1990).

[41] Accrual accounting is used by the management to accurately reflect the underlying firm's performance. In general, accruals represent all adjustments that allocate cash flows to reporting periods in which they are recognized (i.e., accruals filter the volatility of cash flows).

[42] We follow Healy and Wahlen (1999) and define earnings management as all actions taken by managers to intentionally alter financial reports through the use of judgments in financial reporting and in structuring transactions either to mislead some stakeholders about the firm's underlying economic performance or to influence contractual outcomes that base on reported accounting numbers. Therefore, earnings management is inversely related to earnings quality.

[43] Leuz et al. (2003) confirm that the extent of managerial discretion is reflected in accruals.

[44] A desirable relation between smoothness and earnings quality is described, for example, by Schipper and Vincent (2003), whereas Leuz et al. (2003) examine an undesirable relation between smoothness and earnings quality due to management intervention.

accruals (i.e., accruals which cannot be explained by normal business activities) and especially its components (innate and discretionary accruals) are used to capture distortions induced by firm and operating characteristics or earnings management.

Market-based Attributes

Earnings response coefficient (ERC) measures the responsiveness of investors to earnings information that has value implications.[45] Highly informative earnings are regarded as desirable because they are directly linked to decision usefulness in the context of equity valuation purposes.[46] Hence, the ERC is positively related to earnings quality.

Value relevance captures the ability of the level and change in earnings to explain variation in stock returns. Value relevance is closely related to the ERC while it also captures earnings changes.[47] Hence, Earnings with greater explanatory power are regarded as more desirable. Consistent with the ERC, value relevance enhances decision usefulness of earnings and is positively related to earnings quality.

Timeliness measures how timely changes in performance (stock returns) are recognized in current earnings following Basu (1997). Timeliness is desirable because it is one component of relevance in the FASB's Conceptual Framework No. 2 as illustrated in Figure 5. This value relevant (i.e., more timely) information is useful for decision makers such as analysts and investors and thus leads to higher earnings quality.[48]

Conservatism captures the extent to which current earnings asymmetrically reflect economic losses (measured by negative stock returns) relative to economic gains (measured by positive stock returns).[49] Conservative earnings imply a higher degree of verification to recognize economic gains than to recognize economic losses.[50] In consequence, conservative earnings are regarded as desirable because they prevent excessive distributions to shareholders. In this context, Basu (1997) has detected that bad news (i.e., economic losses) are more quickly reflected in earnings than good news (i.e., economic gains), which is also known as asymmetric timeliness. Watts (2003) argues that conservatism constrains opportunistic

[45] See Collins and Kothari (1989).

[46] See Dechow et al. (2010).

[47] See Francis and Schipper (1999) and Francis et al. (2004).

[48] See also Ball et al. (2000).

[49] See Basu (1997).

[50] Watts (2003, p. 287) defines conservatism as the "stronger verifiability requirement for the recognition of gains than for the recognition of losses." In addition, Ball and Shivakumar (2005) explain the distinction between conditional conservatism (i.e., the asymmetric recognition of gains and losses) and unconditional conservatism (i.e., the understatement of book values).

managerial behavior and thus reduces the extent of earnings management. Hence, conservatism is positively related to earnings quality.[51]

Overall, Dechow et al. (2010) reveal that the measurement of earnings quality is context-specific and thus depends on the particular research question. To examine the impact of coinsurance on earnings quality, I select earnings attributes that capture the volatility of a firm's business operations and estimation errors in the accrual process. The selection and calculation of these attributes for my empirical analysis is described in Section 3.4.1.

3.2.3 Determinants

The accounting literature describes a wide range of determinants which are associated with the various measures of earnings quality and the underlying theoretical construct.[52] These determinants (or sources) of earnings quality are commonly grouped into two categories: *innate* sources and *discretionary* sources. For example, Francis et al. (2008b) describe that *innate* sources arise from the business model and operating environment and are of a slow-to-change nature, whereas *discretionary* sources arise from the financial reporting process and rather change period-by-period. Dechow et al. (2010) and Dichev and Tang (2009) confirm that unique firm characteristics (e.g., firm size, performance, growth, debt) and features of the firm's operating environment (e.g., cash flow and sales volatility) are commonly used as *innate* sources of earnings quality.[53] However, Dechow et al. (2010) note that firm characteristics can also be associated with *discretionary* sources. For example, Jensen and Meckling (1976) find that larger firms make income-decreasing accounting method choice in response to greater political or regulatory scrutiny.[54] Therefore, Dechow et al. (2010) emphasize that the fundamental difference in firm characteristics must be controlled before inferring managerial opportunism (e.g., earnings management). The *discretionary* sources, on the other hand, comprise all components which affect the decision-making process of financial reporting: (1) managerial judgments and estimates (e.g., accrual choices);

---

[51] Timeliness and conservatism are both measured using the same regression and are combined also described as the concept of transparency. See Ball et al. (2000) and Francis et al. (2004).

[52] The earnings attribute is the dependent variable in an analysis about determinants of earnings quality.

[53] For example, Francis et al. (2005) use firm size, operating cycle, negative earnings, cash flow and sales volatility as *innate* sources to disentangle the *innate* and *discretionary* components of earnings quality.

[54] Note that the dichotomy between *innate* and *discretionary* sources is imperfect because many determinants of earnings quality have both *innate* and *discretionary* characteristics. For example, the selection of a Big-4 audit firm vs. a non-Big-4 audit firm has been used by researchers as a measure of managerial choice that affects the credibility of financial reporting. However, the choice of a large multi-national firm for a Big-4 audit firm is not *discretionary* but rather required by *innate* factors such as the firm's size and complexity of its operating environment.

(2) information and monitoring activities (e.g., auditors); (3) governance activities (e.g., ownership structure); (4) regulatory scrutiny (e.g., law enforcement); (5) reporting standards (e.g., US GAAP); (6) capital market incentives (e.g., earnings-based targets); and (7) other external factors (e.g., tax regulations).[55]

Overall, *innate* and *discretionary* determinants have considerable influence on the quality of reported earnings and must be controlled – with respect to the specific research question – to avoid erroneous conclusions.

3.2.4 Consequences

One of the most fundamental questions in accounting research is whether accounting information quality (or risk) is priced in the capital market.[56] Prior studies find a theoretical and empirical association between accounting information risk and cost of capital.[57] For example, Easley and O'Hara (2004) argue that information asymmetry between private and public information has a significant impact on the firm's cost of capital. They demonstrate that informed investors (with private information) are more efficient in shifting their portfolio weights to take advantage of new information compared to uninformed investors (with public information only). As a result, uninformed investors demand a higher compensation by a higher risk premium (i.e., higher stock returns) for holding stocks with more private information. Hence, Easley and O'Hara (2004) find that information risk caused by private (i.e., firm-specific) information is a priced risk factor.[58] Following the result that firm-specific information risk and cost of capital are positively related, Francis et al. (2004, 2005) empirically examine whether earnings quality as a source of firm-specific information affects

---

55 For a detailed overview of *innate* and *discretionary* determinants of earnings quality, see Francis et al. (2008b) and Dechow et al. (2010).

56 I follow Francis et al. (2005, p. 296) and define information risk as "the likelihood that firm-specific information that is pertinent to investor pricing decisions is of poor quality", whereby poor quality describes information that is imprecise and low in its extent.

57 I restrict my explanations to the effects on cost of capital because the cost of (equity) capital is the *ex ante* return demanded by investors and thus represents a direct indicator for investment decision making, see Francis et al (2008). However, the stated consequences of accounting information quality (risk) are also positively (negatively) related to other capital market consequences (i.e., higher firms' market valuation or higher accuracy of analysts' earnings forecasts). For example, Hope and Thomas (2008) document that firms which voluntary disclose information (i.e., through conference calls, preannouncements of earnings, or press releases) experience higher firm values by reducing information risk. Note that the earnings attribute is the independent variable in the analysis about consequences of earnings quality.

58 The traditional asset-pricing models such as the three-factor model introduced by Fama and French (1992, 1993) do not include information risk as a systematic risk factor (besides beta, size, and book-to-market). However, Lambert et al. (2007) find that high-quality disclosure reduces the cost of capital by improving analysts' coverage to turn private into public information and thereby confirm that information risk is indeed a priced (systematic) risk factor.

a firms' cost of capital. They find that higher earnings quality imply lower cost of capital and explain this link by a reduced uncertainty (i.e., less information risk) about firms' financial performance.[59]

In contrast, this link has been questioned by a growing number of studies (e.g., Hughes et al. 2007; Core et al. 2008; Caskey et al. 2015). Those studies show that idiosyncratic (firm-specific) risk can be diversified away in the capital market such that no cross-sectional association between idiosyncratic information risk and cost of capital exists. Because accounting information is mainly idiosyncratic in nature, these studies suggest that the link between accounting information risk and cost of capital does not exist in a well-diversified market.[60] However, a recent study by Hou (2015) finds that idiosyncratic information risk is priced when information is subject to managerial discretion, even in a well-diversified market.[61] While he confirms that diversification can largely mitigate the effect of the *innate* component of earnings quality on cost of capital, he shows that the link between the *discretionary* component of earnings quality and cost of capital is hardly affected by diversification. Hou (2015) explains this finding by the ambiguity of discretionary information, because investors do not have complete information whether managers' accrual choices are based on a signaling motive or an opportunistic motive.[62]

Overall, high-quality earnings as proxy for more *useful* accounting information imply low information asymmetry (risk) and thus reduce the cost of capital. In Chapter 4, I further examine the implication of accounting information quality (risk) for diversified and focused firms' valuation (i.e., *excess* value).

3.3 Prior Literature and Hypotheses Development

3.3.1 Literature on Corporate Diversification and Earnings Quality

Diversification as the business strategy underlying a firm's organizational form is subject of research in a wide range of financial economics studies. The firm's combination of different business segments creates diversification-specific effects, which have led to a controversial

---

59 For example, see Francis et al. (2004).

60 Several recent studies show that idiosyncratic risk has a strong association with idiosyncratic volatility. This suggests that a considerable amount of accounting information is idiosyncratic (e.g., Rajgopal and Venkatachalam 2011; Chen et al. 2012).

61 Hou (2015) uses accruals quality as a proxy for accounting information quality (risk).

62 Healy and Wahlen (1999) explain that managers have both a signaling motive (i.e., signal private information to investors) and an opportunistic motive (i.e., maximize their own interests) when choosing reporting methods and estimates.

and ongoing debate whether diversified firms trade at a discount or premium on firm value relative to comparable portfolios of focused firms (e.g., Villalonga 2003; Martin and Sayrak 2003; Maksimovic and Phillips 2007).[63] On one hand, diversified firms are considered as involving a greater level of information asymmetry, which leads to overinvestment problems and inefficient internal investments. These costs of diversification are held responsible for diversified firms trading at an overall discount compared to their focused counterparts (e.g., Lang and Stulz 1994; Berger and Ofek 1995; Denis et al. 1997; Krishnaswami and Subramaniam 1999; Scharfstein and Stein 2000; Rajan et al. 2000).[64] On the other hand, diversification allows firms to take advantage of coinsurance and efficient internal transfers which are counteracting the valuation discount (e.g., Lewellen 1971; Gertner et al. 1994; Stein 1997; Graham et al. 2002; Villalonga 2004; Tong 2012; Hann et al. 2013; Franco et al. 2016).[65]

Despite the large attention on valuation implications of diversification, the accounting implications of this firm-specific characteristic have received little attention in the literature. However, Dechow and Dichev (2002) emphasize the importance to identify observable firm characteristics which act as determinants of earnings quality. Since earnings are the single most important measure of firm performance from financial statements (Graham et al. 2005), earnings quality is a key indicator of the information content of financial reporting which affects the efficient *ex ante* allocation of resources and *ex post* evaluation of firm performance. For example, firms with high earnings quality and thus low accounting information risk are rewarded with a positive market outcome, such as higher market valuation and lower cost of equity and debt capital (e.g., Francis et al. 2004, 2005; Graham et al. 2005; Myers et al. 2007; Barth et al. 2013; Hou 2015). Moreover, earnings are also

63 Corporate diversification is examined under the implicit assumption of imperfect capital markets (e.g., with taxes, bankruptcy costs, or agency costs in contrast to a Modigliani-Miller (1958) world); otherwise firms' diversification strategies would be irrelevant to firm valuation. In order to diversify non-systematic risk, shareholders would be more efficient in diversifying equity risk within their own portfolios by buying and selling different firms' shares. Basically, market imperfections lead to the opposing effects of diversification on firm value. However, these effects cannot be easily mitigated or replicated by shareholders.

64 Alternative explanations for the valuation discount of diversified firms are the endogeneity of diversification decisions (Campa and Kedia 2002), selection bias (Graham et al. 2002), and problems from data and measurement (Whited 2001; Villalonga 2004).

65 Both inefficient investments (cross-subsidization) and efficient transfers (smarter money) are derived from the existence of an internal capital market within diversified firms which additionally enables managers to exploit their considerable discretionary power in operations (i.e., allocation of resources) either opportunistically or efficiently, for example, when financial constraints apply (Kuppuswamy and Villalonga 2010; Dimitrov and Tice 2006; Schoar 2002; Maksimovic and Philips 2002). For an overview of the bright side and the dark side of the internal capital market, see Stein (2003). I assume that such positive or negative operational synergies (e.g., economies of scope or agency costs) will be supplemental to the financial and accounting synergies examined here.

important with regard to their stewardship function in debt contracting or managerial compensation as well as for internal usage to manage the firm (Dichev et al. 2013). Following Dechow and Schrand (2004), I define high quality earnings to be those that accurately reflect companies' current operating performance, truthfully indicate future operating performance, and provide a useful summary measure for evaluating firm performance.

Evidence from Bens and Monahan (2004) suggests that the complex nature of diversified firms delivers a powerful setting to investigate the economic consequences of asymmetric information because this phenomenon will be more pronounced for diversified than for focused firms. Related to this, Berger and Hann (2003) find that more disaggregated information through segment reporting improves the monitoring process and thereby reveals additional agency problems of diversified firms. Berger and Hann (2007) and Bens et al. (2011) also find that managers of diversified firms withhold information on poorly performing segments or inefficient transfers because of an agency cost motive. Consequently, the link of asymmetric information underlying both corporate diversification and earnings quality has been examined by a growing number of studies, which find an agency effect (i.e., more agency problems through diversification) where managers of diversified firms exploit their greater opportunities to engage in earnings management (Lim et al. 2008; Chin et al. 2009; Rodríguez-Pérez and van Hemmen 2010).[66] In particular, Demirkan et al. (2012) document more internal agency problems, measured by lower discretionary accruals quality, in diversified than in focused firms. Their finding supports the view that diversification exacerbates information asymmetry problems and results in more severe agency problems.

While the archival literature in the intersection of corporate diversification and earnings quality has focused on asymmetric information and especially agency problems, the impact of coinsurance on a firm's earnings quality is still unclear. This is surprising because Dechow et al. (2010) argue that firm characteristics are associated with accounting method choices and estimates in earnings and thus must be controlled before inferring managerial opportunism. The notion of coinsurance goes back to Lewellen (1971) and suggests that the combination of imperfectly correlated cash flows reduces a diversified firm's bankruptcy risk (costs) and thereby increases its debt capacity relative to a portfolio of comparable focused firms. Thus, coinsurance can increase firm value through greater optimal leverage and results in higher tax

[66] I follow Healy and Wahlen (1999) and define earnings management as all actions taken by managers to intentionally alter financial reports through the use of judgments in financial reporting and in structuring transactions either to mislead some stakeholders about the firm's underlying economic performance or to influence contractual outcomes that base on reported accounting numbers. Therefore, earnings management is inversely related to earnings quality.

benefits (Lewellen 1971; Leland 2007).[67] In addition, coinsurance can also reduce financial constraints either by providing diversified firms with easier access to credit markets to realize optimal amounts of funding capital (Kuppuswamy and Villalonga 2010), or by allowing diversified firms to hold less cash due to a reduced *ex-ante* probability of financing shortages (Duchin 2010). Supporting this argument, Tong (2012) shows that coinsurance enables diversified firms to hold a higher fraction of corporate liquidity in the form of unused bank lines of credit. Beyond that, Hann et al. (2013) find that coinsurance lowers the cost of capital by reducing a firm's systematic risk. They argue that coinsurance allows resources to be transferred among business units of diversified firms, thereby avoiding some of the countercyclical deadweight costs that focused firms cannot avoid on their own. Franco et al. (2016) also find that high quality segment disclosures allow debt investors to assess the coinsurance effect of diversification more accurately, which reduces the firms' credit risk and thus their cost of debt.

In this chapter, I focus on the question whether coinsurance – the imperfect correlation of business activities – matters for a firm's earnings quality. This is a relevant question because the diversification-specific advantage of coinsurance is an observable firm characteristic, which counteracts agency problems of diversified firms and thus may also have implications for earnings quality. I believe that a firm's organizational form provides an ideal setting to examine potential accounting implications of coinsurance for two reasons. First, coinsurance is an exclusive feature of diversified firms because focused firms do not have a segment level (i.e., operate in only one business segment) and thus simply cannot realize coinsurance benefits. Second, the effect on earnings quality is likely to be stronger for diversified firms with less than perfectly correlated business activities and thus greater coinsurance potential. To the best of my knowledge, this analysis is the first to examine the link of coinsurance between a firm's organizational form and earnings quality.

3.3.2 Development of Testable Hypotheses

I argue that coinsurance among a firm's business units reflects a unique firm characteristic that is associated with a firm's earnings quality through two main channels: (1) less volatile

[67] Leland (2007) finds that such financial synergies can also have a negative effect on firm value. A negative effect from mergers can arise if firms have substantial different activities' volatilities (risks) or bankruptcy costs because of the loss of limited liability protection that discriminates better performing segments. However, the positive effect is more likely when correlations and volatilities of combined activities are low and similar, or bankruptcy costs are jointly high.

operations (financial synergies) and (2) less estimation errors in the accrual process (accounting synergies).

Regarding the first channel, standard portfolio theory suggests that the imperfect correlation of cash flows among a diversified firm's business units likely leads to a lower cash flows volatility at the firm level. Specifically, a diversified firm that consists of at least two different business units with less than perfectly correlated cash flows exhibits less volatile and thus more stable cash flows that the business units would not realize if operated as stand-alone firms. Therefore, coinsurance reduces the volatility of firms' business operations because of the aggregated nature of cash flows, making diversified firms less dependent on a single business and thus less economically risky. For example, Lewellen (1971) and Leland (2007) find that the combination of imperfectly correlated cash flows can in fact create financial synergies through lower bankruptcy risk (costs). Overall, coinsurance is negatively related to cash flow volatility, the latter being an indicator of uncertainty in a firm's operating environment. As prior studies have shown that earnings quality is negatively affected by cash flow volatility (e.g., Dechow and Dichev 2002; Francis et al. 2005; Dichev and Tang 2009), coinsurance should be positively associated with earnings quality.

Regarding the second channel, I extend the model of Dechow (1994) to explain the intuition of how coinsurance can affect the accrual process of diversified firms. Dechow (1994) models the generation of accruals as realized cash flows from sales for a firm with only one accrual (accounts receivable) as follows:

$$C_t = (1 - \varphi)S_t + \varphi S_{t-1}, \tag{1}$$

where C_t is cash collected in accounting period t, S_t is revenues generated from sales in accounting period t, and φ is a constant proportion of the firm's sales which is made on credit and remains uncollected until the next accounting period. Consequently, accruals for accounting period t, A_t, are:

$$A_t = S_t - C_t$$

$$A_t = \varphi S_t - \varphi S_{t-1}, \tag{2}$$

and represent deviations between revenues and cash flows by incorporating future cash flow forecasts (collection of accounts receivable). In the spirit of Equation (2), the variance of accruals for any type of firm is given by:

$$\sigma_{A_t}^2 = \sigma^2(\varphi S_t - \varphi S_{t-1})$$
$$\sigma_{A_t}^2 = \varphi^2(\sigma_{S_t}^2 + \sigma_{S_{t-1}}^2 - 2\sigma_{S_t,S_{t-1}}). \tag{3}$$

Equation (3) reveals that a firm's volatility of accruals is negatively related to the serial correlation of sales. That is, a firm with more persistent sales exhibit lower accruals volatility. In contrast, a firm which operates in a more uncertain environment or which expands its business operations within its segment to realize growth opportunities is likely to have more volatile sales (i.e., lower serial correlation of sales) and thus higher accruals volatility. However, consider for example a firm A which merges with firm B from another business segment. The sales of this industrial diversified firm are then $S_t = S_t^A + S_t^B$. Therefore, the variance of accruals for the diversified firm that consists of two different business units A and B changes to:

$$\sigma_{A_t}^2 = \varphi^2(\sigma_{S_t^A}^2 + \sigma_{S_{t-1}^A}^2 + \sigma_{S_t^B}^2 + \sigma_{S_{t-1}^B}^2 + 2\sigma_{S_t^A,S_t^B} + 2\sigma_{S_{t-1}^A,S_{t-1}^B}$$
$$-2\sigma_{S_t^A,S_{t-1}^A} - 2\sigma_{S_t^B,S_{t-1}^B} - 2\sigma_{S_t^A,S_{t-1}^B} - 2\sigma_{S_{t-1}^A,S_t^B}). \tag{4}$$

Comparing the accruals volatility of a diversified firm to an industry-matched portfolio of focused firms, Equation (4) enables me to motivate the intuition of how coinsurance can affect a firm's accrual process. Assuming that the variances of sales of the single business units A and B (i.e., $\sigma_{S_t^A}^2$, $\sigma_{S_{t-1}^A}^2$, $\sigma_{S_t^B}^2$, and $\sigma_{S_{t-1}^B}^2$) are not affected by the merger, the cross-segment correlation of sales underlying the covariance (e.g., $\sigma_{S_t^A,S_t^B} = \sigma_{S_t^A} \cdot \sigma_{S_t^B} \cdot \rho_{S_t^A,S_t^B}$) is positively related to accruals volatility. That is, less than perfectly correlated segment-level sales (i.e., more sales coinsurance) result in lower firm-level accruals volatility. This is a diversification-specific advantage because focused firms operate in only one business segment and thus cannot benefit from such offsetting effects across different lines of business segments. Moreover, the serial correlation of sales (i.e., $\sigma_{S_t^A,S_{t-1}^A}$ and $\sigma_{S_t^B,S_{t-1}^B}$) but also the cross-serial correlation of sales (i.e., $\sigma_{S_t^A,S_{t-1}^B}$ and $\sigma_{S_{t-1}^A,S_t^B}$) are negatively related to accruals volatility, consistent with such a relation for focused firms shown in Equation (3). Overall, Equation (4) reveals that coinsurance, *ceteris paribus*, decreases the volatility of accruals for diversified firms and thus highlights an unambiguous impact on the properties of accruals.[68]

---

[68] However, the net effect of diversification on accruals volatility is *ex ante* less clear. For example, if firm A and firm B have both less persistent sales and thus tend to merge to realize offsetting effects from diversification (e.g., financial synergies), the sales of the newly formed business units A and B remain less

This understanding is important because Dechow and Dichev (2002) document that the volatility of accruals can be used as an instrument for the propensity to make estimation errors in accruals and as such for accruals and earnings quality. Because a diversified firm operates in different lines of business segments and thus generates revenues from diverse business activities, accruals and its inherent estimation errors are likely to be imperfectly correlated among its business units. For example, Thomas (2002) argues that corporate diversification is not strictly associated with increased asymmetric information, derived from the accuracy of analysts' forecasts. He finds that imperfectly correlated errors in forecasting industry segment cash flows can lead to more accurate consolidated forecasts for diversified firms compared to forecasts for focused firms. In a similar vein, I focus on accrual estimations, namely the extent to which accruals of diversified firms exhibit a lower magnitude of estimation errors than comparable portfolios of focused firms. I argue that less than perfectly correlated estimation errors among a firm's segment-level accruals cancel out which may result in less estimation errors in firm-level accruals. More specifically, even if estimation errors in segment-level accruals are larger than the estimation errors of focused firms, the imperfect correlation of these errors may lead to more accurate accrual estimations of diversified firms relative to comparable portfolios of focused firms. Because of the aggregated nature of accruals in diversified firms, accounting noise is in part diversified away among their business units. Therefore, coinsurance can create accounting synergies through inducing a less noisy accrual process in diversified firms which reduces the relative magnitude of estimation errors in accruals compared to their focused counterparts.[69] Dechow and Dichev (2002) show that a lower magnitude of estimation errors in accruals implies that accruals better map into cash flow realizations, which results in higher accruals quality and more persistent earnings. Moreover, Dichev and Tang (2009) find that the effects of economic volatility (shocks) and larger magnitudes of estimation errors in accruals are negatively related to the predictability of earnings and thus earnings quality. Overall, coinsurance should be positively associated with earnings quality through a lower magnitude of accrual estimation errors and, in turn, a superior mapping of accruals to cash flows and more predictable earnings.

---

persistent and thus may even lead to a higher firm-level accruals volatility when compared to a portfolio of focused firms with more persistent sales (i.e., less incentives to merge).

[69] Accounting synergies leading to higher earnings quality and thus lower accounting information risk may arise because the mutual elimination of errors in accrual estimations and judgments among business units of a diversified firm cannot be replicated by shareholders. For example, Gomes and Livdan (2004) show with their theoretical model that diversification allows a firm to take advantage of synergies which can, if large enough, even eliminate the valuation discount. In my study, I focus on potential synergies created by coinsurance which affect earnings quality. Accounting implications on the diversification discount are not in my focus but provide a potential avenue for future research.

Note that in my main analysis, I do not disentangle accrual errors (i.e., abnormal accruals) into innate and discretionary components because both components imply low accruals and earnings quality. I aim to identify a strong relation between coinsurance benefits and earnings quality, irrespective of whether coinsurance reduces the magnitude of firm-specific (unintentional) or agency-driven (intentional) estimation errors (see Section 3.6.3 for further analysis on this point). This is also important because a greater level of information asymmetry induced by diversification may entail an even larger magnitude of accrual estimation errors for two reasons. First, the complex nature of diversified firms' business operations may make estimating accruals a more difficult task which leads to more unintentional estimation errors. For example, Palepu and Healy (2013) suggest that errors in accrual estimations depend on firm characteristics including the complexity of business activities and the predictability of the firm's environment.[70] Second, higher organizational complexity and resulting monitoring problems in diversified firms may induce managers to use their accounting discretion opportunistically by engaging in accruals manipulation which leads to more intentional estimation errors.[71] For example, managers of diversified firms may use their greater flexibility to make opportunistic accrual choices for simply boosting earnings and thus managerial compensation (Demirkan et al. 2012). Overall, these arguments suggest that asymmetric information problems counteract the beneficial role of coinsurance such that the net effect of diversification on earnings (accruals) quality is an empirical question.

I expect, however, that both of the coinsurance benefits lead to more stable and accurate measures of earnings for diversified firms relative to their stand-alone peers. Following Dechow et al. (2010), earnings quality is commonly determined by properties which measure the fluctuation and magnitude of reported earnings and its components (cash flows and accruals) over time. Because earnings quality is negatively affected by both operating volatility and accounting noise, I expect that coinsurance improves the earnings quality of diversified firms. Accordingly, I expect that reported earnings of diversified firms correspond more closely to the underlying business activities which, all else equal, lead to higher earnings quality. Thus, my first hypothesis is:

---

70 A diversified firm with less than perfectly correlated business activities faces higher complexity of its business operations since such a firm generates earnings (cash flows) from different business segments that require, for example, more and better information and knowledge of its various operating businesses, industry specifics and macro-economic conditions, as well as higher regulatory expertise.

71 The *transparency* hypothesis suggests that diversification increases organizational complexity which leads to larger asymmetric information problems for diversified firms (i.e., reduced transparency to corporate outsiders) compared to their focused counterparts (Thomas 2002).

Hypothesis 1: Diversified firms have higher earnings quality than industry-matched portfolios of focused firms.

In particular, I expect that the effect of diversification on earnings quality depends on the extent of coinsurance among a firm's business units. Thus, my second hypothesis is:

Hypothesis 2: The higher the coinsurance among business units of diversified firms, i.e., the lower the correlation of business activities, the higher the earnings quality.

However, both benefits of coinsurance are not mutually exclusive and may complement each other in affecting earnings quality. For example, Dechow (1994) argues that cash flows of firms that operate in volatile environments have more severe timing and matching problems which lead to larger magnitudes of accruals to shift or adjust the recognition of cash flows over time. Dechow and Dichev (2002) find that the volatility of a firm's business operations is systematically related to the propensity to make accrual estimation errors. More specifically, firms with high cash flow volatility and thus more uncertainty in their operating environment are likely to exhibit a higher level of accrual estimations implying more errors in estimating accruals. Because coinsurance reduces the volatility of diversified firms' business operations, thereby creating a less uncertain operating environment, estimation errors in the accrual process may be explained by systematic differences in operating volatility between diversified and focused firms. Therefore, I extend my analysis and examine whether the marginal effect of coinsurance on earnings quality varies with the level of operating volatility. I expect that the coinsurance effect is stronger for firms that are operating in volatile and uncertain environments since such firms are more likely to exhibit more accrual estimation errors and consequently benefit more from coinsurance on earnings quality. Accordingly, I predict that the positive association between coinsurance and earnings quality increases with higher levels of operating volatility. Thus, my third hypothesis is:

Hypothesis 3: The more volatile and uncertain the environment in which diversified firms operate, the larger the positive effect of coinsurance on earnings quality.

3.4 Research Design and Data

My coinsurance hypotheses relate a diversified firm's earnings quality to the coinsurance effect among its business units. In this section, I explain my main variables and my data and sample selection process to test my hypotheses of coinsurance benefits on earnings quality.

3.4.1 Variable Definition and Methodology

Earnings Attributes

As described in Section 3.2.2, the literature provides a multitude of earnings attributes. To examine the impact of coinsurance on earnings quality, I select earnings predictability and two distinct constructs of accruals quality. The first accruals quality measure is based on the mapping of accruals into cash flows (Dechow and Dichev 2002), while the second measure is based on abnormal accruals from the cross-sectional Jones (1991) model. I select these measures to capture firms' operating volatility and estimation errors in the accrual process, which likely explain cross-sectional variation in earnings quality between diversified and focused firms. Thus, I expect properties of reported earnings that are associated with the volatility of a firm's business operations and accrual estimations to vary with coinsurance among a firm's business units.[72]

My first measure of earnings quality is earnings predictability ($PRED_{i,t}$), which is the standard deviation of firm *i*'s residuals estimated over a 5-year window (*t* - 4 to *t*) from commonly used autoregressive regressions of current on 1-year lagged earnings following Dichev and Tang (2009):

[72] I do not consider earnings smoothness because the relation between less volatile operations and this measure is ambiguous. For example, one might argue that less volatile (more stable) cash flows should directly lead to *naturally* smoothed earnings. However, more smoothed earnings may either be a result of a closer correspondence to the underlying business activity or intentional accruals manipulation (Leuz et al. 2003). It is difficult to disentangle smoothness in terms of these effects (Dechow et al. 2010). I do not consider asymmetric timeliness (conservatism) because it is not obvious whether more or less timely loss recognition underscores the increased correspondence between cash flows and accruals of the firm. For example, Ball and Shivakumar (2005) suggest that timely loss recognition discourages managers from taking poor investments and provides debt holders with more accurate information about firms' performance. In contrast, Penman and Zhang (2002) suggest that conservative accounting facilitates earnings management through a higher amount of hidden reserves, and thus reduces the ability of current earnings to predict firms' future performance. Dechow et al. (2010) note that the results of earnings response coefficients (ERC) highly depend on the information context and are generally not applicable to decisions other than equity valuations. Finally, I do not consider benchmarking (e.g., target beating) and external indicators of earnings misstatements (e.g., restatements) because the role of operating volatility and accrual estimations in these indicators is less clear and more related to opportunistic reporting incentives rather than derived from the firm's organizational form.

$$Earnings_{i,t} = \alpha_0 + \alpha_1 Earnings_{i,t-1} + \varepsilon_{i,t}. \tag{5}$$

PRED is inversely related to earnings quality and thus lower values indicate high quality earnings and vice versa (see Table 3 for variable descriptions). Earnings predictability measures the remaining variation in earnings after accounting for the effect of earnings persistence (α_1) and sends an unambiguous signal of earnings quality. Higher predictability is associated with a lower degree of uncertainty (e.g., accounting information risk) about a firm's business operations for corporate outsiders and thus improves the assessment of a firm's future performance.[73] I expect the coinsurance benefits to reduce both operating volatility and accounting noise, thereby leading to more stable and accurate measures of earnings for diversified firms. As a result, I expect more predictable earnings in diversified firms through fewer problems in explaining future earnings from current earnings and consequently less variability of the earnings series compared to focused firms.

My second measure of earnings quality is accruals quality ($ACQ1_{i,t}$) measured by the standard deviation of firm *i*'s residuals over a 5-year window (*t* - 4 to *t*) from the cross-sectional Dechow and Dichev (2002) model and modified with the fundamental variables from the Jones (1991) model following McNichols (2002):

$$TCA_{i,t} = \beta_0 + \beta_1 CFO_{i,t-1} + \beta_2 CFO_{i,t} + \beta_3 CFO_{i,t+1} + \beta_4 \Delta Rev_{i,t} + \beta_5 PPE_{i,t} + \varepsilon_{i,t}. \tag{6}$$

I estimate Equation (6) for 48 industry groups (Fama and French 1997) with at least 20 firms in any given year (see Table 3 for variable descriptions). *ACQ1* measures how well a firm's current accruals map into past, present, and future cash flows, where lower values are associated with higher accruals quality and vice versa.

My third measure of earnings quality is accruals quality ($ACQ2_{i,t}$) measured by the absolute value of firm *i*'s residuals from the cross-sectional Jones (1991) model, where firm *i*'s residuals are performance-matched following Kothari et al. (2005):[74]

---

[73] Because earnings persistence and earnings predictability are derived from the same regression and thus are closely related (Dichev and Tang 2009), I concentrate my discussion on earnings predictability since it captures more directly the variability of the earnings series and is also an important component for valuation purposes (Lipe 1990). However, my inferences of unreported results for earnings persistence are comparable.

[74] Kothari et al. (2005) suggest a "performance matching" of residuals from the Jones (1991) model because of the correlations between performance and those residuals. Performance-matched residuals are determined by matching a sample firm to another firm from the same industry and year with the closest return on assets

$$TA_{i,t} = \gamma_0 + \gamma_1(1/ASSETS_{i,t-1}) + \gamma_2 \Delta SALES_{i,t} + \gamma_3 PPE_{i,t} + \varepsilon_{i,t}. \quad (7)$$

I estimate Equation (7) for each two-digit Standard Industrial Classification (SIC) industry group with at least 20 firms in any given year (see Table 3 for variable descriptions). *ACQ2* measures the absolute value of abnormal accruals of a firm, where lower values indicate higher accruals quality and vice versa. High quality accruals are positively associated with earnings quality because they either succeed in filtering the volatility of cash flows or lower the likelihood of artificial measurement errors in the accrual process. I use both measures of accruals quality to examine the accrual patterns of diversified firms compared to focused firms, especially the errors in accrual estimations. I expect coinsurance to reduce the magnitude of estimation errors in accruals through the imperfect correlation of these errors among a diversified firm's business units. Because less estimation errors indicate that accruals correspond more closely to cash flow realizations (Dechow and Dichev 2002), accruals of diversified firms may better map into realized cash flows. As a result, I expect higher earnings (accruals) quality in diversified firms through a superior mapping of accruals to cash flows and a lower absolute value of abnormal accruals compared to their focused counterparts.

Excess Earnings Quality

To compare the extent of a diversified firm's earnings quality to the earnings quality that its business units would have if operated as stand-alone firms, I adapt the procedure of Berger and Ofek (1995) and compute a firm- and year-specific measure of *excess* earnings quality (hereafter, *excess* EQ). For all three *actual* earnings attributes (i.e., *PRED*, *ACQ1*, and *ACQ2*), $excess\ EQ_{i,t}$ is the difference between a firm's *actual* earnings quality (hereafter, *actual* EQ) and its *imputed* earnings quality (hereafter, *imputed* EQ) in year *t*:

$$excess\ EQ_{i,t} = actual\ EQ_{i,t} - imputed\ EQ_{i,t}. \quad (8)$$

Consistent with the inverse relation of my *actual* earnings attributes, a negative (positive) *excess* EQ value indicates that diversification improves (deteriorates) the firm's earnings quality beyond their focused counterparts. I compute my *imputed* EQ measure

(ROA) and then deduct the control firm's residuals from those of the sample firm. I follow Kothari et al. (2005) because performance differences between diversified and focused firms are an important concern in the financial economics literature.

($imputed\ EQ_{i,t}$) for firm i in year t as a sales-weighted average of the *imputed* stand-alone EQ of its n business units (segments):

$$imputed\ EQ_{i,t} = \sum_{k=1}^{n} \frac{Sales_{i,t,k}}{\sum_{j=1}^{n} Sales_{i,t,j}} impEQ_{i,t,k}\ , \tag{9}$$

where $Sales_{i,t,k}$ is the total sales of segment k of firm i in year t, and $impEQ_{i,t,k}$ is the *imputed* stand-alone EQ of segment k of firm i in year t.[75] The *imputed* stand-alone EQ of each business unit is the median earnings quality of focused firms from the same industry-year. The industry medians are based on the narrowest SIC grouping that includes at least five focused firms with at least \$20 million of sales and has non-missing earnings quality values. The *imputed* EQ of a firm estimates the firm's earnings quality as if all of its business units were operated as typical focused firms in their respective industry and thus ensures an industry-matched comparison to the firm's *actual* EQ. *Excess* EQ captures the extent to which the firm's *actual* EQ value is below (above) the earnings quality estimate of a comparable portfolio of focused firms, or simply the advantage (disadvantage) from diversification. However, *excess* EQ provides not only a direct estimate of the overall diversification effect on earnings quality, but also enables further investigation at the segment level to identify potential sources of such an effect (Berger and Ofek 1995). In my analysis, I focus on identifying the relation between coinsurance among a firm's business units and earnings quality.

Coinsurance Measures

My measures of coinsurance quantify the effect of imperfect correlation of business activities among a firm's business units. The empirical challenge of measuring the extent of coinsurance among a firm's business units is that the joint distribution of future business unit earnings is not observable and historical business unit earnings are problematic because firm composition changes over time (Hann et al. 2013). Thus, I follow Hann et al. (2013) by using correlations of industry-level earnings based on focused firms. Industry definitions are based on the narrowest SIC grouping that includes at least five focused firms with at least \$20 million in sales over the last ten years. For each year in my sample, I estimate pairwise

[75] Calculating excess earnings quality as the natural logarithm of the ratio of a firm's actual EQ to its imputed EQ yields qualitatively and statistically similar results. I also calculate the excess EQ using imputed $Sales_{i,t,k}$ by using median total sales of focused firms in the same segment's industry rather than actual $Sales_{i,t,k}$ as robustness check and draw the same conclusions.

industry correlations using prior ten-year average industry earnings. I use earnings as my primary output of business activities because earnings are considered as the single most important indicator of firm performance (Graham et al. 2005). As coinsurance of cash flows is used as the standard measure in the financial economics literature (Duchin 2010; Tong 2012; Hann et al. 2013), I also estimate pairwise industry correlations using prior ten-year average industry cash flows.

I use the estimated correlations to construct my inverse measure of coinsurance, which I compute as a sales-weighted portfolio correlation measure ($\rho_{i,t}$) for firm *i* in year *t* following Hann et al. (2013):

$$\rho_{i,t} = \sum_{p=1}^{n}\sum_{q=1}^{n} w_{i,t,p(h)} w_{i,t,q(j)} Corr_{[t-10,t-1]}(h,j), \tag{10}$$

where *n* is the number of business units (segments), $w_{i,t,p(h)}$ is the sales share of segment *p* of firm *i* in year *t* operating in industry *h* (respectively for segment *q* of firm *i* in year *t* operating in industry *j*), and $Corr_{[t-10,t-1]}(h,j)$ is the estimated correlation of industry earnings (cash flows) between industries *h* and *j* over the prior ten-year period. In accordance with the inverse relation to coinsurance, less cross-segment earnings (cash flow) correlations imply more coinsurance and vice versa.[76] Note that the sales-weighted cross-segment earnings (cash flow) correlation measure equals one by construction for focused firms and for diversified firms whose business units operate in the same industry (Hann et al. 2013).

Volatility Measures

I use measures of earnings volatility and cash flow volatility as proxies for operating volatility to test my hypothesis 3 of whether the positive association between coinsurance and earnings quality increases for firms that operate in volatile and uncertain environments (Dechow and Dichev 2002; Francis et al. 2005; Dichev and Tang 2009). The imperfect correlation of segment-level earnings (cash flows) reduces the volatility of firm-level earnings (cash flows) in diversified firms by construction (portfolio effect).[77] Thus, coinsurance helps diversified firms to absorb economic shocks or to mitigate problems in the accounting determination of

---

[76] As an alternative coinsurance measure, Duchin (2010) computes a firm's cross-segment correlation in cash flow by additionally including the respective standard deviations of industry-level cash flow. This alternative measure of coinsurance, both for earnings and for cash flows, leads to similar results.

[77] I also compute the volatility of accruals and contemporaneous correlation between cash flows and accruals to provide a coherent picture of all single earnings variability components, see Table 3.

income which leads to less operating volatility compared to their focused counterparts (Dichev and Tang 2008, 2009). Moreover, the volatility of a firm's business operations is positively related to the propensity to make accrual estimation errors. As argued by Dechow and Dichev (2002) and Francis et al. (2005), high cash flow volatility indicates high uncertainty in the operating environment and the likelihood of more accrual estimations, with corresponding larger estimation errors and lower accruals quality.[78] Dichev and Tang (2009) find that the volatility of earnings dominates the volatility of cash flows because it combines economic volatility and accounting-based volatility with regard to earnings predictability. For example, firms operating in environments exposed to large economic shocks exhibit more volatile and less predictable earnings. Consequently, both earnings and cash flow volatility measures are directly linked to earnings quality. I interact my measures for coinsurance (i.e., cross-segment correlations) and my measures for operating volatility to examine whether the positive effect of coinsurance on earnings quality is stronger for firms operating in volatile and uncertain environments. Following Dichev and Tang (2009), earnings and cash flow volatility are calculated as the standard deviation of firm *i*'s earnings (cash flows) scaled by average total assets over a 5-year window (*t* - 4 to *t*).

Control Variables

To ensure that my results are not contaminated by non-operational and other mechanically related effects, I control for previously identified determinants of earnings quality. I follow Dechow et al. (2010) and control for different firm-specific characteristics including size, growth, performance, and leverage.[79] I also control for prospect of litigation, auditors, mergers and acquisitions, proportion of losses, and lagged total accruals which are potentially correlated with my measures of earnings quality (Demirkan et al. 2012). Including a measure of the operating cycle captures the speed with which accruals are converted into cash flows (Dechow and Dichev 2002). To mitigate concerns about a mechanical effect on earnings quality, I further account for factors known to reflect a firm's operating environment. Following Dichev and Tang (2008, 2009), I control for sales volatility as an economic factor

[78] High uncertainty in the operating environment is reflected by large standard deviations of residuals from accrual models. For example, if a firm has a high variability in residuals (e.g., by industry effects) so that the standard deviation of residuals is large, this firm has relatively low accruals quality because of high uncertainty about its accruals and thus its operations compared to a firm with consistently large residuals.

[79] For example, firm size often serves in the literature as an alternative proxy for diversification because diversified firms are on average larger in size (e.g., Dechow and Dichev 2002; Dichev and Tang 2009). In this context, larger firms may have more imperfectly correlated projects and thus experience greater benefits from coinsurance (Hann et al. 2013). However, Berger and Ofek (1995) note that firm size is a poor proxy for the complex nature of the diversification decision and the ambiguous diversification effects because the magnitude of these effects is not entirely determined by the size of the firm.

and for the correlation between expenses and revenues as an accounting factor to rule out that my results are driven by these effects. All variables are winsorized at the 1st and 99th percentiles (see Table 3 for variable descriptions).

Table 3: Variable Descriptions

Variable name	*Description*
Earnings attributes	
$PRED_{i,t}$	The (inverse) measure for predictability is the standard deviation of firm *i*'s residuals estimated over a 5-year window (*t* - 4 to *t*) from commonly used autoregressive regressions: see Equation (5).
$ACQ1_{i,t}$	The first (inverse) measure for accruals quality is the standard deviation of firm *i*'s residuals estimated over a 5-year window (*t* - 4 to *t*) by the cross-sectional Dechow and Dichev (2002) model and modified with the fundamental variables from the Jones (1991) model following McNichols (2002) and Francis et al. (2005): see Equation (6).
$ACQ2_{i,t}$	The second (inverse) measure for accruals quality is the absolute value of the cross-sectional Jones (1991) model performance-matched abnormal accruals for firm *i* in year *t* following Kothari et al. (2005): see Equation (7).
Excess earnings quality	
$excess\ EQ_{i,t}$	Firm *i*'s *excess* earnings quality is defined as the difference between its *actual* earnings quality and its *imputed* earnings quality of the earnings attribute (*PRED*, *ACQ1*, and *ACQ2* respectively) in year *t*: see Equation (8).
$imputed\ EQ_{i,t}$	Firm *i*'s *imputed* earnings quality is a sales-weighted average of the *imputed* stand-alone earnings quality of the respective business units in year *t*. The *imputed* stand-alone earnings quality is the median value of the *actual* earnings attribute (*PRED*, *ACQ1*, and *ACQ2* respectively) of focused firms from the same industry-year: see Equation (9).
Coinsurance measures	
$EAR\_correlations_{i,t}$	As (inverse) measure for earnings coinsurance, cross-segment earnings correlations for firm *i* in year *t* is a sales-weighted portfolio correlation of pairwise segment correlations estimated using prior 10-year industry earnings based on focused firms: see Equation (10).
$CF\_correlations_{i,t}$	As (inverse) measure for cash flow coinsurance, cross-segment cash flow correlations for firm *i* in year *t* is a sales-weighted portfolio correlation of pairwise segment correlations estimated using prior 10-year industry cash flows based on focused firms following Hann et al. (2013): see Equation (10).
Volatility measures	
$EAR\_vola_{i,t}$	Earnings volatility is the standard deviation of firm *i*'s earnings scaled by average total assets calculated over a 5-year window (*t* - 4 to *t*) following Dichev and Tang (2009).
$CF\_vola_{i,t}$	Cash flow volatility is the standard deviation of firm *i*'s cash flow from operations scaled by average total assets calculated over a 5-year window (*t* - 4 to *t*) following Dichev and Tang (2009).
$AC\_vola_{i,t}$	Accruals volatility is the standard deviation of firm *i*'s *total* accruals scaled by average total assets calculated over a 5-year window (*t* - 4 to *t*).
$Corr\_CF\_AC_{i,t}$	Correlation between cash flow from operations and *total* accruals is calculated pairwise for firm *i* over a 5-year window (*t* - 4 to *t*).
Control variables	
$Size_{i,t}$	Natural logarithm of firm *i*'s market value of equity (*MVE*) in year *t*. *MVE* is calculated as the stock price at the fiscal year-end times the number of shares outstanding.
$Growth_{i,t}$	Firm *i*'s ratio of *MVE* over book value of equity (market-to-book) in year *t*.
$Performance_{i,t}$	Firm *i*'s ratio of earnings to its average total assets (return on assets) in year *t*.
$Leverage_{i,t}$	Firm *i*'s ratio of total debt to its average total assets in year *t*.

Table 3 (continued)

Variable name	*Description*
$Litigation_{i,t}$	Indicator that equals 1 if firm *i* in year *t* operates in a high-litigation industry (SIC codes of 2833-2836, 3570-3577, 3600-3674, 5200-5961, and 7370), and 0 otherwise.
$Auditors_{i,t}$	Indicator that equals 1 if firm *i* in year *t* is audited by one of the Big Five auditors and 0 otherwise.
$Mergers_{i,t}$	Indicator that equals 1 if firm *i* had a merger in year *t* and 0 otherwise.
$Negearn_{i,t}$	Indicator that equals 1 if firm *i* reported negative (non-zero) earnings in year *t*, and 0 otherwise.
$Lagaccrual_{i,t}$	Lagged total accruals of firm *i* in year *t* scaled by average total assets.
$Opcycle_{i,t}$	Natural logarithm of firm *i*'s length of the operating *Cycle* [360 / (SALE / Average Account Receivables [RECT]) + 360 / (COGS / Average Inventory [INVT])] in year *t*.
$Ecofactor_{i,t}$	Sales volatility is the standard deviation of firm *i*'s sales scaled by average total assets calculated over a 5-year window (*t* - 4 to *t*).
$Accfactor_{i,t}$	Correlation between revenues and expenses is calculated pairwise for firm *i* over a 5-year window (*t* - 4 to *t*).

This table presents the description of all variables used in my main analysis. Following Francis et al. (2005), *Earnings* is defined as net income before extraordinary items [IB] for firm *i* in year *t*. Total current accruals for firm *i* in year *t* is defined as $TCA_{i,t} = \Delta CA_{i,t} - \Delta CL_{i,t} - \Delta Cash_{i,t} + \Delta STDEBT_{i,t}$, where $\Delta CA_{i,t}$ is change in current assets, $\Delta CL_{i,t}$ is change in current liabilities, $\Delta Cash_{i,t}$ is change in cash, and $\Delta STDEBT_{i,t}$ is change in debt in current liabilities for firm *i* between year *t* - 1 and *t* (respectively). Cash flow from operations ($CFO_{i,t}$) is defined as difference between firm *i*'s earnings and total accruals ($TA_{i,t}$) in year *t*. Total accruals for firm *i* in year *t* is calculated as $TA_{i,t} = TCA_{i,t} - DEPN_{i,t}$, where $DEPN_{i,t}$ is firm *i*'s depreciation and amortization expense in year *t*. $\Delta Rev_{i,t}$ is the change in revenue for firm *i* between year *t* - 1 and *t*. $PPE_{i,t}$ is the gross value of property, plant, and equipment for firm *i* in year *t*. $\Delta SALES_{i,t}$ is the change in total sales for firm *i* between year *t* - 1 and *t*. All variables are scaled by average total assets [AT] for firm *i* ($ASSETS_i$). I calculate total accruals using the balance sheet (indirect) approach rather than the statement of cash flows (direct) approach because statement of cash flows data is not available prior to 1988. However, while estimating total accruals I control for mergers/acquisitions and divestitures as suggested by Hribar and Collins (2002).

3.4.2 Data and Sample Selection

I obtain data of U.S. companies from the Compustat Annual Industrial files and calculate earnings attributes, correlation and volatility measures, and control variables, and from the Compustat Industrial Segment files to calculate *excess* earnings quality and coinsurance measures for the period from 1979 to 2011.[80] In my sample selection, I follow Berger and Ofek (1995) to avoid distorted *excess* value calculations: I require that (1) all firms have total sales of at least \$20 million in any given year; (2) the sum of segment sales must be within 1% of total sales of the diversified firm to ensure completely allocated sales among reported segments; (3) all firms with at least one segment in the financial service industry (SIC codes between 6000 and 6999) are eliminated from the sample; (4) all of the diversified firm's business units for a given year have at least five focused firms in the same 2-digit SIC industry with non-missing values for my earnings attributes. To be included in the final

[80] The Compustat database is provided by Wharton Research Data Services (WRDS). Standard & Poor's Compustat database provides a broad range of data of publicly-traded companies for financial analysis.

sample, I also require that each firm-year observation has data on all featured measures and variables from both the Compustat Annual Industrial and Industrial Segment files to provide sample integrity. After all restrictions, the final sample contains 40,520 firm-year observations, of which 24,738 (15,782) observations are focused (diversified) firms.

Panel A of Table 4 summarizes the selection process. Panel B (Panel C) of Table 4 reports systematic differences in firm-level (segment-level) characteristics of selected accounting variables between diversified and focused firms. I emphasize median values rather than mean values because of skewness in the distribution. At the firm level, diversified firms are more than twice as large as focused firms in terms of total assets ($473.8 to $206.6 million) and total sales ($538.0 to $247.3 million). Diversified firms compared to focused firms report higher median earnings ($16.36 to $6.89 million), cash flows ($30.25 to $12.48 million) and accruals ($-9.96 to $-5.50 million). Note that the matching level, as measured by the ratio of the absolute value of total accruals to cash flows, is lower for diversified firms (58.68%) than for focused firms (80.29%) which provides initial support that diversification leads to a relatively lower level of accruals and indicates, on average, less timing and matching problems of cash flows. At the segment level, diversified firms' business units tend to be smaller than focused firms, which is in part due to an incomplete allocation of resources by diversified firms to their business units (Berger and Ofek 1995).[81] In addition, business units of diversified firms are on average less likely to report losses compared to focused firms, which is consistent with lower operational risks for diversified firms. All median (mean) differences between diversified firms and focused firms are statistically significant at the 1% level.

[81] However, I find that the segment values of diversified firms are more comparable to the *imputed* values of focused firms which support the view that the median industry values of focused firms provide a reasonable benchmark to the diversified firms' business units. For example, the *imputed* stand-alone sales which are the median sales of focused firms in the same segment's industry amount to $142.6 million compared to $151.4 million of median sales for diversified firms' business units. Therefore, diversified and focused firms are more comparable at the segment level in contrast to the firm level.

Table 4: Sample Selection and Sample Characteristics

Panel A: Sample selection

Compustat merged annual industrial and segment file: firm-years over 1970-2012	502,424
Firm-years without duplicates from segment file	309,234
Firm-years with available data to calculate *predictability* and *accruals quality*	78,008
Firm-years with available data on *excess predictability* and *excess accruals quality*	57,919
Firm-years with available data to calculate earnings and cash flow *coinsurance*	50,148
Firm-years with available data on all *volatility measures*	50,148
Firm-years with available data on all *control variables*	40,520
Final sample size (1979-2011)	40,520

Panel B: Sample characteristics at the firm level

	Diversified firms			Focused firms			Difference	
	Mean	SD	Med.	Mean	SD	Med.	Mean	Med.
No. of segments	2.784	1.026	2.000	1.000	0.000	1.000	1.784***	1.000***
Assets ($ millions)	2,459	5,976	473.8	1,659	6,144	206.6	800***	267.2***
Sales ($ millions)	2,365	6,142	538.0	1,575	6,122	247.3	790***	290.7***
Earnings ($ millions)	108.4	310.9	16.36	78.0	493.6	6.89	30.4***	9.47***
Cash flow ($ millions)	208.2	554.2	30.25	153.5	811.8	12.48	54.7***	17.76***
Accruals ($ millions)	-99.9	351.4	-9.96	-75.5	463.8	-5.50	-24.4***	-4.46***
|Accruals| ($ millions)	118.3	345.6	17.75	90.7	461.1	10.02	27.6***	7.72***
Observations	15,782			24,738				

Panel C: Sample characteristics at the segment level

	Diversified firms			Focused firms			Difference	
	Mean	SD	Med.	Mean	SD	Med.	Mean	Med.
Segment assets ($ millions)	703.8	2,400	95.7	1,653	6,121	205.6	-949.2***	-109.9***
Segment sales ($ millions)	849.4	2.828	151.4	1,575	6,122	247.3	-725.6***	-95.9***
Negative earnings	0.007	0.084	0.000	0.210	0.407	0.000	-0.203***	0.000***
Observations	43,937			24,738				

I obtain data from the Compustat Annual Industrial file for calculating my earnings attributes, volatility measures, and control variables and data from the Compustat Industrial Segment file for my *excess* EQ and coinsurance calculations. Panel A reports the sample selection process for the analysis of *excess* EQ and coinsurance. Panel B and Panel C display systematic differences in accounting measurement and operating characteristics between diversified and focused firms. Accruals are total accruals, |Accruals| is the absolute value of total accruals, and Negative earnings is an indicator that equals 1 if a segment has negative earnings and 0 otherwise. For variable descriptions, see Table 3. Significance levels are stated for the difference between diversified and focused firms. The mean difference is based on a t-test and the median difference is based on a Wilcoxon Rank-Sum test. Asterisks indicate significance at the 1% (***), 5% (**), or 10% (*) level (respectively).

3.5 Empirical Results

3.5.1 Summary Statistics

Table 5 presents summary statistics for all basic variables (earnings attributes, coinsurance measures, volatility measures, and control variables) for diversified and focused firms. In

Panel A of Table 5, both mean and median differences between diversified and focused firms for all three *actual* EQ measures (*PRED*, *ACQ1*, and *ACQ2*) are negative and significant. This finding provides initial support that earnings quality for diversified firms is significantly higher compared to focused firms.

The coinsurance measures for focused firms equal one by construction because without an existing segment level, focused firms do not realize coinsurance benefits. The mean (median) earnings and cash flow correlations for diversified firms are 0.6672 and 0.6628 (0.6710 and 0.6667). This indicates a strong and consistent coinsurance effect within diversified firms since my measures of coinsurance are inversely related to cross-segment correlations. In terms of my volatility measures, earnings, cash flows, and accruals of diversified firms are consistently less volatile compared to focused firms, and thus both mean and median differences are negative and significant. In addition, the contemporaneous correlation between cash flows and accruals is stronger (more negative) for diversified firms. These results suggest less volatility in firm-level earnings and its components (cash flows and accruals) and initially indicate an increased correspondence between cash flows and accruals within diversified firms. Overall, these statistics are in line with the view that corporate diversification leads to less volatile operations and less accrual estimations.

Finally, among my controls I find that diversified firms are larger in size, have lower growth opportunities, are higher leveraged, have less litigation risk, engage in more mergers, and are less likely to report losses than focused firms. Among others, these factors reveal differences in firm characteristics between diversified and focused firms and have been identified as determinants of earnings quality in the preceding literature (Dechow et al. 2010).

In Panel B (Panel C) of Table 5, I show the correlation between my earnings attributes (volatility measures). As expected, all measures are positively correlated except for the correlation of cash flows and accruals and accruals volatility, which are slightly negatively correlated.

Table 5: Earnings Quality, Cross-segment Correlations, Volatility measures and Control Variables

Panel A: Basic variables

	Diversified firms			Focused firms			Difference	
	Mean	SD	Med.	Mean	SD	Med.	Mean	Med.
Earnings attributes								
PRED	0.0336	0.0310	0.0241	0.0626	0.0711	0.0377	-0.0272***	-0.0136***
ACQ1	0.0354	0.0291	0.0276	0.0550	0.0525	0.0389	-0.0196***	-0.0113***
ACQ2	0.0588	0.0655	0.0382	0.0864	0.1080	0.0511	-0.0276***	-0.0129***
Coinsurance measures								
EAR_correlations	0.6672	0.2599	0.6710	1.0000	0.0000	1.0000	-0.3328***	-0.3290***
CF_correlations	0.6628	0.2627	0.6667	1.0000	0.0000	1.0000	-0.3372***	-0.3333***
Volatility measures								
EAR_vola	0.0318	0.0283	0.0233	0.0535	0.0552	0.0330	-0.0217***	-0.0097***
CF_vola	0.0589	0.0371	0.0498	0.0764	0.0572	0.0597	-0.0175***	-0.0099***
AC_vola	0.0536	0.0355	0.0452	0.0658	0.0483	0.0523	-0.0122***	-0.0071***
Corr_CF_AC	-0.7950	0.2609	-0.9079	-0.6736	0.4057	-0.8598	-0.1214***	-0.0481***
Control variables								
Size	5.6843	2.2148	5.7881	5.2113	2.0557	5.0866	0.4730***	0.7015***
Growth	1.9475	1.6669	1.5175	2.1689	2.3931	1.5629	-0.2214***	-0.0454***
Performance	0.0408	0.0667	0.0475	0.0301	0.1110	0.0454	0.0107**	0.0021**
Leverage	0.2730	0.1847	0.2630	0.2668	0.2244	0.2387	0.0062***	0.0243***
Litigation	0.1685	0.3743	0.0000	0.2919	0.4546	0.0000	-0.1234***	0.0000***
Auditors	0.8759	0.3297	1.0000	0.8348	0.3713	1.0000	0.0411***	0.0000***
Mergers	0.1691	0.3748	0.0000	0.1165	0.3208	0.0000	0.0526***	0.0000***
Negearn	0.1474	0.3546	0.0000	0.2094	0.4069	0.0000	-0.0620***	0.0000***
Lagaccrual	-0.0323	0.0626	-0.0321	-0.0367	0.0833	-0.0332	0.0044***	0.0011***
Opcycle	4.7760	0.5207	4.8153	4.6944	0.7144	4.7936	0.0816***	0.0217***
Ecofactor	0.1410	0.0976	0.1165	0.1729	0.1348	0.1339	-0.0319***	-0.0174***
Accfactor	0.9454	0.1187	0.9896	0.8996	0.1868	0.9826	0.0458***	0.0070***
Observations	15,782			24,738				

Panel B: Pearson correlation coefficients for earnings attributes

Variable	*PRED*	*ACQ1*	*ACQ2*
PRED	1.0000		
ACQ1	0.6079 (.0000)	1.0000	
ACQ2	0.2639 (.0000)	0.3564 (.0000)	1.0000

Table 5 (continued)

Panel C: Pearson correlation coefficients for volatility measures

Variable	*EAR_vola*	*CF_vola*	*AC_vola*	*Corr_CF_AC*
EAR_vola	1.0000			
CF_vola	0.7008 (.0000)	1.0000		
AC_vola	0.4589 (.0000)	0.7601 (.0000)	1.0000	
Corr_CF_AC	0.6139 (.0000)	0.1133 (.0000)	-0.0822 (.0000)	1.0000

This table reports summary statistics for all basic variables used in my analysis. The three *actual* EQ measures, namely *PRED, ACQ1*, and *ACQ2*, are used to calculate my measures of *excess* EQ, see Equations (8) and (9). The sample includes 40,520 observations between 1979 and 2011. For variable descriptions, see Table 3. Significance levels are stated for the difference between diversified and focused firms. The mean difference is based on a t-test and the median difference is based on a Wilcoxon Rank-Sum test. Asterisks indicate significance at the 1% (***), 5% (**), or 10% (*) level (respectively).

The results in Table 5 provide initial support that a firm's organizational form leads to higher earnings quality. However, this simple comparison between both types of firms does not consider that diversified firms are not directly comparable to focused firms due to different firm characteristics and diversification effects (Berger and Ofek 1995; Bens and Monahan 2004; Hann et al. 2013). To compare a diversified firm's earnings quality to the earnings quality that its business units would have if operated as stand-alone firms, I use the *actual* earnings quality of focused firms to compute *imputed* earnings quality of industry-matched portfolios. In a more demanding comparison, the *imputed* EQ represents the benchmark for a diversified firm as if its business units were each operated as an industry-typical focused firm. Thus, *excess* EQ allows examining the difference between a diversified firm's earnings quality to the earnings quality estimate of a comparable portfolio of their focused counterparts.

In Table 6, I report summary statistics for all three *excess* EQ estimates (*excess PRED*, *excess ACQ1*, and *excess ACQ2*) for diversified and focused firms in Panel A, Panel B, and Panel C, respectively.[82] Because the results for all *excess* EQ measures are consistent and qualitatively similar, I focus my discussion on the results for *excess PRED* in Panel A of Table 6. For the diversified subsample, both mean and median *excess* EQ are negative and

[82] In line with prior literature, I include focused firms in my main analysis because they can be treated – from a diversification perspective – as firms without coinsurance but still may have some degree of diversification and operate in more than one industry not reported in the Compustat data (e.g., Duchin 2010; Hann et al. 2013). However, in my robustness section I exclude all focused firms and repeat my main analysis for the subsample of diversified firms.

significant (-0.0095 and -0.0106). For the focused subsample, the mean *excess* EQ value is positive (0.0086) and the median *excess* EQ value is zero (0.0000) by construction, moreover both are statistically significant.[83] The difference in mean and median *excess* EQ values between both subsamples is negative and significant (-0.0181 and -0.0106), which indicates that the firm's organizational form positively influences its earnings quality. In addition, note that the difference in *excess* EQ between diversified and focused firms is smaller compared to the difference in the *actual* EQ measures of both types of firms (in Table 5). In Panel D of Table 6 I show the correlation between my measures of *excess* EQ. As expected, all measures are positively correlated and similar to the correlation between the *actual* EQ measures (in Table 5).

Table 6: *Excess* Earnings Quality

Panel A: excess PRED

	Mean	SD	10%	25%	Median	75%	90%	Obs.
Diversified	-0.0095***	0.0330	-0.0441	-0.0249	-0.0106***	0.0030	0.0259	15,782
Focused	0.0086***	0.0382	-0.0317	-0.0123	0.0000***	0.0183	0.0687	24,738
Div – Foc	-0.0181***				-0.0106***			

Panel B: excess ACQ1

	Mean	SD	10%	25%	Median	75%	90%	Obs.
Diversified	-0.0074***	0.0260	-0.0360	-0.0221	-0.0088***	0.0047	0.0248	15,782
Focused	0.0052***	0.0277	-0.0258	-0.0109	0.0000***	0.0141	0.0475	24,738
Div – Foc	-0.0126***				-0.0088***			

Panel C: excess ACQ2

	Mean	SD	10%	25%	Median	75%	90%	Obs.
Diversified	-0.0122***	0.0702	-0.0839	-0.0518	-0.0199***	0.0165	0.0723	15,782
Focused	0.0122***	0.0666	-0.0607	-0.0276	0.0000***	0.0349	0.1113	24,738
Div – Foc	-0.0244***				-0.0199***			

[83] As proof of the validity of my benchmark approach, all measures of *excess* earnings quality are constructed with median values of zero for focused firms because the *imputed* values are computed by using median focused firms in each industry and year (Berger and Ofek 1995).

Table 6 (continued)

Panel D: Pearson correlation coefficients for excess earnings quality

Variable	*excess PRED*	*excess ACQ1*	*excess ACQ2*
excess PRED	1.0000		
excess ACQ1	0.4897 (.0000)	1.0000	
excess ACQ2	0.1706 (.0000)	0.2248 (.0000)	1.0000

This table reports summary statistics for my *excess* EQ estimates, namely *excess_PRED*, *excess_ACQ1*, and *excess_ACQ2* in Panel A, B, and C (respectively). Panel D presents Pearson correlation coefficients with two-sided p-values (below the coefficients) for all three *excess* earnings quality estimates. The statistics are computed over a time period of 1979 to 2011 for a sample of diversified and focused firms. For variable descriptions, see Table 3. The significance of mean values is based on a t-test and that of median values is based on a Wilcoxon signed-rank test. Asterisks indicate significance at the 1% (***), 5% (**), or 10% (*) level (respectively).

3.5.2 Results of Diversification on Earnings Quality

To ensure that my results are not driven by other factors influencing earnings quality, I start my analysis by examining the impact of corporate diversification on *excess* EQ for my sample of diversified and focused firms and include each of the control variables discussed above (see Table 3 for variable descriptions). The diversification indicator, which takes the value of 1 for diversified firms (i.e., firms that operate in at least two different four-digit SIC codes) and 0 otherwise, captures the overall effect of diversification (e.g., agency problems and coinsurance benefits) on earnings quality. Table 7 presents the results of this initial analysis with year and industry fixed effects and robust standard errors clustered by firm in parentheses.[84] Industry dummies are specified for each Fama and French (1997) 48 industry groups.

I find a significant negative relation between corporate diversification and all of my three measures of *excess* EQ. The coefficient estimates on diversification with *excess PRED*, *excess ACQ1*, and *excess ACQ2* as dependent variables are -0.0089, -0.0071 and -0.0204 and all significant at the 1% level.[85] Because a negative *excess* EQ value indicates that diversification improves earnings quality, I find that diversified firms have on average a higher earnings quality compared to industry-matched portfolios of their focused counterparts. Thus, after controlling for previously identified determinants of earnings quality, agency problems in diversified firms are not predominantly affecting earnings quality.[86] In most

84 Robust standard errors clustered by firm and year (two-way) lead to similar inferences (Petersen 2009).

85 Variance inflation factors (VIF) are all below common cut-off values.

86 In terms of construct validity, I also perform tests using measures of *actual* EQ for a naive comparison between diversified and focused firms (see Section 3.6.4). The coefficients on the diversification indicators

cases, the control variables have the expected signs. Overall, these results are consistent with hypothesis 1.

Table 7: Regressions of *Excess* Earnings Quality on Diversification Indicator

$$excess\ EQ_{i,t} = \alpha_0 + \boldsymbol{\alpha_1 Div\_Dummy_{i,t}} + \alpha_2 Size_{i,t} + \alpha_3 Growth_{i,t} + \alpha_4 Performance_{i,t} + \alpha_5 Leverage_{i,t} + \alpha_6 Litigation_{i,t} + \alpha_7 Auditors_{i,t} + \alpha_8 Mergers_{i,t} + \alpha_9 Negearn_{i,t} + \alpha_{10} Lagaccrual_{i,t} + \alpha_{11} Opcycle_{i,t} + \alpha_{12} Ecofactor_{i,t} + \alpha_{13} Accfactor_{i,t} + \sum INDUSTRY_t + \sum YEAR + \varepsilon_{i,t}$$

		Dependent variable		
	Pred.	*excess PRED*	*excess ACQ1*	*excess ACQ2*
Div_Dummy	-	-0.0089***	-0.0071***	-0.0204***
		(0.0006)	(0.0005)	(0.0008)
Size	-	-0.0035***	-0.0024***	-0.0022***
		(0.0002)	(0.0001)	(0.0002)
Growth	+	0.0017***	0.0010***	0.0015***
		(0.0002)	(0.0001)	(0.0002)
Performance	-	-0.0218***	-0.0096***	-0.0306***
		(0.0040)	(0.0028)	(0.0067)
Leverage	+	0.0021	0.0015	-0.0018
		(0.0017)	(0.0012)	(0.0020)
Litigation	+	-0.0015	-0.0023**	-0.0022
		(0.0015)	(0.0010)	(0.0018)
Auditors	-	-0.0012	-0.0021***	-0.0006
		(0.0009)	(0.0007)	(0.0012)
Mergers	+	0.0007	0.0008*	0.0013
		(0.0005)	(0.0004)	(0.0010)
Negearn	+	0.0057***	0.0014**	0.0071***
		(0.0008)	(0.0006)	(0.0014)
Lagaccrual	+	0.0002	-0.0175***	-0.0142**
		(0.0027)	(0.0022)	(0.0055)
Opcycle	+	-0.0005	0.0033***	0.0019**
		(0.0007)	(0.0005)	(0.0009)
Ecofactor	+	0.1016***	0.0767***	0.0480***
		(0.0032)	(0.0023)	(0.0038)
Accfactor	-	-0.0758***	-0.0340***	-0.0170***
		(0.0022)	(0.0016)	(0.0026)
Constant	?	0.0908***	0.0033	0.0178
		(0.0161)	(0.0067)	(0.0131)
Industry dummies		Yes	Yes	Yes
Year dummies		Yes	Yes	Yes
Observations		40,520	40,520	40,520
R-squared		0.3326	0.2513	0.0594

This table presents regressions of *excess* earnings quality on an indicator variable *Div_Dummy* which takes the value of 1 for diversified firms (i.e., firms that operate in at least two different four-digit SIC codes) and 0 otherwise. The predicted sign for *Div_Dummy* is negative because diversified firms are expected to have higher quality earnings and thus a negative *excess* EQ value. The regressions are estimated over a time period of 1979 to 2011. Industry dummies are specified for each Fama and French's (1997) 48 industry groups. For variable descriptions, see Table 3. Robust standard errors clustered by firm are in parentheses. Asterisks indicate significance at the 1% (***), 5% (**), or 10% (*) level (respectively).

using *actual* EQ measures as dependent variable are slightly above the coefficients using *excess* EQ measures, which indicate that the effect of diversification on earnings quality is less pronounced when comparing diversified firms with industry-matched portfolios of focused firms.

3.5.3 Results of Coinsurance on Earnings Quality

After confirming that diversified firms have on average higher earnings quality compared to industry-matched portfolios of their focused counterparts, I next examine whether these findings can be explained by coinsurance benefits. Table 8 presents the mean values of *excess PRED*, *excess ACQ1*, and *excess ACQ2* sorted into coinsurance quintiles in Panel A, Panel B, and Panel C, respectively. Diversified firms are divided into quintiles based on their cross-segment earnings (cash flow) correlations, where the lowest correlation quintile contains diversified firms with the highest coinsurance effect and vice versa. I also report the results for focused firms useful for comparison, even though they do not realize coinsurance benefits. Because the results for all *excess* EQ measures across the two correlation sorts are consistent and qualitatively similar, I focus my discussion on the first sort based on cross-segment earnings correlations for *excess PRED* in Panel A of Table 8.

I find a monotonic increase in *excess PRED* from the lowest correlation quintile (Q1) with the highest coinsurance effect to the highest correlation quintile (Q5) with the lowest coinsurance effect. The mean difference between Q1 and Q5 is -0.0262 and statistically significant. Consistently, the mean difference between the earnings quality of diversified firms in the lowest correlation quintile (Q1) and focused firms is -0.0309 and statistically significant. These results show that diversified firms realize coinsurance benefits which incrementally improve the extent of their earnings quality. Thus, consistent with hypothesis 2, diversified firms with less correlated business activities and thus greater coinsurance potential have higher earnings quality.

Table 8: *Excess* Earnings Quality and Cross-segment Correlations

Panel A: excess PRED

	Firms sorted by					
	EAR_correlations			*CF_correlations*		
	Sort Variable	*excess PRED*	Obs.	Sort Variable	*excess PRED*	Obs.
Diversified firms						
Q1 (Lowest)	0.4158	-0.0223	3,157	0.4100	-0.0229	3,157
Q2	0.5600	-0.0134	3,156	0.5532	-0.0136	3,156
Q3	0.6687	-0.0094	3,157	0.6655	-0.0086	3,157
Q4	0.7798	-0.0061	3,156	0.7754	-0.0059	3,156
Q5 (Highest)	0.9116	0.0039	3,156	0.9100	0.0037	3,156
Focused firms	1.0000	0.0086	24,738	1.0000	0.0086	24,738
Q1 – Q5		-0.0262***			-0.0266***	
Q1 – Focused		-0.0309***			-0.0315***	

Table 8 (continued)

Panel B: excess ACQ1

	Firms sorted by					
	EAR_correlations			***CF_correlations***		
	Sort Variable	*excess ACQ1*	Obs.	Sort Variable	*excess ACQ1*	Obs.
Diversified firms						
Q1 (Lowest)	0.4158	-0.0159	3,157	0.4100	-0.0159	3,157
Q2	0.5600	-0.0103	3,156	0.5532	-0.0106	3,156
Q3	0.6687	-0.0077	3,157	0.6655	-0.0068	3,157
Q4	0.7798	-0.0053	3,156	0.7754	-0.0053	3,156
Q5 (Highest)	0.9116	0.0023	3,156	0.9100	0.0018	3,156
Focused firms	1.0000	0.0052	24,738	1.0000	0.0052	24,738
Q1 – Q5		-0.0182***			-0.0177***	
Q1 – Focused		-0.0211***			-0.0211***	

Panel C: excess ACQ2

	Firms sorted by					
	EAR_correlations			***CF_correlations***		
	Sort Variable	*excess ACQ2*	Obs.	Sort Variable	*excess ACQ2*	Obs.
Diversified firms						
Q1 (Lowest)	0.4158	-0.0290	3,157	0.4100	-0.0303	3,157
Q2	0.5600	-0.0184	3,156	0.5532	-0.0180	3,156
Q3	0.6687	-0.0149	3,157	0.6655	-0.0135	3,157
Q4	0.7798	-0.0080	3,156	0.7754	-0.0081	3,156
Q5 (Highest)	0.9116	0.0092	3,156	0.9100	0.0089	3,156
Focused firms	1.0000	0.0122	24,738	1.0000	0.0122	24,738
Q1 – Q5		-0.0382***			-0.0392***	
Q1 – Focused		-0.0412***			-0.0425***	

This table presents *excess* earnings quality sorts based on cross-segment earnings (cash flows) correlations. Diversified firms are sorted into quintiles based on their cross-segment earnings (cash flow) correlations. For variable descriptions, see Table 3. The significance of mean values is based on a t-test. Asterisks indicate significance at the 1% (***), 5% (**), or 10% (*) level (respectively).

In my main regression analysis, I examine the impact of coinsurance (i.e., cross-segment earnings and cash flow correlations) on *excess* EQ for my sample of diversified and focused firms. Similar to Table 7, I control for previously identified determinants of earnings quality. Table 9 presents the results of this analysis with year and industry fixed effects and robust standard errors clustered by firm in parentheses.[87]

As in my univariate analysis, I document a positive relation between cross-segment correlations and all three measures of *excess* EQ, consistent with hypothesis 2 that coinsurance benefits are associated with higher quality earnings.[88] The coefficient estimates

[87] Robust standard errors clustered by firm and year (two-way) lead to similar inferences (Petersen 2009).

[88] The positive relation between coinsurance and earnings quality is explained by the fact that my measures of *excess* EQ and cross-segment correlations are each inversely related to earnings quality and coinsurance,

on cross-segment earnings correlations with *excess PRED*, *excess ACQ1*, and *excess ACQ2* as dependent variables are 0.0136, 0.0108 and 0.0304 and significant, respectively. Accordingly, the coefficient estimates on cross-segment cash flow correlations are 0.0134, 0.0104 and 0.0309 and significant, respectively.[89] Thus, I find that diversified firms have on average higher quality earnings compared to industry-matched portfolios of their focused counterparts. The results for the control variables are comparable to Table 7. Overall, these results confirm hypothesis 2 that firms with less correlated business activities among their business units and thus greater coinsurance potential have a higher earnings quality, even after controlling for other factors influencing earnings quality.[90]

Table 9: Regressions of *Excess* Earnings Quality on Cross-segment Correlations

$$excess\ EQ_{i,t} = \alpha_0 + \boldsymbol{\alpha_1 Correlations_{i,t}} + \alpha_2 Size_{i,t} + \alpha_3 Growth_{i,t} + \alpha_4 Performance_{i,t} + \alpha_5 Leverage_{i,t} + \alpha_6 Litigation_{i,t} + \alpha_7 Auditors_{i,t} + \alpha_8 Mergers_{i,t} + \alpha_9 Negearn_{i,t} + \alpha_{10} Lagaccrual_{i,t} + \alpha_{11} Opcycle_{i,t} + \alpha_{12} Ecofactor_{i,t} + \alpha_{13} Accfactor_{i,t} + \sum INDUSTRY_t + \sum YEAR + \varepsilon_{i,t}$$

		Dependent variable					
		excess PRED		*excess ACQ1*		*excess ACQ2*	
	Pred.	Model 1	Model 2	Model 1	Model 2	Model 1	Model 2
EAR_correlations	+	0.0136***		0.0108***		0.0304***	
		(0.0011)		(0.0009)		(0.0018)	
CF_correlations	+		0.0134***		0.0104***		0.0309***
			(0.0011)		(0.0009)		(0.0018)
Size	-	-0.0036***	-0.0036***	-0.0024***	-0.0024***	-0.0023***	-0.0023***
		(0.0002)	(0.0002)	(0.0001)	(0.0001)	(0.0002)	(0.0002)
Growth	+	0.0017***	0.0017***	0.0010***	0.0010***	0.0015***	0.0015***
		(0.0002)	(0.0002)	(0.0001)	(0.0001)	(0.0002)	(0.0002)
Performance	-	-0.0219***	-0.0220***	-0.0097***	-0.0098***	-0.0306***	-0.0311***
		(0.0040)	(0.0040)	(0.0028)	(0.0028)	(0.0067)	(0.0068)
Leverage	+	0.0019	0.0019	0.0014	0.0014	-0.0022	-0.0022
		(0.0017)	(0.0017)	(0.0012)	(0.0012)	(0.0020)	(0.0020)
Litigation	+	-0.0011	-0.0011	-0.0020*	-0.0020**	-0.0013	-0.0014
		(0.0015)	(0.0015)	(0.0010)	(0.0010)	(0.0018)	(0.0018)
Auditors	-	-0.0012	-0.0012	-0.0021***	-0.0021***	-0.0007	-0.0007
		(0.0009)	(0.0009)	(0.0007)	(0.0007)	(0.0012)	(0.0012)
Mergers	+	0.0005	0.0005	0.0006	0.0006	0.0008	0.0008
		(0.0005)	(0.0005)	(0.0004)	(0.0004)	(0.0010)	(0.0011)
Negearn	+	0.0056***	0.0056***	0.0013**	0.0013**	0.0070***	0.0070***
		(0.0008)	(0.0008)	(0.0006)	(0.0006)	(0.0014)	(0.0014)

respectively. For example, lower (i.e., more negative) values of *excess* EQ indicate higher earnings quality. Similarly, less than perfectly correlated earnings (cash flows) among a firm's business units (i.e., less cross-segment correlations) indicate more coinsurance.

89 Variance inflation factors (VIF) are all below common cut-off values.

90 I also perform tests using measures of *actual* EQ for a naive comparison between diversified and focused firms (see Section 3.6.4). The coefficients on cross-segment correlations using *PRED* and *ACQ1* as dependent variable are slightly above the coefficients using *excess PRED* and *excess ACQ1*, while the coefficient using *ACQ2* is slightly below the coefficient using *excess ACQ2*.

Table 9 (continued)

	Pred.	*excess PRED* Model 1	*excess PRED* Model 2	*excess ACQ1* Model 1	*excess ACQ1* Model 2	*excess ACQ2* Model 1	*excess ACQ2* Model 2
Lagaccrual	+	0.0001	0.0001	-0.0176***	-0.0175***	-0.0144***	-0.0143***
		(0.0027)	(0.0027)	(0.0023)	(0.0023)	(0.0055)	(0.0055)
Opcycle	+	-0.0005	-0.0005	0.0032***	0.0032***	0.0018**	0.0018**
		(0.0007)	(0.0007)	(0.0005)	(0.0005)	(0.0009)	(0.0009)
Ecofactor	+	0.1037***	0.1037***	0.0783***	0.0784***	0.0529***	0.0528***
		(0.0032)	(0.0032)	(0.0023)	(0.0023)	(0.0038)	(0.0038)
Accfactor	-	-0.0776***	-0.0776***	-0.0354***	-0.0354***	-0.0213***	-0.0210***
		(0.0022)	(0.0022)	(0.0016)	(0.0016)	(0.0026)	(0.0026)
Constant	?	0.0790***	0.0791***	-0.0061	-0.0058	-0.0083	-0.0092
		(0.0164)	(0.0164)	(0.0067)	(0.0067)	(0.0137)	(0.0137)
Industry dummies		Yes	Yes	Yes	Yes	Yes	Yes
Year dummies		Yes	Yes	Yes	Yes	Yes	Yes
Observations		40,520	40,520	40,520	40,520	40,520	40,520
R-squared		0.3269	0.3268	0.2448	0.2445	0.0502	0.0507

This table presents regressions of *excess* earnings quality on cross-segment earnings (cash flow) correlations for a sample of diversified and focused firms. The regressions are estimated over a time period of 1979 to 2011. Industry dummies are specified for each Fama and French's (1997) 48 industry groups. For variable descriptions, see Table 3. Robust standard errors clustered by firm are in parentheses. Asterisks indicate significance at the 1% (***), 5% (**), or 10% (*) level (respectively).

3.5.4 Results of Coinsurance and Operating Volatility on Earnings Quality

To examine whether the coinsurance effect on earnings quality is more pronounced for diversified firms operating in volatile and uncertain environments, I use two measures associated with the uncertainty in the firm's operating environment: Earnings volatility and cash flow volatility.

Table 10 presents for all three *excess* EQ measures two-way sorts based on cross-segment earnings (cash flow) correlations and earnings volatility in Panel A, Panel B, and Panel C, respectively. All observations are first sorted into above and below median earnings volatility.[91] Subsequently, diversified firms are second sorted within each volatility partition into quintiles based on their cross-segment earnings (cash flow) correlations. Similar to Table 8, the lowest correlation quintile (Q1) contains diversified firms with the highest coinsurance effect and vice versa. Because the results for all *excess* EQ measures across the two-way sorts are consistent and qualitatively similar, I focus my discussion on the second sort based on cross-segment earnings correlations for *excess PRED* in Panel A of Table 10.[92] The results in Table 10 show that the "Q1-Q5" and "Q1-focused firms" differences of earnings quality are stronger for the subsample of firms that operate in a high volatility

91 To facilitate my discussion, I only report the results for earnings volatility as sorting variable. Cash flow volatility as alternative sorting variable leads to unchanged inferences.

92 The results for all *excess* EQ measures across the two-way sorts are consistent and qualitatively similar.

regime, and that these firms have consistently lower earnings quality compared to the subsample of firms in the low volatility regime. Consistent with hypothesis 3, I conclude that diversified firms realize higher coinsurance benefits when operating in volatile and uncertain environments. I further document that earnings volatility and earnings quality are negatively related, consistent with existing literature (Dichev and Tang 2009).

Table 10: *Excess* Earnings Quality, Cross-segment Correlations, and Earnings Volatility

Panel A: excess PRED and earnings volatility

	Firms sorted by							
excess PRED	***EAR_correlations***				***CF_correlations***			
	Low Vola.	Obs.	High Vola.	Obs.	Low Vola.	Obs.	High Vola.	Obs.
Diversified firms								
Q1 (Lowest)	-0.0285	1,857	-0.0102	1,300	-0.0289	1,858	-0.0108	1,300
Q2	-0.0205	1,857	-0.0009	1,300	-0.0208	1,856	-0.0025	1,300
Q3	-0.0169	1,856	0.0019	1,300	-0.0166	1,857	0.0034	1,300
Q4	-0.0157	1,857	0.0074	1,300	-0.0153	1,856	0.0085	1,300
Q5 (Highest)	-0.0095	1,856	0.0173	1,299	-0.0096	1,856	0.0169	1,299
Focused firms	-0.0083	10,977	0.0222	13,761	-0.0083	10,977	0.0222	13,761
Q1 – Q5	-0.0190***		-0.0275***		-0.0193***		-0.0277***	
Q1 – Focused	-0.0202***		-0.0324***		-0.0206***		-0.0330***	

Panel B: excess ACQ1 and earnings volatility

	Firms sorted by							
excess ACQ1	***EAR_correlations***				***CF_correlations***			
	Low Vola.	Obs.	High Vola.	Obs.	Low Vola.	Obs.	High Vola.	Obs.
Diversified firms								
Q1 (Lowest)	-0.0192	1,857	-0.0092	1,300	-0.0188	1,858	-0.0095	1,300
Q2	-0.0140	1,857	-0.0041	1,300	-0.0150	1,856	-0.0047	1,300
Q3	-0.0114	1,856	-0.0021	1,300	-0.0107	1,857	-0.0008	1,300
Q4	-0.0100	1,857	0.0016	1,300	-0.0099	1,856	0.0021	1,300
Q5 (Highest)	-0.0053	1,856	0.0097	1,299	-0.0055	1,856	0.0089	1,299
Focused firms	-0.0037	10,977	0.0122	13,761	-0.0037	10,977	0.0122	13,761
Q1 – Q5	-0.0139***		-0.0189***		-0.0133***		-0.0184***	
Q1 – Focused	-0.0155***		-0.0214***		-0.0151***		-0.0217***	

Table 10 (continued)

Panel C: excess ACQ2 and earnings volatility

	Firms sorted by							
excess ACQ2	***EAR_correlations***				***CF_correlations***			
	Low Vola.	Obs.	High Vola.	Obs.	Low Vola.	Obs.	High Vola.	Obs.
Diversified firms								
Q1 (Lowest)	-0.0294	1,857	-0.0257	1,300	-0.0304	1,858	-0.0289	1,300
Q2	-0.0204	1,857	-0.0166	1,300	-0.0203	1,856	-0.0125	1,300
Q3	-0.0173	1,856	-0.0091	1,300	-0.0161	1,857	-0.0119	1,299
Q4	-0.0126	1,857	-0.0036	1,300	-0.0114	1,856	-0.0023	1,300
Q5 (Highest)	0.0042	1,856	0.0147	1,299	0.0029	1,856	0.0153	1,299
Focused firms	0.0051	10,977	0.0179	13,761	0.0051	10,977	0.0179	13,761
Q1 – Q5	-0.0336***		-0.0404***		-0.0333***		-0.0442***	
Q1 – Focused	-0.0345***		-0.0436***		-0.0355***		-0.0468***	

This table presents *excess* earnings quality two-way sorts based on cross-segment earnings (cash flow) correlations and earnings volatility. Observations are first sorted into above and below median earnings volatility and second sorted within each volatility partition into quintiles based on cross-segment earnings (cash flow) correlations. For variable descriptions, see Table 3. The significance of mean values is based on a t-test. Asterisks indicate significance at the 1% (***), 5% (**), or 10% (*) level (respectively).

Table 11 presents regression results of *excess* EQ on cross-segment earnings (cash flow) correlations and interactions with earnings volatility for my sample of diversified and focused firms.[93] Again, I control for previously identified determinants of earnings quality and include year and industry fixed effects and cluster standard errors by firm in parentheses.[94] The earnings volatility is measured as quintile rank that ranges from 0 for firms in the lowest volatility quintile (lowest uncertainty) to 4 for firms in the highest volatility quintile (highest uncertainty). In this analysis, I examine the link between coinsurance and uncertainty in the firm's operating environment. Thus, my main variable of interest is *EAR_Interaction* (*CF_Interaction*), which is the interaction term between cross-segment earnings (cash flow) correlations and my measure of earnings volatility. The coefficient estimate on *EAR_Interaction* (*CF_Interaction*) captures the marginal effect of coinsurance on earnings quality depending on the level of operating volatility. I document a positive and significant interrelationship between both cross-segment correlation measures and earnings volatility.[95] The coefficient estimates on *EAR_Interaction* (*CF_Interaction*) with *excess PRED*, *excess ACQ1*, and *excess ACQ2* as dependent variables are 0.0060 (0.0060), 0.0023 (0.0023) and 0.0056 (0.0061) and significant, respectively. I find that the marginal effect of coinsurance on earnings quality increases with higher levels of operating volatility after

93 I only present the results for earnings volatility. In unreported tests, interaction with cash flow volatility leads to unchanged inferences.

94 Robust standard errors clustered by firm and year (two-way) lead to similar inferences (Petersen 2009).

95 Variance inflation factors (VIF) are all below common cut-off values.

controlling for previously identified determinants of earnings quality.[96] In most cases, the control variables have the expected signs. Overall, diversified firms that operate in volatile and uncertain environments benefit more from coinsurance on earnings quality, which is consistent with hypothesis 3.

Table 11: Regressions of *Excess* Earnings Quality on Cross-segment Correlations and Earnings Volatility

$$excess\ EQ_{i,t} = \alpha_0 + \alpha_1 Correlations_{i,t} + \alpha_2 EAR\_vola_{i,t} + \boldsymbol{\alpha_{12} Interaction} + \delta_1 Size_{i,t} + \delta_2 Growth_{i,t} + \delta_3 Performance_{i,t} + \delta_4 Leverage_{i,t} + \delta_5 Litigation_{i,t} + \delta_6 Auditors_{i,t} + \delta_7 Mergers_{i,t} + \delta_8 Negearn_{i,t} + \delta_9 Lagaccrual_{i,t} + \delta_{10} Opcycle_{i,t} + \delta_{11} Ecofactor_{i,t} + \delta_{12} Accfactor_{i,t} + \sum INDUSTRY_t + \sum YEAR + \varepsilon_{i,t}$$

		Dependent variable					
		excess PRED		*excess ACQ1*		*excess ACQ2*	
	Pred.	Model 1	Model 2	Model 1	Model 2	Model 1	Model 2
EAR_correlations	+	0.0015		0.0063***		0.0207***	
		(0.0013)		(0.0012)		(0.0026)	
EAR_vola	+	0.0044***		0.0012**		-0.0030**	
		(0.0007)		(0.0006)		(0.0012)	
EAR_Interaction	+	0.0060***		0.0023***		0.0056***	
		(0.0008)		(0.0006)		(0.0013)	
CF_correlations	+		0.0013		0.0059***		0.0203***
			(0.0013)		(0.0012)		(0.0026)
EAR_vola	+		0.0044***		0.0012**		-0.0033***
			(0.0007)		(0.0006)		(0.0012)
CF_Interaction	+		0.0060***		0.0023***		0.0061***
			(0.0007)		(0.0006)		(0.0013)
Size	-	-0.0026***	-0.0026***	-0.0021***	-0.0021***	-0.0022***	-0.0021***
		(0.0002)	(0.0002)	(0.0001)	(0.0001)	(0.0002)	(0.0002)
Growth	+	0.0014***	0.0014***	0.0009***	0.0009***	0.0015***	0.0015***
		(0.0001)	(0.0001)	(0.0001)	(0.0001)	(0.0002)	(0.0002)
Performance	-	-0.0261***	-0.0264***	-0.0110***	-0.0112***	-0.0307***	-0.0312***
		(0.0039)	(0.0039)	(0.0028)	(0.0028)	(0.0067)	(0.0067)
Leverage	+	0.0026	0.0025	0.0016	0.0016	-0.0020	-0.0020
		(0.0016)	(0.0016)	(0.0011)	(0.0012)	(0.0020)	(0.0020)
Litigation	+	-0.0027*	-0.0027*	-0.0026**	-0.0025**	-0.0017	-0.0018
		(0.0015)	(0.0015)	(0.0010)	(0.0010)	(0.0018)	(0.0018)
Auditors	-	-0.0014	-0.0013	-0.0022***	-0.0022***	-0.0008	-0.0008
		(0.0009)	(0.0009)	(0.0007)	(0.0007)	(0.0012)	(0.0012)
Mergers	+	0.0011**	0.0011**	0.0008*	0.0008*	0.0009	0.0009
		(0.0005)	(0.0005)	(0.0004)	(0.0004)	(0.0011)	(0.0011)
Negearn	+	-0.0017**	-0.0017**	-0.0011*	-0.0011**	0.0056***	0.0055***
		(0.0007)	(0.0007)	(0.0006)	(0.0006)	(0.0014)	(0.0014)
Lagaccrual	+	0.0092***	0.0093***	-0.0145***	-0.0144***	-0.0124**	-0.0122**
		(0.0026)	(0.0026)	(0.0022)	(0.0022)	(0.0055)	(0.0055)
Opcycle	+	-0.0024***	-0.0024***	0.0026***	0.0026***	0.0014	0.0014
		(0.0007)	(0.0007)	(0.0005)	(0.0005)	(0.0009)	(0.0009)

[96] I also perform tests using measures of *actual* EQ for a naive comparison between diversified and focused firms (see Section 3.6.4). The coefficients on the interaction terms using measures of *actual* EQ as dependent variable are substantially above the coefficients using measures of *excess* EQ, which indicates that the naive comparison overstates the effect of coinsurance on earnings quality for firms that are operating in volatile and uncertain environments.

Table 11 (continued)

	Pred.	*excess PRED* Model 1	*excess PRED* Model 2	*excess ACQ1* Model 1	*excess ACQ1* Model 2	*excess ACQ2* Model 1	*excess ACQ2* Model 2
Ecofactor	+	0.0618***	0.0617***	0.0642***	0.0642***	0.0432***	0.0429***
		(0.0031)	(0.0031)	(0.0024)	(0.0024)	(0.0042)	(0.0042)
Accfactor	-	-0.0473***	-0.0471***	-0.0252***	-0.0252***	-0.0143***	-0.0139***
		(0.0023)	(0.0023)	(0.0017)	(0.0017)	(0.0029)	(0.0029)
Constant	?	0.0594***	0.0594***	-0.0123	-0.0121	-0.0068	-0.0071
		(0.0128)	(0.0128)	(0.0076)	(0.0076)	(0.0134)	(0.0134)
Industry dummies		Yes	Yes	Yes	Yes	Yes	Yes
Year dummies		Yes	Yes	Yes	Yes	Yes	Yes
Observations		40,520	40,520	40,520	40,520	40,520	40,520
R-squared		0.3842	0.3844	0.2566	0.2563	0.0514	0.0520

This table presents regressions of *excess* earnings quality on cross-segment earnings (cash flow) correlations, earnings volatility (ranked in quintiles from 0 to 4), and an interaction with the respective correlations and earnings volatility ($\alpha_{12} Correlations_{i,t} * EAR\_vola_{i,t}$) for a sample of diversified and focused firms. The regressions are estimated over a time period of 1979 to 2011. Industry dummies are specified for each Fama and French's (1997) 48 industry groups. For variable descriptions, see Table 3. Robust standard errors clustered by firm are in parentheses. Asterisks indicate significance at the 1% (***), 5% (**), or 10% (*) level (respectively).

3.6 Robustness Checks and Additional Results

In this section, I check the robustness of my main results. First, I repeat my coinsurance analysis for the subsample of diversified firms. Second, I address potential endogeneity concerns by testing whether the inclusion of firm-fixed effects changes the inferences of my results, and by investigating whether my estimates of coinsurance are biased due to self-selection emerging from a firm's decision to diversify. In addition, I examine whether the coinsurance effect on accruals quality can be explained by innate and discretionary sources. Finally, I use *actual* earnings quality instead of *excess* earnings quality to check the validity of my approach to compare the earnings quality between diversified and focused firms.

3.6.1 Subsample of Diversified Firms

In contrast to focused firms, diversified firms can realize coinsurance benefits by cross-correlation on their segment level, which is impossible for focused firms. Accordingly, the extent of the coinsurance benefits should be more distinct for diversified firms with less correlated business activities and thus greater coinsurance potential. I test this coinsurance effect by repeating my main regression analyses for the subsample of diversified firms.

Table 12 presents regression results with year and industry fixed effects and robust standard errors clustered by firm in parentheses. The results are comparable to those for the full-sample. Consistently, I document a significant positive relation between earnings (cash flows) coinsurance and *excess* earnings quality. However, the relation is less pronounced compared to the full-sample because I exclude focused firms which – by construction – do not have any coinsurance potential and thus do not enhance the difference in earnings quality in this analysis.[97]

Table 12: Regressions of *Excess* Earnings Quality on Cross-segment Correlations: Diversified Sample

$$excess\ EQ_{i,t} = \alpha_0 + \boldsymbol{\alpha_1 Correlations_{i,t}} + \alpha_2 Size_{i,t} + \alpha_3 Growth_{i,t} + \alpha_4 Performance_{i,t} + \alpha_5 Leverage_{i,t} + \alpha_6 Litigation_{i,t} + \alpha_7 Auditors_{i,t} + \alpha_8 Mergers_{i,t} + \alpha_9 Negearn_{i,t} + \alpha_{10} Lagaccrual_{i,t} + \alpha_{11} Opcycle_{i,t} + \alpha_{12} Ecofactor_{i,t} + \alpha_{13} Accfactor_{i,t} + \sum INDUSTRY_t + \sum YEAR + \varepsilon_{i,t}$$

		Dependent variable					
		excess PRED		*excess ACQ1*		*excess ACQ2*	
	Pred.	Model 1	Model 2	Model 1	Model 2	Model 1	Model 2
EAR_correlations	+	0.0074***		0.0043***		0.0084***	
		(0.0013)		(0.0010)		(0.0020)	
CF_correlations	+		0.0073***		0.0037***		0.0095***
			(0.0013)		(0.0010)		(0.0020)
Size	-	-0.0034***	-0.0034***	-0.0023***	-0.0023***	-0.0020***	-0.0020***
		(0.0002)	(0.0002)	(0.0002)	(0.0002)	(0.0003)	(0.0003)
Growth	+	0.0016***	0.0016***	0.0006***	0.0006***	0.0015***	0.0015***
		(0.0003)	(0.0003)	(0.0002)	(0.0002)	(0.0005)	(0.0004)
Performance	-	-0.0096	-0.0101	0.0010	0.0008	-0.0075	-0.0083
		(0.0074)	(0.0074)	(0.0061)	(0.0061)	(0.0151)	(0.0149)
Leverage	+	0.0029	0.0029	0.0013	0.0013	-0.0000	-0.0001
		(0.0023)	(0.0023)	(0.0019)	(0.0019)	(0.0034)	(0.0034)
Litigation	+	-0.0004	0.0004	-0.0033**	-0.0033**	-0.0063**	-0.0063**
		(0.0019)	(0.0019)	(0.0014)	(0.0014)	(0.0025)	(0.0024)
Auditors	-	-0.0000	-0.0000	-0.0001	-0.0001	0.0009	0.0010
		(0.0013)	(0.0013)	(0.0010)	(0.0010)	(0.0019)	(0.0019)
Mergers	+	0.0003	0.0003	0.0003	0.0003	-0.0005	-0.0005
		(0.0006)	(0.0006)	(0.0005)	(0.0005)	(0.0014)	(0.0014)
Negearn	+	0.0053***	0.0053***	0.0010	0.0010	0.0073***	0.0072***
		(0.0010)	(0.0010)	(0.0009)	(0.0009)	(0.0024)	(0.0024)
Lagaccrual	+	-0.0012	-0.0011	-0.0046	-0.0046	-0.0121	-0.0120
		(0.0045)	(0.0045)	(0.0037)	(0.0037)	(0.0092)	(0.0091)
Opcycle	+	-0.0028***	-0.0028***	0.0025***	0.0025***	0.0008	0.0009
		(0.0011)	(0.0011)	(0.0009)	(0.0009)	(0.0016)	(0.0015)
Ecofactor	+	0.0508***	0.0508***	0.0469***	0.0470***	0.0159**	0.0159**
		(0.0041)	(0.0041)	(0.0035)	(0.0035)	(0.0069)	(0.0068)
Accfactor	-	-0.0486***	-0.0484***	-0.0169***	-0.0168***	-0.0102*	-0.0099*
		(0.0035)	(0.0035)	(0.0024)	(0.0024)	(0.0053)	(0.0052)
Constant	?	0.0618***	0.0617***	-0.0151***	-0.0148***	-0.0795***	-0.0805***
		(0.0059)	(0.0059)	(0.0044)	(0.0044)	(0.0095)	(0.0094)
Industry dummies		Yes	Yes	Yes	Yes	Yes	Yes
Year dummies		Yes	Yes	Yes	Yes	Yes	Yes
Observations		15,782	15,782	15,782	15,782	15,782	15,782
R-squared		0.2101	0.2100	0.1577	0.1572	0.0283	0.0286

[97] For example, focused firms that operate in the same industry as diversified firms have a relatively higher operating volatility and thus lower earnings quality. This increases the difference in *excess* earnings quality between diversified and focused firms.

Table 12 (continued)

This table presents regressions of *excess* earnings quality on cross-segment earnings (cash flow) correlations for the subsample of diversified firms. The regressions are estimated over a time period of 1979 to 2011. Industry dummies are specified for each Fama and French's (1997) 48 industry groups. For variable descriptions, see Table 3. Robust standard errors clustered by firm are in parentheses. Asterisks indicate significance at the 1% (***), 5% (**), or 10% (*) level (respectively).

Table 13 presents regression results of the analysis whether the coinsurance effect on earnings quality is stronger for diversified firms that operate in volatile and uncertain environments. In accordance with the results of Table 11, I document a significant positive interaction between both coinsurance measures and earnings volatility. This indicates that the positive association between coinsurance and earnings quality is stronger for higher levels of operating volatility. Thus, the coinsurance effect on earnings quality remains stronger for diversified firms facing higher operating volatility.

Table 13: Regressions of *Excess* Earnings Quality on Cross-segment Correlations and Earnings Volatility: Diversified Sample

$$excess\ EQ_{i,t} = \alpha_0 + \alpha_1 Correlations_{i,t} + \alpha_2 EAR\_vola_{i,t} + \boldsymbol{\alpha_{12} Interaction} + \delta_1 Size_{i,t} + \delta_2 Growth_{i,t} + \delta_3 Performance_{i,t} + \delta_4 Leverage_{i,t} + \delta_5 Litigation_{i,t} + \delta_6 Auditors_{i,t} + \delta_7 Mergers_{i,t} + \delta_8 Negearn_{i,t} + \delta_9 Lagaccrual_{i,t} + \delta_{10} Opcycle_{i,t} + \delta_{11} Ecofactor_{i,t} + \delta_{12} Accfactor_{i,t} + \Sigma INDUSTRY_t + \Sigma YEAR + \varepsilon_{i,t}$$

		Dependent variable					
		excess PRED		*excess ACQ1*		*excess ACQ2*	
	Pred.	Model 1	Model 2	Model 1	Model 2	Model 1	Model 2
EAR_correlations	+	-0.0191***		-0.0178***		-0.0656***	
		(0.0018)		(0.0015)		(0.0036)	
EAR_vola	+	0.0022***		-0.0012**		-0.0125***	
		(0.0006)		(0.0005)		(0.0013)	
EAR_Interaction	+	0.0104***		0.0102***		0.0346***	
		(0.0009)		(0.0007)		(0.0018)	
CF_correlations	+		-0.0187***		-0.0179***		-0.0659***
			(0.0018)		(0.0015)		(0.0037)
EAR_vola	+		0.0024***		-0.0010*		-0.0129***
			(0.0006)		(0.0006)		(0.0013)
CF_Interaction	+		0.0102***		0.0100***		0.0354***
			(0.0009)		(0.0007)		(0.0018)
Size	-	-0.0029***	-0.0029***	-0.0020***	-0.0020***	-0.0015***	-0.0015***
		(0.0002)	(0.0002)	(0.0002)	(0.0002)	(0.0004)	(0.0004)
Growth	+	0.0014***	0.0014***	0.0005**	0.0005**	0.0013**	0.0013***
		(0.0003)	(0.0003)	(0.0002)	(0.0002)	(0.0005)	(0.0005)
Performance	-	-0.0200***	-0.0212***	0.0001	-0.0010	-0.0057	-0.0097
		(0.0074)	(0.0074)	(0.0061)	(0.0061)	(0.0158)	(0.0158)
Leverage	+	0.0053**	0.0050**	0.0020	0.0017	0.0017	0.0007
		(0.0024)	(0.0024)	(0.0019)	(0.0019)	(0.0037)	(0.0037)
Litigation	+	-0.0018	-0.0016	-0.0042***	-0.0041***	-0.0073***	-0.0069***
		(0.0020)	(0.0020)	(0.0014)	(0.0014)	(0.0026)	(0.0026)
Auditors	-	-0.0001	-0.0000	-0.0006	-0.0005	0.0010	0.0013
		(0.0013)	(0.0013)	(0.0011)	(0.0011)	(0.0020)	(0.0020)

Table 13 (continued)

	Pred.	*excess PRED* Model 1	Model 2	*excess ACQ1* Model 1	Model 2	*excess ACQ2* Model 1	Model 2
Mergers	+	0.0012*	0.0011*	0.0008	0.0008	-0.0001	-0.0002
		(0.0006)	(0.0006)	(0.0005)	(0.0005)	(0.0015)	(0.0015)
Negearn	+	-0.0002	-0.0002	-0.0016*	-0.0017*	0.0029	0.0028
		(0.0010)	(0.0010)	(0.0009)	(0.0009)	(0.0025)	(0.0025)
Lagaccrual	+	0.0062	0.0066	-0.0024	-0.0021	-0.0077	-0.0068
		(0.0044)	(0.0044)	(0.0037)	(0.0037)	(0.0099)	(0.0098)
Opcycle	+	-0.0042***	-0.0042***	0.0018**	0.0017**	-0.0006	-0.0008
		(0.0010)	(0.0010)	(0.0009)	(0.0009)	(0.0017)	(0.0017)
Ecofactor	+	0.0241***	0.0244***	0.0334***	0.0336***	-0.0123	-0.0109
		(0.0040)	(0.0040)	(0.0037)	(0.0037)	(0.0076)	(0.0076)
Accfactor	-	-0.0281***	-0.0277***	-0.0045*	-0.0040	0.0122**	0.0134**
		(0.0035)	(0.0035)	(0.0025)	(0.0025)	(0.0058)	(0.0058)
Constant	?	0.0606***	0.0603***	-0.0137***	-0.0138***	-0.0559***	-0.0558***
		(0.0059)	(0.0059)	(0.0045)	(0.0045)	(0.0104)	(0.0103)
Industry dummies		Yes	Yes	Yes	Yes	Yes	Yes
Year dummies		Yes	Yes	Yes	Yes	Yes	Yes
Observations		15,782	15,782	15,782	15,782	15,782	15,782
R-squared		0.3684	0.3684	0.2635	0.2630	0.1012	0.1034

This table presents regressions of *excess* earnings quality on cross-segment earnings (cash flow) correlations, earnings volatility (ranked in quintiles from 0 to 4), and an interaction with the respective correlations and earnings volatility ($\alpha_{12} Correlations_{i,t} * EAR\_vola_{i,t}$) for the subsample of diversified firms. The regressions are estimated over a time period of 1979 to 2011. Industry dummies are specified for each Fama and French's (1997) 48 industry groups. For variable descriptions, see Table 3. Robust standard errors clustered by firm are in parentheses. Asterisks indicate significance at the 1% (***), 5% (**), or 10% (*) level (respectively).

3.6.2 Endogeneity of Diversification Decision

To examine firm-specific beyond industry-wide effects, I use the firm-fixed effect estimator to control for unobserved firm heterogeneity.[98] Firm-fixed effects models control for all time-invariant differences across firms while considering only those characteristics that vary over time within each firm. Thus, I check the robustness of my main results by investigating the causes of changes in earnings quality within a firm. Table 14 shows results from this modification of my main regression analysis. Similar to the regression results in Table 9, the coefficient estimates on cross-segment earnings (cash flows) correlations are all positive, significant and similar with respect to their magnitudes. These results confirm that firms with more coinsurance exhibit higher earnings quality.

98 The application of the firm-fixed effects model is confirmed by the Hausman (1978) specification test.

Table 14: Regressions of *Excess* Earnings Quality on Cross-segment Correlations: Controlling for Unobserved Heterogeneity

$$excess\ EQ_{i,t} = \alpha_0 + \alpha_1 \boldsymbol{Correlations}_{i,t} + \alpha_2 Size_{i,t} + \alpha_3 Growth_{i,t} + \alpha_4 Performance_{i,t} + \alpha_5 Leverage_{i,t} + \alpha_6 Litigation_{i,t} + \alpha_7 Auditors_{i,t} + \alpha_8 Mergers_{i,t} + \alpha_9 Negearn_{i,t} + \alpha_{10} Lagaccrual_{i,t} + \alpha_{11} Opcycle_{i,t} + \alpha_{12} Ecofactor_{i,t} + \alpha_{13} Accfactor_{i,t} + \sum INDUSTRY_t + \sum YEAR + \varepsilon_{i,t}$$

		Dependent variable					
		excess PRED		*excess ACQ1*		*excess ACQ2*	
	Pred.	Model 1	Model 2	Model 1	Model 2	Model 1	Model 2
EAR_correlations	+	0.0114***		0.0124***		0.0236***	
		(0.0015)		(0.0012)		(0.0028)	
CF_correlations	+		0.0116***		0.0120***		0.0250***
			(0.0015)		(0.0012)		(0.0028)
Size	-	-0.0059***	-0.0059***	-0.0030***	-0.0030***	-0.0023***	-0.0023***
		(0.0005)	(0.0005)	(0.0004)	(0.0004)	(0.0008)	(0.0007)
Growth	+	0.0011***	0.0011***	0.0009***	0.0009***	0.0014***	0.0014***
		(0.0001)	(0.0001)	(0.0001)	(0.0001)	(0.0003)	(0.0003)
Performance	-	-0.0029	-0.0030	-0.0042	-0.0043	-0.0306***	-0.0309***
		(0.0035)	(0.0035)	(0.0027)	(0.0027)	(0.0080)	(0.0080)
Leverage	+	-0.0006	-0.0006	-0.0009	-0.0009	-0.0050	-0.0049
		(0.0019)	(0.0019)	(0.0014)	(0.0014)	(0.0032)	(0.0032)
Litigation	+	-0.0009	-0.0010	-0.0015	-0.0015	-0.0082**	-0.0083**
		(0.0025)	(0.0025)	(0.0019)	(0.0019)	(0.0040)	(0.0040)
Auditors	-	-0.0005	-0.0005	-0.0011	-0.0011	-0.0013	-0.0013
		(0.0011)	(0.0011)	(0.0009)	(0.0009)	(0.0018)	(0.0018)
Mergers	+	0.0005	0.0005	0.0007**	0.0007**	0.0020*	0.0020*
		(0.0004)	(0.0004)	(0.0004)	(0.0004)	(0.0011)	(0.0011)
Negearn	+	-0.0003	-0.0003	0.0001	0.0001	0.0055***	0.0055***
		(0.0006)	(0.0006)	(0.0005)	(0.0005)	(0.0015)	(0.0015)
Lagaccrual	+	0.0014	0.0014	-0.0128***	-0.0127***	-0.0085	-0.0083
		(0.0020)	(0.0020)	(0.0020)	(0.0020)	(0.0062)	(0.0060)
Opcycle	+	-0.0043***	-0.0043***	0.0002	0.0002	0.0005	0.0005
		(0.0012)	(0.0012)	(0.0010)	(0.0010)	(0.0021)	(0.0021)
Ecofactor	+	0.0463***	0.0463***	0.0524***	0.0524***	0.0314***	0.0312***
		(0.0028)	(0.0028)	(0.0025)	(0.0025)	(0.0051)	(0.0051)
Accfactor	-	-0.0343***	-0.0342***	-0.0242***	-0.0241***	-0.0105***	-0.0104***
		(0.0018)	(0.0018)	(0.0016)	(0.0016)	(0.0032)	(0.0032)
Constant	?	0.0632***	0.0630***	0.0175***	0.0178***	0.0023	0.0012
		(0.0061)	(0.0062)	(0.0053)	(0.0053)	(0.0114)	(0.0114)
Year dummies		Yes	Yes	Yes	Yes	Yes	Yes
Observations		40,520	40,520	40,520	40,520	40,520	40,520
R-squared		0.1207	0.1209	0.0901	0.0898	0.0129	0.0132

This table presents firm-fixed effects regressions of *excess* earnings quality on cross-segment earnings (cash flow) correlations for a sample of diversified and focused firms to control for unobserved firm characteristics. The regressions are estimated over a time period of 1979 to 2011. For variable descriptions, see Table 3. Robust standard errors clustered by firm are in parentheses. Asterisks indicate significance at the 1% (***), 5% (**), or 10% (*) level (respectively).

An important concern in the diversification discount literature is the firms' *ex ante* decision to diversify. Campa and Kedia (2002) argue that diversification strategies are determined by the same firm-specific characteristics, which cause diversified firms to be discounted. Because firms choose their organizational form and thus to diversify when the benefits outweigh the costs of diversification, the same unobserved firm characteristics that affect the diversification decision may also cause firms to have higher earnings quality. To control for these self-selection effects, I test whether the effect of coinsurance on earnings quality is driven by firm-specific characteristics which influence both earnings quality and the decision to diversify. I follow Heckman's (1979) two-stage procedure to overcome potential misspecification from firms' self-selection into the diversified status through the inclusion of a correction term, also known as inverse Mills ratio. I estimate the inverse Mills ratio from a first-stage probit model (selection equation) to account for firms' decisions to diversify. The dependent variable in the probit model is equal to 1 for diversified firms and 0 otherwise. Following Hann et al. (2013), I estimate the first-stage probit model in two ways. First, I include all control variables from my main regression analysis without additional controls ("No Instrument"). Second, I include two instruments ("With Instruments") for industry attractiveness (*PNDIV* and *PSDIV*) from Campa and Kedia (2002). *PNDIV* is the fraction of all firms in the industry, which are diversified, and *PSDIV* is the fraction of sales in the industry accounted for by diversified firms. In the second-stage regressions (structural equation), the inverse Mills ratio is included as additional control to correct for potential self-selection bias.

Table 15 presents results of second-stage regressions that control for the inverse Mills ratio from first-stage probit models for all three *excess* EQ measures (*excess PRED*, *excess ACQ1*, and *excess ACQ2*) in Panel A, Panel B, and Panel C, respectively. The coefficient of the inverse Mills ratio is positive and significant in the "No Instrument" model but only significant for *excess ACQ1* in the "With Instrument" model. This indicates that the firm characteristics that cause firms to self-select into diversification are positively correlated with earnings quality. Thus, firms with a higher probability of diversifying also tend to have higher earnings quality. However, estimated coefficients on cross-segment correlations remain all consistently positive and significant. Overall, the obtained results support the conclusions drawn from my main analysis after controlling for self-selection.

Table 15: Regressions of *Excess* Earnings Quality on Cross-segment Correlations: Controlling for Self-selection Effects

Panel A: Heckman's second stage regression – excess PRED

		No instrument		With instruments	
	Pred.	Model 1	Model 2	Model 1	Model 2
EAR_correlations	+	0.0159***		0.0152***	
		(0.0011)		(0.0011)	
CF_correlations	+		0.0159***		0.0151***
			(0.0011)		(0.0011)
Size	-	0.0021***	0.0021**	-0.0034***	-0.0034***
		(0.0009)	(0.0009)	(0.0002)	(0.0002)
Growth	+	-0.0026***	-0.0026***	0.0014***	0.0014***
		(0.0007)	(0.0007)	(0.0002)	(0.0002)
Performance	-	-0.0279***	-0.0281***	-0.0233***	-0.0235***
		(0.0041)	(0.0041)	(0.0040)	(0.0040)
Leverage	+	0.0166***	0.0166***	0.0082***	0.0081***
		(0.0021)	(0.0021)	(0.0017)	(0.0017)
Litigation	+	-0.0360***	-0.0361***	-0.0046***	-0.0045***
		(0.0049)	(0.0049)	(0.0010)	(0.0010)
Auditors	-	0.0062***	0.0062***	-0.0009	-0.0009
		(0.0015)	(0.0015)	(0.0010)	(0.0010)
Mergers	+	0.0160***	0.0160***	-0.0009	-0.0009
		(0.0027)	(0.0027)	(0.0006)	(0.0006)
Negearn	+	0.0023***	0.0023***	0.0040***	0.0040***
		(0.0008)	(0.0008)	(0.0008)	(0.0008)
Lagaccrual	+	-0.0059*	-0.0058*	0.0029	0.0029
		(0.0030)	(0.0030)	(0.0027)	(0.0027)
Opcycle	+	0.0111***	0.0112***	-0.0044***	-0.0043***
		(0.0024)	(0.0024)	(0.0006)	(0.0006)
Ecofactor	+	-0.0218	-0.0220	0.0892***	0.0894***
		(0.0177)	(0.0177)	(0.0037)	(0.0037)
Accfactor	-	0.0543***	0.0564***	-0.0702***	-0.0702***
		(0.0200)	(0.0200)	(0.0030)	(0.0030)
Inverse Mills ratio	+	0.1227***	0.1230***	0.0024	0.0023
		(0.0192)	(0.0192)	(0.0021)	(0.0021)
Constant	?	-0.2444***	-0.2452***	0.0719***	0.0719***
		(0.0501)	(0.0502)	(0.0065)	(0.0065)
Observations		40,520	40,520	40,520	40,520
R-squared		0.3039	0.3041	0.3011	0.3013

Panel B: Heckman's second stage regression – excess ACQ1

		No instrument		With instruments	
	Pred.	Model 1	Model 2	Model 1	Model 2
EAR_correlations	+	0.0123***		0.0117***	
		(0.0009)		(0.0009)	
CF_correlations	+		0.0120***		0.0115***
			(0.0009)		(0.0009)
Size	-	0.0002	0.0002	-0.0021***	-0.0021***
		(0.0006)	(0.0006)	(0.0001)	(0.0001)
Growth	+	-0.0009*	-0.0009*	0.0007***	0.0007***
		(0.0005)	(0.0005)	(0.0001)	(0.0001)

Table 15 (continued)

	Pred.	No instrument Model 1	No instrument Model 2	With instruments Model 1	With instruments Model 2
Performance	-	-0.0138***	-0.0139***	-0.0119***	-0.0120***
		(0.0029)	(0.0029)	(0.0028)	(0.0028)
Leverage	+	0.0089***	0.0088***	0.0053***	0.0052***
		(0.0015)	(0.0015)	(0.0012)	(0.0012)
Litigation	+	-0.0159***	-0.0159***	-0.0026***	-0.0026***
		(0.0037)	(0.0037)	(0.0007)	(0.0007)
Auditors	-	0.0007	0.0007	-0.0023***	-0.0023***
		(0.0011)	(0.0011)	(0.0007)	(0.0007)
Mergers	+	0.0070***	0.0070***	-0.0001	-0.0001
		(0.0020)	(0.0020)	(0.0005)	(0.0005)
Negearn	+	0.0002	0.0002	0.0009	0.0009
		(0.0006)	(0.0006)	(0.0006)	(0.0006)
Lagaccrual	+	-0.0198***	-0.0197***	-0.0160***	-0.0160***
		(0.0024)	(0.0024)	(0.0023)	(0.0023)
Opcycle	+	0.0062***	0.0062***	-0.0004	-0.0004
		(0.0018)	(0.0018)	(0.0004)	(0.0004)
Ecofactor	+	0.0195	0.0196	0.0665***	0.0666***
		(0.0132)	(0.0132)	(0.0026)	(0.0026)
Accfactor	-	0.0220	0.0220	-0.0307***	-0.0306***
		(0.0146)	(0.0146)	(0.0021)	(0.0021)
Inverse Mills ratio	+	0.0538***	0.0538***	0.0029**	0.0028**
		(0.0143)	(0.0143)	(0.0014)	(0.0014)
Constant	?	-0.1171***	-0.1170***	0.0169***	0.0171***
		(0.0372)	(0.0372)	(0.0046)	(0.0046)
Observations		40,520	40,520	40,520	40,520
R-squared		0.2199	0.2197	0.2192	0.2190

Panel C: Heckman's second stage regression – excess ACQ2

	Pred.	No instrument Model 1	No instrument Model 2	With instruments Model 1	With instruments Model 2
EAR_correlations	+	0.0314***		0.0306***	
		(0.0018)		(0.0018)	
CF_correlations	+		0.0318***		0.0310***
			(0.0017)		(0.0018)
Size	-	0.0007	0.0007	-0.0024***	-0.0024***
		(0.0010)	(0.0010)	(0.0002)	(0.0002)
Growth	+	-0.0009	-0.0009	0.0014***	0.0014***
		(0.0008)	(0.0008)	(0.0002)	(0.0002)
Performance	-	-0.0323***	-0.0327***	-0.0298***	-0.0301***
		(0.0067)	(0.0067)	(0.0067)	(0.0067)
Leverage	+	0.0074***	0.0074***	0.0026	0.0026
		(0.0026)	(0.0026)	(0.0019)	(0.0019)
Litigation	+	-0.0210***	-0.0212***	-0.0033***	-0.0032***
		(0.0061)	(0.0061)	(0.0011)	(0.0011)
Auditors	-	0.0041**	0.0042**	0.0001	0.0001
		(0.0018)	(0.0018)	(0.0011)	(0.0011)
Mergers	+	0.0101***	0.0102***	0.0006	0.0006
		(0.0034)	(0.0034)	(0.0011)	(0.0011)
Negearn	+	0.0049***	0.0049***	0.0059***	0.0059***
		(0.0014)	(0.0014)	(0.0014)	(0.0014)

Table 15 (continued)

	Pred.	No instrument Model 1	Model 2	With instruments Model 1	Model 2
Lagaccrual	+	-0.0146**	-0.0145**	-0.0096*	-0.0095*
		(0.0057)	(0.0057)	(0.0054)	(0.0054)
Opcycle	+	0.0085***	0.0086***	-0.0003	-0.0002
		(0.0030)	(0.0030)	(0.0007)	(0.0007)
Ecofactor	+	-0.0199	-0.0205	0.0428***	0.0431***
		(0.0215)	(0.0215)	(0.0042)	(0.0042)
Accfactor	-	0.0567**	0.0578**	-0.0135***	-0.0136***
		(0.0239)	(0.0239)	(0.0035)	(0.0035)
Inverse Mills ratio	+	0.0718***	0.0752***	0.0039	0.0036
		(0.0232)	(0.0232)	(0.0024)	(0.0024)
Constant	?	-0.1906***	-0.1933***	-0.0117	-0.0118
		(0.0608)	(0.0608)	(0.0078)	(0.0078)
Observations		40,520	40,520	40,520	40,520
R-squared		0.0434	0.0439	0.0432	0.0437

This table presents second-stage *excess* earnings quality regressions that control for the inverse Mills ratio (i.e., the correction for self-selection) from first-stage probit models for three measures of *excess* EQ: *excess PRED*, *excess ACQ1*, and *excess ACQ2* in Panel A, B, and C (respectively). Under "No Instrument", the inverse Mills ratio is from a first-stage probit model with all of the control variables in the second stage. Under "With Instruments", the first-stage probit model additionally includes *PNDIV* and *PSDIV* following Campa and Kedia (2002). *PNDIV* is the fraction of all firms in the industry which are diversified, and *PSDIV* is the fraction of sales in the industry accounted for by diversified firms. The regressions are estimated over a time period of 1979 to 2011. For variable descriptions, see Table 3. Robust standard errors clustered by firm are in parentheses. Asterisks indicate significance at the 1% (***), 5% (**), or 10% (*) level (respectively).

3.6.3 Innate and Discretionary Components of Accruals Quality

I examine the relation between the diversification-specific advantage of coinsurance and estimation errors in the accrual process, regardless of the sources of these estimation errors. However, Dechow and Dichev (2002) and Francis et al. (2005) assign the sources of accruals quality into innate (unintentional) and discretionary (intentional) components. Innate accruals quality represents firm and industry characteristics, which arise from the business model and operating environment, whereas discretionary accruals quality arises from managerial reporting choices. To explain the source of coinsurance, I further disentangle both of my accruals quality measures (*ACQ1* and *ACQ2*) into innate and discretionary components. Because the organizational form as firm-specific characteristic is attributable to the innate component of accruals quality, I examine whether coinsurance explains a significant portion of innate accruals quality. In addition, the discretionary component of accruals quality enables me to examine whether the complex nature of diversified firms explains more opportunistic accrual choices caused by more agency problems in diversified firms.[99]

[99] For example, the *transparency* hypothesis suggests that diversification increases organizational complexity which leads to larger asymmetric information problems for diversified firms (i.e., reduced transparency to corporate outsiders) compared to their focused counterparts (Thomas 2002). As a result, managers may

Thus, I decompose my total accruals quality measures from Equations (6) and (7) into an innate component and a discretionary component following Francis et al. (2005):

$$ACQ_{i,t} = \delta_0 + \delta_1 LogAsset_{i,t} + \delta_2 StdCFO_{i,t} + \delta_3 StdSALES_{i,t} + \delta_4 LogCycle_{i,t} + \delta_5 NegEarn_{i,t} + \varepsilon_{i,t}. \tag{11}$$

I estimate Equation (11) for any given year; variables are described in Table 16. The predicted value from the regression yields an estimate of the innate component of accruals quality for firm i in year t, whereas the predicted residual $\varepsilon_{i,t}$ is the estimate of the discretionary component of accruals quality for firm i in year t. Both innate and discretionary components are inversely measured with higher values indicating lower accruals quality and vice versa. The innate component of accruals quality reflects a set of observable firm and industry characteristics that proxy for the firm's economic fundamentals and the propensity to make unintentional estimation errors (Dechow and Dichev 2002; Francis et al. 2005). I expect that a firm's organizational form explains the documented positive effect on accruals quality which is likely reflected by a positive association between cross-segment earnings (cash flow) correlations and measures of innate accruals quality. In contrast, the discretionary component of accruals quality captures intentional estimation errors and thus signals unobservable managerial opportunism.[100] Following prior literature, I expect that managers of diversified firms use their increased discretionary power to engage in opportunistic accrual choices which likely leads to a negative relation between cross-segment earnings (cash flow) correlations and measures of discretionary accruals quality.

Table 16 presents summary statistics for the decomposition of total accruals quality measures into innate and discretionary components. Panel A of Table 16 reports the innate factors used to estimate Equation (11) for diversified and focused firms. Consistent with the literature, diversified firms are larger in size, show considerably less volatility in cash flows and total sales and are less likely to experience a loss. However, the mean (median) operating *CYCLE* is very similar with 135 (123) days for diversified firms and 135 (121) days for focused firms.

---

engage in agency behavior by using their accounting discretion opportunistically to make accruals manipulation for simply boosting earnings and thus managerial compensation (Demirkan et al. 2012). This would lead to more intentional estimation errors in accruals for diversified firms.

100 Besides an opportunistic motive, Healy and Wahlen (1999) summarize that managers also have a signaling motive when making accrual estimations. For example, managers may be more accurate when estimating accruals to signal private information about the firm's future performance and thereby reduce the level of information asymmetry with corporate outsiders. Guay et al. (1996) show that managers tend to use accruals to improve earnings as an information signal. In this case, more accurate and less erroneous accruals would lead to less intentional estimation errors in accruals (less earnings management) and thus higher discretionary accruals quality. However, which motive (opportunistic vs. signaling) prevails is an empirical question.

Panel B of Table 16 presents the mean coefficient estimates from annual regressions of Equation (11) with t-statistics based on robust standard errors clustered by firm. In line with Francis et al. (2005), I find the predicted signs on the innate factors, where size is negatively related and all other innate factors are positively related to accruals quality. Panel C of Table 16 provides *actual* values and *excess* values of the innate and discretionary components for both measures of accruals quality. The results suggest that diversified firms have both higher *actual* innate and *excess* innate accruals quality than focused firms. However, *actual* discretionary and *excess* discretionary accruals are of lower quality compared to focused firms. This finding suggests that a firm's organizational form positively influences the innate component of accruals quality, but this effect is slightly diminished by opportunistic accrual choices captured in the discretionary component. Therefore, the majority of variation in accruals quality is explained by innate sources that managers cannot intentionally affect by managerial discretion, consistent with Francis et al. (2005). In addition, Panel D (Panel E) of Table 16 shows the correlation between the *actual* (*excess*) innate and discretionary components of accruals quality. Both *actual* (*excess*) innate components are positively correlated. Similarly, both *actual* (*excess*) discretionary components exhibit positive correlations. As expected, the correlations between the *actual* (*excess*) innate and discretionary components are all negative and significant.

Table 16: Disentangling Innate and Discretionary Accruals Quality

Panel A: Innate factors

	Diversified firms			**Focused firms**			**Difference**	
	Mean	SD	Med.	Mean	SD	Med.	Mean	Med.
Innate factors								
LogAsset	6.1004	2.0300	6.1608	5.5391	1.8170	5.3310	0.5613***	0.8288***
StdCFO	0.0578	0.0598	0.0459	0.0807	0.1197	0.0547	-0.0229***	-0.0088***
StdSALES	0.3057	0.2473	0.2577	0.3693	0.4247	0.2878	-0.0637***	-0.0301***
CYCLE	135	67	123	135	81	121	0	3***
LogCycle	4.7760	0.5207	4.8153	4.6944	0.7144	4.7936	0.0816***	0.0217***
NegEarn	0.1225	0.1849	0.0000	0.1890	0.2372	0.1000	-0.0665***	-0.1000***
Observations	15,782			24,738				

Panel B: Mean results of annual regressions of total accruals quality on innate factors

$$ACQ_{i,t} = \delta_0 + \delta_1 LogAsset_{i,t} + \delta_2 StdCFO_{i,t} + \delta_3 StdSALES_{i,t} + \delta_4 LogCycle_{i,t} + \delta_5 NegEarn_{i,t} + \varepsilon_{i,t}$$

		Dependent variable			
		ACQ1		*ACQ2*	
	Pred.	Coeff. estimate	t-statistics	Coeff. estimate	t-statistics
LogAsset	-	-0.0019	-6.67	-0.0024	-6.32
StdCFO	+	0.1002	6.23	0.1021	5.98
StdSALES	+	0.0107	2.44	0.1007	2.10
LogCycle	+	0.0065	9.35	0.0154	15.71
NegEarn	+	0.0706	21.27	0.0655	15.77
Observations		40,520		40,520	
R-squared		0.3031		0.0822	

Table 16 (continued)

Panel C: Innate and discretionary components

	Diversified firms			Focused firms			Difference	
	Mean	SD	Med.	Mean	SD	Med.	Mean	Med.
Actual Innate and discretionary accruals quality								
IACQ1	0.0386	0.0228	0.0320	0.0572	0.0387	0.0445	-0.0186***	-0.0125***
IACQ2	0.0667	0.0468	0.0541	0.0984	0.0829	0.0707	-0.0317***	-0.0166***
DACQ1	-0.0033	0.0226	-0.0052	-0.0045	0.0350	-0.0078	0.0012***	0.0026***
DACQ2	-0.0074	0.0127	-0.0066	-0.0147	0.0244	-0.0106	0.0073***	0.0040***
Excess innate and discretionary accruals quality								
excess IACQ1	-0.0062	0.0256	-0.0089	0.0062	0.0249	0.0000	-0.0124***	-0.0089***
excess IACQ2	-0.0083	0.1052	-0.0166	0.0215	0.1043	0.0000	-0.0298***	-0.0166***
excess DACQ1	0.0017	0.0229	0.0019	-0.0005	0.0220	0.0000	0.0022***	0.0019***
excess DACQ2	0.0070	0.1132	0.0060	-0.0107	0.1078	0.0000	0.0177***	0.0060***
Observations	15,782			24,738				

Panel D: Pearson correlation coefficients for actual innate and actual discretionary components

Variable	*IACQ1*	*IACQ2*	*DACQ1*	*DACQ2*
IACQ1	1.0000			
IACQ2	0.9203	1.0000		
	(.0000)			
DACQ1	-0.2584	-0.2414	1.0000	
	(.0000)	(.0000)		
DACQ2	-0.6775	-0.7713	0.3083	1.0000
	(.0000)	(.0000)	(.0000)	

Panel E: Pearson correlation coefficients for excess innate and excess discretionary components

Variable	*excess IACQ1*	*excess IACQ2*	*excess DACQ1*	*excess DACQ2*
excess IACQ1	1.0000			
excess IACQ2	0.8876	1.0000		
	(.0000)			
excess DACQ1	-0.3573	-0.3706	1.0000	
	(.0000)	(.0000)		
excess DACQ2	-0.6395	-0.7463	0.3632	1.0000
	(.0000)	(.0000)	(.0000)	

This table reports summary statistics for the distinction between innate and discretionary accruals quality. Innate factors are calculated following Francis et al. (2005). $ACQ_{i,t}$ is *ACQ1* (*ACQ2*). $LogAsset_{i,t}$ is the natural logarithm of firm *i*'s total assets in year *t*. $StdCFO_{i,t}$ is the standard deviation of firm *i*'s cash flows from operations calculated over prior 10 years. $StdSales_{i,t}$ is the standard deviation of firm *i*'s sales calculated over prior 10 years. $LogCycle_{i,t}$ is the natural logarithm of firm *i*'s operating *Cycle* [360 / (SALE / Average Account Receivables [RECT]) + 360 / (COGS / Average Inventory [INVT])]. $NegEarn_{i,t}$ is an indicator of firm *i*'s negative earnings over prior 10 years. Panel B reports mean values from regressions of both *total* accruals quality measures (*ACQ1* and *ACQ2*) on innate factors. t-statistics are based on robust standard errors clustered by firm. $IACQ1_{i,t}$ is firm *i*'s predicted value of innate accruals quality of $ACQ1_{i,t}$ in year *t* (*IACQ2* respectively for $ACQ2_{i,t}$). $DACQ1_{i,t}$ is firm *i*'s predicted residual as an estimate of discretionary accruals quality of $ACQ1_{i,t}$ in year *t* (*DACQ2* respectively for $ACQ2_{i,t}$). Both measures of innate and discretionary accruals quality are inversely related to earnings quality. The *actual* innate and discretionary accruals quality measures, namely *IACQ1, IACQ2, DACQ1,* and *DACQ2*, are used to calculate my measures of *excess* innate and discretionary accruals quality, see Equations (8) and (9). The statistics are computed over a time period of 1979 to 2011 for a sample of diversified and focused firms. For variable descriptions, see Table 3. Significance levels are stated for the difference between diversified and focused firms. The mean difference is based on a t-test and the median difference is based on a Wilcoxon signed-rank test. Asterisks indicate significance at the 1% (***), 5% (**), or 10% (*) level (respectively).

Panel A of Table 17 presents regression results of *excess* innate accruals quality on cross-segment earnings (cash flow) correlations. I find a positive and significant relation between cross-segment correlations and my measures of *excess* innate accruals quality, consistent with the prediction that coinsurance leads to higher innate accruals quality. This finding underscores my main results that the coinsurance benefits for accruals quality arise from firm fundamentals (i.e., innate component) which are not distorted by managerial discretion. Moreover, this empirical finding supports the survey result of Dichev et al. (2013) who report that the firm's business model is the most important innate source affecting earnings quality, even more than accounting standards.[101] Demirkan et al. (2012) also find higher innate accruals quality for diversified firms than for focused firms, which they explain by fundamental differences in the firms' business models.[102] In this context, I provide evidence that the imperfect correlation of business activities within diversified firms explains less unintentional estimation errors in accruals and thus the difference in innate and total accruals quality between diversified and focused firms.

Panel B of Table 17 presents regression results of *excess* discretionary accruals quality on cross-segment earnings (cash flow) correlations. I find that the relation between cross-segment correlations and my measures of *excess* discretionary accruals quality is negative but insignificant. This result indicates that coinsurance does not explain more opportunistic accrual choices and thus lower discretionary accruals quality of diversified firms. However, the imperfect correlation of estimation errors among segment-level accruals also reduces the magnitude of intentional estimation errors in firm-level accruals and thus may decrease the likelihood for detecting earnings management in diversified firms.

Overall, my results highlight the importance of coinsurance in explaining higher innate and total accruals quality and support the view that coinsurance is a fundamental firm characteristic that is positively related to earnings (accruals) quality of diversified firms.

---

[101] Other subordinate factors are the company's industry, macro-economic conditions, firm's internal controls, the board of directors, reporting choices, and how fast the operating cycle converts accruals to cash flows (Dichev et al. 2013).

[102] Dechow and Dichev (2002) and Francis et al. (2005) argue that differences between firms' business models likely leads to differences in accruals quality.

Table 17: Regressions of *Excess* Innate and *Excess* Discretionary Accruals Quality on Cross-segment Correlations

Panel A: excess innate accruals quality

$$excess\ IACQ_{i,t} = \alpha_0 + \boldsymbol{\alpha_1 Correlations_{i,t}} + \alpha_2 Size_{i,t} + \alpha_3 Growth_{i,t} + \alpha_4 Performance_{i,t} + \alpha_5 Leverage_{i,t} + \alpha_6 Litigation_{i,t} + \alpha_7 Auditors_{i,t} + \alpha_8 Mergers_{i,t} + \alpha_9 Negearn_{i,t} + \alpha_{10} Lagaccrual_{i,t} + \alpha_{11} Opcycle_{i,t} + \alpha_{12} Ecofactor_{i,t} + \alpha_{13} Accfactor_{i,t} + \sum INDUSTRY_t + \sum YEAR + \varepsilon_{i,t}$$

		excess IACQ1		*excess IACQ2*	
	Pred.	Model 1	Model 2	Model 1	Model 2
EAR_correlations	+	0.0090***		0.0134***	
		(0.0008)		(0.0037)	
CF_correlations	+		0.0085***		0.0116***
			(0.0008)		(0.0037)
Size	-	-0.0043***	-0.0043***	-0.0021***	-0.0021***
		(0.0001)	(0.0001)	(0.0006)	(0.0006)
Growth	+	0.0011***	0.0011***	0.0020***	0.0020***
		(0.0001)	(0.0001)	(0.0004)	(0.0004)
Performance	-	-0.0052**	-0.0052**	-0.0531***	-0.0531***
		(0.0023)	(0.0023)	(0.0102)	(0.0102)
Leverage	+	0.0029*	0.0029**	0.0463***	0.0462***
		(0.0011)	(0.0011)	(0.0051)	(0.0051)
Litigation	+	-0.0013	-0.0013	-0.0100**	-0.0099**
		(0.0009)	(0.0009)	(0.0041)	(0.0041)
Auditors	-	-0.0006	-0.0006	-0.0003	-0.0004
		(0.0006)	(0.0006)	(0.0027)	(0.0027)
Mergers	+	-0.0019***	-0.0019***	-0.0087***	-0.0088***
		(0.0004)	(0.0003)	(0.0016)	(0.0016)
Negearn	+	0.0112***	0.0112***	0.0619***	0.0619***
		(0.0005)	(0.0005)	(0.0023)	(0.0022)
Lagaccrual	+	-0.0321***	-0.0320***	-0.1470***	-0.1470***
		(0.0017)	(0.0017)	(0.0076)	(0.0076)
Opcycle	+	0.0011**	0.0011**	0.0206***	0.0206***
		(0.0005)	(0.0005)	(0.0021)	(0.0021)
Ecofactor	+	0.0506***	0.0506***	0.1971***	0.1974***
		(0.0018)	(0.0018)	(0.0082)	(0.0082)
Accfactor	-	-0.0333***	-0.0333***	-0.1440***	-0.1442***
		(0.0012)	(0.0012)	(0.0056)	(0.0056)
Constant	?	0.0387***	0.0391***	0.0078	0.0096
		(0.0082)	(0.0036)	(0.0322)	(0.0322)
Industry dummies		Yes	Yes	Yes	Yes
Year dummies		Yes	Yes	Yes	Yes
Observations		40,520	40,520	40,520	40,520
R-squared		0.3979	0.3974	0.2747	0.2745

Table 17 (continued)

Panel B: excess discretionary accruals quality

$$excess\ DACQ_{i,t} = \alpha_0 + \boldsymbol{\alpha_1 Correlations_{i,t}} + \alpha_2 Size_{i,t} + \alpha_3 Growth_{i,t} + \alpha_4 Performance_{i,t} + \alpha_5 Leverage_{i,t} + \alpha_6 Litigation_{i,t} + \alpha_7 Auditors_{i,t} + \alpha_8 Mergers_{i,t} + \alpha_9 Negearn_{i,t} + \alpha_{10} Lagaccrual_{i,t} + \alpha_{11} Opcycle_{i,t} + \alpha_{12} Ecofactor_{i,t} + \alpha_{13} Accfactor_{i,t} + \sum INDUSTRY_t + \sum YEAR + \varepsilon_{i,t}$$

		excess DACQ1		*excess DACQ2*	
	Pred.	Model 1	Model 2	Model 1	Model 2
EAR_correlations	-	-0.0011		-0.0033	
		(0.0008)		(0.0037)	
CF_correlations	-		-0.0010		-0.0013
			(0.0008)		(0.0036)
Size	-	0.0019***	0.0019***	-0.0007	-0.0007
		(0.0001)	(0.0001)	(0.0006)	(0.0006)
Growth	+	-0.0002*	-0.0002*	-0.0002	-0.0002
		(0.0001)	(0.0001)	(0.0004)	(0.0004)
Performance	-	-0.0046*	-0.0046*	0.0095	0.0093
		(0.0026)	(0.0026)	(0.0114)	(0.0114)
Leverage	+	-0.0014	-0.0014	-0.0455***	-0.0455***
		(0.0011)	(0.0011)	(0.0049)	(0.0049)
Litigation	+	-0.0009	-0.0009	0.0080**	0.0079**
		(0.0009)	(0.0009)	(0.0040)	(0.0040)
Auditors	-	-0.0015**	-0.0015**	-0.0011	-0.0011
		(0.0006)	(0.0006)	(0.0027)	(0.0027)
Mergers	+	0.0023***	0.0023***	0.0086***	0.0087***
		(0.0004)	(0.0004)	(0.0017)	(0.0017)
Negearn	+	-0.0089***	-0.0089***	-0.0540***	-0.0541***
		(0.0005)	(0.0005)	(0.0024)	(0.0024)
Lagaccrual	+	0.0165***	0.0165***	0.1330***	0.1330***
		(0.0020)	(0.0020)	(0.0088)	(0.0088)
Opcycle	+	0.0018***	0.0018***	-0.0190***	-0.0190***
		(0.0004)	(0.0004)	(0.0020)	(0.0020)
Ecofactor	+	0.0225***	0.0225***	-0.1394***	-0.1397***
		(0.0019)	(0.0019)	(0.0081)	(0.0081)
Accfactor	-	-0.0010	-0.0010	0.1165***	0.1168***
		(0.0013)	(0.0013)	(0.0054)	(0.0054)
Constant	?	-0.0304***	-0.0304***	0.0148	0.0128
		(0.0088)	(0.0088)	(0.0300)	(0.0300)
Industry dummies		Yes	Yes	Yes	Yes
Year dummies		Yes	Yes	Yes	Yes
Observations		40,520	40,520	40,520	40,520
R-squared		0.0758	0.0758	0.1399	0.1398

This table presents regressions of *excess* innate (discretionary) accruals quality on cross-segment earnings (cash flow) correlations in Panel A (Panel B) for a sample of diversified and focused firms. The regressions are estimated over a time period of 1979 to 2011. Industry dummies are specified for each Fama and French's (1997) 48 industry groups. For variable descriptions, see Table 3. Robust standard errors clustered by firm are in parentheses. Asterisks indicate significance at the 1% (***), 5% (**), or 10% (*) level (respectively).

3.6.4 Naive Comparison between Diversified and Focused Firms

In my regression analyses, I use *excess* earnings quality to benchmark the *actual* earnings quality of a diversified firm against the *imputed* earnings quality that its business units would have if operated as stand-alone firms. Subsequently, I check the validity of this approach by using measures of *actual* earnings quality instead of *excess* earnings quality.

Table 18 presents regression results of *actual* earnings quality on a diversification indicator, which takes the value of 1 for diversified firms (i.e., firms that operate in at least two different four-digit SIC codes) and 0 otherwise.[103] Similar to Table 7, I find a negative relation between the diversification indicator and all three measures of *actual* EQ. The coefficient estimates on diversification with *PRED*, *ACQ1*, and *ACQ2* as dependent variables are -0.0111, -0.0089 and -0.0237 and all significant at the 1% level.[104] Remember, a negative *actual* EQ (i.e., *PRED*, *ACQ1*, and *ACQ2)* value indicates that diversification improves earnings quality. Therefore, by using a *naive* comparison of earnings quality between diversified and focused firms, I find that diversified firms have on average higher earnings quality compared to their stand-alone peers. Note that the coefficient estimates are even more negative compared to my results in Table 7 using *excess* earnings quality, which suggests that my benchmark approach successfully enhances the comparison of earnings quality between diversified and focused firms.

Table 18: Regressions of *Actual* Earnings Quality on Diversification Indicator: Naive Comparison

$$EQ_{i,t} = \alpha_0 + \boldsymbol{\alpha_1 Div\_Dummy_{i,t}} + \alpha_2 Size_{i,t} + \alpha_3 Growth_{i,t} + \alpha_4 Performance_{i,t} + \alpha_5 Leverage_{i,t} + \alpha_6 Litigation_{i,t} + \alpha_7 Auditors_{i,t} + \alpha_8 Mergers_{i,t} + \alpha_9 Negearn_{i,t} + \alpha_{10} Lagaccrual_{i,t} + \alpha_{11} Opcycle_{i,t} + \alpha_{12} Ecofactor_{i,t} + \alpha_{13} Accfactor_{i,t} + \sum INDUSTRY_t + \sum YEAR + \varepsilon_{i,t}$$

		Dependent variable		
	Pred.	*PRED*	*ACQ1*	*ACQ2*
Div_Dummy	-	-0.0111***	-0.0089***	-0.0237***
		(0.0007)	(0.0006)	(0.0010)
Size	-	-0.0039***	-0.0029***	-0.0025***
		(0.0003)	(0.0002)	(0.0003)
Growth	+	0.0030***	0.0017***	0.0020***
		(0.0003)	(0.0002)	(0.0003)
Performance	-	-0.0538***	-0.0224***	-0.0585***
		(0.0073)	(0.0052)	(0.0113)
Leverage	+	-0.0053**	-0.0029	-0.0043
		(0.0026)	(0.0018)	(0.0031)
Litigation	+	0.0092***	0.0010**	0.0033
		(0.0022)	(0.0016)	(0.0024)
Auditors	-	-0.0047***	-0.0047***	-0.0009
		(0.0015)	(0.0010)	(0.0016)
Mergers	+	0.0018**	0.0025***	0.0024*
		(0.0008)	(0.0006)	(0.0013)

[103] Robust standard errors clustered by firm and year (two-way) lead to similar inferences (Petersen 2009).
[104] Variance inflation factors (VIF) are all below common cut-off values.

Table 18 (continued)

	Pred.	*PRED*	*ACQ1*	*ACQ2*
Negearn	+	0.0052***	0.0014*	0.0077***
		(0.0011)	(0.0008)	(0.0019)
Lagaccrual	+	0.0054	-0.0213***	-0.0237***
		(0.0041)	(0.0034)	(0.0077)
Opcycle	+	0.0010	0.0045***	0.0059***
		(0.0011)	(0.0008)	(0.0013)
Ecofactor	+	0.1797***	0.1277***	0.0815***
		(0.0061)	(0.0040)	(0.0055)
Accfactor	-	-0.1342***	-0.0586***	-0.0338***
		(0.0043)	(0.0028)	(0.0044)
Constant	?	0.1421***	0.0330***	0.0691***
		(0.0084)	(0.0091)	(0.0141)
Industry dummies		Yes	Yes	Yes
Year dummies		Yes	Yes	Yes
Observations		40,520	40,520	40,520
R-squared		0.5029	0.4657	0.1614

This table presents regressions of *actual* earnings quality on an indicator variable *Div_Dummy* which takes the value of 1 for diversified firms (i.e., firms that operate in at least two different four-digit SIC codes) and 0 otherwise. The predicted sign for *Div_Dummy* is negative because diversified firms are expected to have higher quality earnings and thus smaller values of my earnings attributes compared to focused firms. The regressions are estimated for a sample of diversified and focused firms over a time period of 1979 to 2011. Industry dummies are specified for each Fama and French's (1997) 48 industry groups. For variable descriptions, see Table 3. Robust standard errors clustered by firm are in parentheses. Asterisks indicate significance at the 1% (***), 5% (**), or 10% (*) level (respectively).

Table 19 shows the robustness of the results of my main analysis regarding the impact of coinsurance (i.e., cross-segment earnings and cash flow correlations) on *actual* EQ. Similar to Table 9, I document a positive relation between cross-segment correlations and all three measures of *actual* EQ. That is, less cross-segment correlations (i.e., more coinsurance) lead to lower *actual* EQ values (i.e., higher earnings quality). The coefficient estimates on cross-segment earnings correlations with *PRED*, *ACQ1*, and *ACQ2* as dependent variables are 0.0143, 0.0112 and 0.0293 and significant, respectively. Accordingly, the coefficient estimates on cross-segment cash flow correlations are 0.0139, 0.0109 and 0.0296 and significant, respectively.[105] Thus, I find that diversified firms have on average higher quality earnings compared to their focused counterparts, which is explained by coinsurance benefits.

[105] Variance inflation factors (VIF) are all below common cut-off values.

Table 19: Regressions of *Actual* Earnings Quality on Cross-segment Correlations: Naive Comparison

$$EQ_{i,t} = \alpha_0 + \boldsymbol{\alpha_1 Correlations_{i,t}} + \alpha_2 Size_{i,t} + \alpha_3 Growth_{i,t} + \alpha_4 Performance_{i,t} + \alpha_5 Leverage_{i,t} + \alpha_6 Litigation_{i,t} + \alpha_7 Auditors_{i,t} + \alpha_8 Mergers_{i,t} + \alpha_9 Negearn_{i,t} + \alpha_{10} Lagaccrual_{i,t} + \alpha_{11} Opcycle_{i,t} + \alpha_{12} Ecofactor_{i,t} + \alpha_{13} Accfactor_{i,t} + \sum INDUSTRY_t + \sum YEAR + \varepsilon_{i,t}$$

		Dependent variable					
		PRED		*ACQ1*		*ACQ2*	
	Pred.	Model 1	Model 2	Model 1	Model 2	Model 1	Model 2
EAR_correlations	+	0.0143***		0.0112***		0.0293***	
		(0.0013)		(0.0011)		(0.0019)	
CF_correlations	+		0.0139***		0.0109***		0.0296***
			(0.0013)		(0.0010)		(0.0019)
Size	-	-0.0040***	-0.0040***	-0.0030***	-0.0030***	-0.0027***	-0.0027***
		(0.0003)	(0.0003)	(0.0002)	(0.0002)	(0.0003)	(0.0003)
Growth	+	0.0030***	0.0030***	0.0018***	0.0018***	0.0022***	0.0022***
		(0.0003)	(0.0003)	(0.0002)	(0.0002)	(0.0004)	(0.0004)
Performance	-	-0.0536***	-0.0537***	-0.0222***	-0.0223***	-0.0580***	-0.0584***
		(0.0073)	(0.0073)	(0.0053)	(0.0053)	(0.0114)	(0.0114)
Leverage	+	-0.0056**	-0.0056**	-0.0032*	-0.0032*	-0.0049	-0.0049
		(0.0026)	(0.0026)	(0.0018)	(0.0018)	(0.0031)	(0.0031)
Litigation	+	0.0098***	0.0098***	0.0016	0.0015	0.0048**	0.0047*
		(0.0022)	(0.0022)	(0.0016)	(0.0016)	(0.0024)	(0.0024)
Auditors	-	-0.0048***	-0.0048***	-0.0047***	-0.0047***	-0.0010	-0.0010
		(0.0015)	(0.0015)	(0.0010)	(0.0010)	(0.0017)	(0.0017)
Mergers	+	0.0015*	0.0015*	0.0022***	0.0022***	0.0016	0.0017
		(0.0008)	(0.0008)	(0.0006)	(0.0006)	(0.0013)	(0.0013)
Negearn	+	0.0052***	0.0052***	0.0013*	0.0013*	0.0077***	0.0077***
		(0.0011)	(0.0011)	(0.0008)	(0.0008)	(0.0019)	(0.0019)
Lagaccrual	+	0.0053	0.0054	-0.0213***	-0.0213***	-0.0239***	-0.0239***
		(0.0041)	(0.0041)	(0.0035)	(0.0035)	(0.0078)	(0.0078)
Opcycle	+	0.0009	0.0009	0.0045***	0.0045***	0.0058***	0.0058***
		(0.0011)	(0.0011)	(0.0008)	(0.0008)	(0.0013)	(0.0013)
Ecofactor	+	0.1827***	0.1827***	0.1302***	0.1302***	0.0882***	0.0881***
		(0.0061)	(0.0061)	(0.0040)	(0.0040)	(0.0056)	(0.0056)
Accfactor	-	-0.1368***	-0.1367***	-0.0607***	-0.0607***	-0.0396***	-0.0394***
		(0.0044)	(0.0044)	(0.0028)	(0.0028)	(0.0045)	(0.0045)
Constant	?	0.1302***	0.1304***	0.0237***	0.0240***	0.0451***	0.0470***
		(0.0150)	(0.0150)	(0.0092)	(0.0092)	(0.0143)	(0.0147)
Industry dummies		Yes	Yes	Yes	Yes	Yes	Yes
Year dummies		Yes	Yes	Yes	Yes	Yes	Yes
Observations		40,520	40,520	40,520	40,520	40,520	40,520
R-squared		0.4985	0.4984	0.4605	0.4604	0.1525	0.1527

This table presents regressions of *actual* earnings quality on cross-segment earnings (cash flow) correlations for a sample of diversified and focused firms. The regressions are estimated over a time period of 1979 to 2011. Industry dummies are specified for each Fama and French's (1997) 48 industry groups. For variable descriptions, see Table 3. Robust standard errors clustered by firm are in parentheses. Asterisks indicate significance at the 1% (***), 5% (**), or 10% (*) level (respectively).

Table 20 presents regression results of *actual* EQ on cross-segment earnings (cash flow) correlations and interactions with earnings volatility. Here I examine the link between coinsurance and uncertainty in the firm's operating environment. Thus, my main variable of interest is *EAR_Interaction* (*CF_Interaction*), which is the interaction term between cross-segment earnings (cash flow) correlations and earnings volatility. Similar to Table 11, I find a positive and significant interrelationship between both cross-segment correlation measures and earnings volatility.[106] The coefficient estimates on *EAR_Interaction* (*CF_Interaction*) with *excess PRED*, *excess ACQ1*, and *excess ACQ2* as dependent variables are 0.0183 (0.0180), 0.0087 (0.0086) and 0.0130 (0.0132) and significant, respectively. Accordingly, I find that the marginal effect of coinsurance on earnings quality increases with higher levels of operating volatility. However, the coefficients on the interaction term are substantially above the coefficients when using measures of *excess* EQ which suggests that a naive comparison overstates the effect of coinsurance on earnings quality for firms that operate in more volatile and uncertain environments.

Overall, these robustness checks confirm the validity of the obtained results using my benchmark approach to compare the earnings quality of diversified firms to similar constructed portfolios of their focused counterparts.

Table 20: Regressions of *Actual* Earnings Quality on Cross-segment Correlations and Earnings Volatility: Naive Comparison

$$EQ_{i,t} = \alpha_0 + \alpha_1 Correlations_{i,t} + \alpha_2 EAR\_vola_{i,t} + \boldsymbol{\alpha_{12} Interaction} + \delta_1 Size_{i,t} + \delta_2 Growth_{i,t} + \delta_3 Performance_{i,t} + \delta_4 Leverage_{i,t} + \delta_5 Litigation_{i,t} + \delta_6 Auditors_{i,t} + \delta_7 Mergers_{i,t} + \delta_8 Negearn_{i,t} + \delta_9 Lagaccrual_{i,t} + \delta_{10} Opcycle_{i,t} + \delta_{11} Ecofactor_{i,t} + \delta_{12} Accfactor_{i,t} + \sum INDUSTRY_t + \sum YEAR + \varepsilon_{i,t}$$

		Dependent variable					
		PRED		*ACQ1*		*ACQ2*	
	Pred.	Model 1	Model 2	Model 1	Model 2	Model 1	Model 2
EAR_correlations	+	-0.0186***		-0.0041***		0.0072***	
		(0.0017)		(0.0015)		(0.0027)	
EAR_vola	+	-0.0037***		-0.0036***		-0.0089***	
		(0.0008)		(0.0007)		(0.0011)	
EAR_Interaction	+	0.0183***		0.0087***		0.0130***	
		(0.0009)		(0.0008)		(0.0013)	
CF_correlations	+		-0.0187***		-0.0043***		0.0070**
			(0.0017)		(0.0015)		(0.0028)
EAR_vola	+		-0.0034***		-0.0034***		-0.0090***
			(0.0007)		(0.0007)		(0.0011)
CF_Interaction	+		0.0180***		0.0086***		0.0132***
			(0.0009)		(0.0008)		(0.0013)
Size	-	-0.0029***	-0.0029***	-0.0026***	-0.0026***	-0.0026***	-0.0026***
		(0.0003)	(0.0003)	(0.0002)	(0.0002)	(0.0003)	(0.0003)
Growth	+	0.0026***	0.0026***	0.0016***	0.0016***	0.0021***	0.0021***
		(0.0003)	(0.0003)	(0.0002)	(0.0002)	(0.0004)	(0.0004)
Performance	-	-0.0572***	-0.0576***	-0.0229***	-0.0231***	-0.0570***	-0.0576***
		(0.0072)	(0.0072)	(0.0053)	(0.0053)	(0.0113)	(0.0113)
Leverage	+	-0.0047*	-0.0048*	-0.0028	-0.0029	-0.0046	-0.0047
		(0.0025)	(0.0025)	(0.0018)	(0.0018)	(0.0031)	(0.0031)

[106] Variance inflation factors (VIF) are all below common cut-off values.

Table 20 (continued)

	Pred.	*PRED* Model 1	*PRED* Model 2	*ACQ1* Model 1	*ACQ1* Model 2	*ACQ2* Model 1	*ACQ2* Model 2
Litigation	+	0.0075***	0.0076***	0.0007	0.0007	0.0040*	0.0040*
		(0.0021)	(0.0021)	(0.0016)	(0.0016)	(0.0024)	(0.0024)
Auditors	-	-0.0052***	-0.0051***	-0.0049***	-0.0049***	-0.0012	-0.0011
		(0.0014)	(0.0014)	(0.0010)	(0.0010)	(0.0017)	(0.0017)
Mergers	+	0.0021***	0.0020***	0.0024***	0.0023***	0.0016	0.0016
		(0.0007)	(0.0007)	(0.0006)	(0.0006)	(0.0013)	(0.0013)
Negearn	+	-0.0040***	-0.0041***	-0.0017**	-0.0017**	0.0060***	0.0059***
		(0.0010)	(0.0010)	(0.0008)	(0.0008)	(0.0019)	(0.0019)
Lagaccrual	+	0.0173***	0.0175***	-0.0173***	-0.0172***	-0.0212***	-0.0210***
		(0.0040)	(0.0040)	(0.0034)	(0.0034)	(0.0078)	(0.0078)
Opcycle	+	-0.0015	-0.0016	0.0037***	0.0036***	0.0053***	0.0053***
		(0.0010)	(0.0010)	(0.0008)	(0.0008)	(0.0013)	(0.0013)
Ecofactor	+	0.1267***	0.1267***	0.1110***	0.1110***	0.0745***	0.0743***
		(0.0062)	(0.0062)	(0.0044)	(0.0044)	(0.0061)	(0.0061)
Accfactor	-	-0.0964***	-0.0961***	-0.0469***	-0.0468***	-0.0299***	-0.0294***
		(0.0047)	(0.0047)	(0.0031)	(0.0031)	(0.0050)	(0.0050)
Constant	?	0.1186***	0.1184***	0.0233**	0.0233**	0.0545***	0.0540***
		(0.0109)	(0.0109)	(0.0107)	(0.0107)	(0.0146)	(0.0147)
Industry dummies		Yes	Yes	Yes	Yes	Yes	Yes
Year dummies		Yes	Yes	Yes	Yes	Yes	Yes
Observations		40,520	40,520	40,520	40,520	40,520	40,520
R-squared		0.5396	0.5396	0.4699	0.4698	0.1547	0.1550

This table presents regressions of *actual* earnings quality on cross-segment earnings (cash flow) correlations, earnings volatility (ranked in quintiles from 0 to 4), and an interaction with the respective correlations and earnings volatility ($\alpha_{12} Correlations_{i,t} * EAR\_vola_{i,t}$) for a sample of diversified and focused firms. The regressions are estimated over a time period of 1979 to 2011. Industry dummies are specified for each Fama and French's (1997) 48 industry groups. For variable descriptions, see Table 3. Robust standard errors clustered by firm are in parentheses. Asterisks indicate significance at the 1% (***), 5% (**), or 10% (*) level (respectively).

3.7 Conclusion

In this chapter, I examine whether organizational form matters for firms' earnings quality. I argue that coinsurance among a firm's business units changes the properties of reported earnings through less volatile operations (financial synergies) and less estimation errors in the accrual process (accounting synergies). My empirical analysis provides evidence of a significant positive association between coinsurance and *excess* earnings quality. I find that diversified firms have on average more predictable earnings, superior mapping between accruals and cash flows, and a lower absolute value of abnormal accruals compared to industry-matched portfolios of focused firms. I further find that diversified firms benefit even more from coinsurance on *excess* earnings quality when operating in volatile and uncertain environments. This supports the important role of the coinsurance effect for firms facing higher operating volatility. Overall, my results illustrate that the coinsurance effect is a diversification-specific advantage, which allows diversified firms to create financial synergies (e.g., less bankruptcy risk) as well as accounting synergies (e.g., less information risk).

My findings are relevant for both the earnings quality and the financial economics literature. I contribute to the earnings quality literature by revealing that coinsurance is a unique characteristic that is not captured in previously identified determinants of earnings quality (e.g., firm size, growth, performance, leverage, and operating cycle). The role of coinsurance in accounting information quality (risk) has not been examined in the financial economics literature. Therefore, I contribute by adding evidence related to the fundamental economic question of why so many firms remain diversified as diversification is often an ex-ante value-reducing and thus an inefficient strategy. This analysis explains in part the reluctance of diversified firms to adopt a more focused organizational form.

Moreover, I contribute to the debate on the value consequence of corporate diversification. I reveal a new dimension on how coinsurance can affect firm valuation that thus far has received little attention, namely, accounting information quality (risk). Because accounting information is a priced risk factor and thus affects firm value (Francis et al. 2005; Lambert et al. 2007; Hou 2015), coinsurance can be value-enhancing for diversified firms through reducing the level of accounting information risk. I examine whether diversified firms benefit from higher earnings quality (i.e., reduced information risk) by higher market valuation in the following chapter.

4 Implication for the Excess Value of Corporate Diversification

This chapter covers the economic implications of corporate diversification. Specifically, I explore whether coinsurance benefits on earnings quality (operating volatility) affect the excess value of diversified firms through less accounting information risk.

4.1 Introduction

As presented in Chapter 3 of this doctoral thesis, diversified firms benefit from coinsurance by higher earnings quality, that is, less volatile operations and less estimation errors in the accrual process. Because higher earnings quality (lower operating volatility) leads to less uncertainty about firms' financial performance (Francis et al. 2004, 2005; Hou 2015), the coinsurance effect of diversification implies less accounting information risk.[107] In this chapter, I combine accounting information risk with firm value by investigating the valuation implications of differences in firm's earnings quality (operating volatility) for diversified and focused firms. As pointed out in Section 2.3, the effects of corporate diversification on firm value have been a focus of significant scientific research over the past decades. In particular, agency and behavioral problems are popular explanations for the so-called "diversification discount", which refers to the empirical observation that diversified firms are, on average, valued less than comparable portfolios of their focused peers (Lang and Stulz 1994; Berger and Ofek 1995). In this context, evidence from prior research suggests that accounting information of high-quality (low-risk) reduces agency costs, which arise from information asymmetries between managers and corporate outsiders regarding firm performance (e.g., Lambert 2001; Leuz and Verrecchia 2000). Consequently, because Lambert et al. (2007) show that the quality of accounting information is priced in the capital market, I argue that less accounting information risk (i.e., higher earnings quality or lower operating volatility) reduces agency costs of diversified firms and thus the diversification discount.[108]

In order to test my hypothesis that the association between accounting information quality (risk) and firm value differs for diversified and focused firms, I use a large sample of U.S.

[107] For example, I assume that coinsurance among a firm's business units counteracts agency problems by aggravating circumstances for managers to behave opportunistically in use of their accounting discretion. This would lead to a reduction in accrual manipulations and thus less accrual estimation errors (i.e., less private information about the firm's true financial performance).

[108] In contrast to Chapter 3, I examine the effects earnings volatility and all of its components (besides cash flow volatility) on firm value in my main analysis (see Section 4.5), while I still use the term operating volatility for consistency reasons.

firms for the time period from 1979 to 2011. I follow Berger and Ofek (1995) and compute *Excess Value*, a measure that represents the value of a diversified firm relative to its stand-alone peers. In addition, I focus on earnings quality (operating volatility) as measures of accounting information risk that may affect the value of diversification.

I find that diversified firms benefit from higher (lower) earnings quality (operating volatility) by higher firm valuation. More specifically, I find that for a given level of operating (i.e., earnings and its components) volatility, the firm excess value of diversified firms is higher compared with focused firms.[109] Correspondingly, I also find that for a given level of earnings quality, diversified firms have a higher excess value than focused firms. My evidence suggests that diversified firms with less accounting information risk and thus less agency costs have a relatively lower discount in firm value. However, the documented discount in diversified firms' value is reduced but not eliminated by this accounting dimension. In addition, my results remain robust to potential endogeneity concerns (i.e., firm-fixed effects regressions and Heckman (1979) two-stage procedure), changes in the determinants that affect firm value and alternative estimation techniques.

My investigation in this chapter contributes to the literature in the following two ways. First, it shows the association between agency costs as proxied by the diversification discount and accounting information risk as proxied by earnings quality (operating volatility). Accordingly, I reveal that accounting information of high-quality (low-risk) reduces the discount in diversified firms' value. Second, my empirical results offer a new perspective to better understand the valuation implications of corporate diversification. Thereby, it provides insights into the interrelationship between agency costs, information risk, and firm valuation.

The remainder of this chapter is structured as follows. Section 4.2 presents a preliminary analysis that validates the impact of corporate diversification (coinsurance) on operating volatility. Section 4.3 provides the theoretical background and the development of testable hypotheses. Section 4.4 describes the research design and sample. Section 4.5 reports the main results and Section 4.6 checks for robustness. Section 4.7 concludes this chapter.

4.2 Preliminary Analysis: Operating Volatility of Diversified Firms

The objective of this section is to validate the coinsurance effect of corporate diversification on the firms' operating (i.e., earnings and cash flow) volatility. As stated in Chapter 3,

[109] In line with Berger and Ofek (1995), the excess value of focused firms is computed by using multipliers for the median focused firm in each industry-year (see Section 4.4.1 for more details).

diversified firms are known to create financial synergies (e.g., less bankruptcy risk) through less than perfectly correlated segment-level earnings (cash flows). In the following, I first present the underlying theory and hypothesis. Then I explain my methodological approach and sample restriction process. Finally, I empirically examine the effect of diversification and coinsurance on a firm's operating volatility.

4.2.1 Theory and Hypothesis

The financial advantage of corporate diversification is first described by Lewellen (1971) who finds that less than perfectly correlated earnings (cash flows) reduce diversified firms' bankruptcy risk (costs) by enabling these firms to exploit additional leverage possibilities through improved satisfaction of contractual debt criteria. Besides potential capital market implications, this coinsurance effect suggests that diversification basically leads to a lower volatility of earnings (cash flows).[110] The financial economics literature confirms such a direct consequence of coinsurance and finds that diversified firms generally exhibit less volatility than focused firms (e.g., Comment and Jarell 1995; Thomas 2002; Leland 2007; Kuppuswamy and Villalonga 2010; Duchin 2010). The rationale behind this observation follows the notion of standard portfolio theory which suggests that the combination of imperfectly correlated segment-level earnings (cash flows) entails lower firm-level earnings (cash flow) volatility. Consequently, coinsurance reduces the volatility of firms' business operations because of the aggregated nature of earnings (cash flows), making diversified firms less dependent on a single business and thus less economically risky.[111] For example, consider a firm A which merges with firm B from another business segment. The earnings of this newly created industrial diversified firm F and the variance of its earnings are now as follows:

$$Ear_{i,t}^{F} = Ear_{i,t}^{A} + Ear_{i,t}^{B}$$
$$\sigma^2_{Ear_{i,t}^{F}} = \sigma^2_{Ear_{i,t}^{A}} + \sigma^2_{Ear_{i,t}^{B}} + 2\sigma_{Ear_t^A, Ear_t^B} \quad (12)$$

where $\sigma_{Ear_t^A, Ear_t^B}$ is equal to $\sigma_{Ear_{i,t}^{A}} \cdot \sigma_{Ear_{i,t}^{B}} \cdot \rho_{Ear_t^A, Ear_t^B}$. The imperfect cross-segment correlation of earnings between business units A and B, expressed by $\rho_{Ear_t^A, Ear_t^B} < 1$, leads to a lower firm-level volatility of earnings for diversified firm F (this is also true when using

110 See Section 4.3.1 for a literature review of potential capital market implications.

111 By assumption, those business units of a diversified firm which operate in different business segments (industries) are less than perfectly correlated.

cash flows instead of earnings).[112] Therefore, the earnings (cash flow) volatility of diversified firms should be lower compared to focused firms (or industry-matched portfolios of focused firms) because those firms operate in only one business segment (industry) and thus cannot benefit from such offsetting effects across different business units.[113] Thus, my hypothesis is:

Hypothesis 4: Corporate diversification, and especially the coinsurance effect, leads to a decrease in earnings and cash flow volatility.

However, lower earnings volatility of diversified firms is not necessarily a *mechanical* effect but could also indicate earnings smoothing because earnings are subject to measurement errors and potential manipulations through its accrual component (i.e., agency problems). Moreover, even if the negative relation between corporate diversification and earnings volatility is rather evident from Equation (12), the link between both is still interesting to be examined because earnings (cash flow) volatility is often used as a measure of business (operating) risk (e.g., Shin and Stulz 2000; Dichev and Tang 2009; Rountree et al. 2008). Therefore, coinsurance implies that diversified firms are inherently less risky than focused firms (see Section 4.3 for this matter).

4.2.2 Methodology and Sample

My research design is based on the hypothesis that corporate diversification (coinsurance) is a determinant of a firm's operating volatility. I follow Dichev and Tang (2009) and use measures of earnings (cash flow) volatility as proxy for operating volatility which are calculated as the standard deviation of firm *i*'s earnings (cash flows) scaled by average total assets over a 5-year window (*t* - 4 to *t*). In my empirical analysis, I use *excess* operating volatility to compare the earnings (cash flow) volatility of a diversified firm to the earnings (cash flow) volatility that its business units would have if operated as stand-alone firms. Similar to Section 3.4.1, I follow Berger and Ofek (1995) and compute a firm- and year-specific measure of *excess* earnings (cash flow) volatility (hereafter, *EX_vola*) which is the difference between a firm's *actual* earnings (cash flow) volatility (hereafter, *actual* Vola) and its *imputed* earnings (cash flow) volatility (hereafter, *imputed* Vola) in year *t*:

---

[112] While the theoretical construct is the variance of earnings (i.e., $\sigma^2_{Ear^F_{i,t}}$), we operationalize this measure by using earnings volatility as our variability proxy which is simply the square root of the variance of earnings.

[113] It is important to understand that the coinsurance benefit of diversification has an effect on the segment level which changes the properties of earnings and its components on the firm level.

$$EX\_vola_{i,t} = actual\ Vola_{i,t} - imputed\ Vola_{i,t}. \tag{13}$$

A negative (positive) *EX_vola* value indicates that diversification decreases (increases) the firm's earnings (cash flow) volatility beyond their focused counterparts. I calculate my *imputed* Vola measure ($imputed\ Vola_{i,t}$) for firm *i* in year *t* as a sales-weighted average of the *imputed* stand-alone volatility of its *n* business units (segments):

$$imputed\ Vola_{i,t} = \sum_{k=1}^{n} \frac{Sales_{i,t,k}}{\sum_{j=1}^{n} Sales_{i,t,j}} impVola_{i,t,k}\ , \tag{14}$$

where $Sales_{i,t,k}$ is the total sales of segment *k* of firm *i* in year *t*, and $impVola_{i,t,k}$ is the *imputed* stand-alone volatility of segment *k* of firm *i* in year *t*. The *imputed* stand-alone volatility of each business unit is the median earnings (cash flow) volatility of focused firms from the same industry-year. The industry medians are based on the narrowest SIC grouping that includes at least five focused firms with at least $20 million of sales and has non-missing earnings (cash flow) volatility values. The *imputed* volatility of a firm estimates the firm's earnings (cash flow) volatility as if all of its business units were operated as typical focused firms in their respective industry and thus ensures an industry-matched comparison to the firm's *actual* volatility.

I use the same coinsurance measures as in my investigation in Chapter 3. In addition, I select control variables following Dechow and Dichev (2002), Rountree et al. (2008) and Dichev and Tang (2009) which I list and define in Table 21. These controls ensure that my results are not contaminated by previously identified determinants (e.g., economic shocks and accounting factors as explained in Dichev and Tang 2009) affecting operating volatility. All variables are winsorized at the 1st and 99th percentiles.

Table 21: Variable Descriptions

Variable name	*Description*
Volatility measures	
$EAR\_vola_{i,t}$	Earnings volatility is the standard deviation of firm *i*'s earnings scaled by average total assets calculated over a 5-year window (*t* - 4 to *t*) following Dichev and Tang (2009).
$CF\_vola_{i,t}$	Cash flow volatility is the standard deviation of firm *i*'s cash flow from operations scaled by average total assets calculated over a 5-year window (*t* - 4 to *t*) following Dichev and Tang (2009).
$AC\_vola_{i,t}$	Accruals volatility is the standard deviation of firm *i*'s *total* accruals scaled by average total assets calculated over a 5-year window (*t* - 4 to *t*).
$Corr\_CF\_AC_{i,t}$	Correlation between cash flow from operations and *total* accruals is calculated pairwise for firm *i* over a 5-year window (*t* - 4 to *t*).

Table 21 (continued)

Variable name	*Description*
$AC\_vola_{i,t}$	Accruals volatility is the standard deviation of firm *i*'s *total* accruals scaled by average total assets calculated over a 5-year window (*t* - 4 to *t*).
$Corr\_CF\_AC_{i,t}$	Correlation between cash flow from operations and *total* accruals is calculated pairwise for firm *i* over a 5-year window (*t* - 4 to *t*).
Excess volatility measures	
$EX\_EAR\_vola_{i,t}$	Firm *i*'s *excess* earnings volatility is defined as the difference between its *actual* earnings volatility and its *imputed* earnings volatility in year *t*: see Equations (13) and (14).
$EX\_CF\_vola_{i,t}$	Firm *i*'s *excess* cash flow volatility is defined as the difference between its *actual* cash flow volatility and its *imputed* cash flow volatility in year *t*: see Equations (13) and (14).
$EX\_AC\_vola_{i,t}$	Firm *i*'s *excess* accruals volatility is defined as the difference between its *actual* accruals volatility and its *imputed* accruals volatility in year *t*: see Equations (13) and (14).
$EX\_Corr\_CF\_AC_{i,t}$	Firm *i*'s *excess* correlation between cash flow and accruals is defined as the difference between its *actual* correlation and its *imputed* correlation in year *t*: see Equations (13) and (14).
Coinsurance measures	
$EAR\_correlations_{i,t}$	As (inverse) measure for earnings coinsurance, cross-segment earnings correlations for firm *i* in year *t* is a sales-weighted portfolio correlation of pairwise segment correlations estimated using prior 10-year industry earnings based on focused firms: see Equation (10).
$CF\_correlations_{i,t}$	As (inverse) measure for cash flow coinsurance, cross-segment cash flow correlations for firm *i* in year *t* is a sales-weighted portfolio correlation of pairwise segment correlations estimated using prior 10-year industry cash flows based on focused firms following Hann et al. (2013): see Equation (10).
Control variables	
$LogAsset_{i,t}$	Natural logarithm of firm *i*'s total asset (AT) in year *t*.
$SalesGrowth_{i,t}$	Firm *i*'s change in total sales (SALE) between year *t* - 1 and *t*.
$ROA_{i,t}$	Firm *i*'s ratio of earnings (IB) to its average total assets (return on assets) in year *t*.
$NegEarn_{i,t}$	Indicator that equals 1 if firm *i* reported negative (non-zero) earnings in year *t*, and 0 otherwise.
$Opcycle_{i,t}$	Natural logarithm of firm *i*'s length of the operating *Cycle* [360 / (SALE / Average Account Receivables [RECT]) + 360 / (COGS / Average Inventory [INVT])] in year *t*.
$Mergers_{i,t}$	Indicator that equals 1 if firm *i* had a merger in year *t* and 0 otherwise.
$R\&D_{i,t}$	Firm *i*'s ratio of research and development expenses (XRD) to sales (SALE) in year *t*.
$Abs(Acc)_{i,t}$	Absolute value of total accruals for firm *i* in year *t* scaled by average total assets.
$Sales\_Vola_{i,t}$	Sales volatility is the standard deviation of firm *i*'s sales scaled by average total assets calculated over a 5-year window (*t* - 4 to *t*).
$Corr\_Rev\_Exp_{i,t}$	Correlation between revenues and expenses is calculated pairwise for firm *i* over a 5-year window (*t* - 4 to *t*).

This table presents the description of all variables used in this preliminary analysis. Following Francis et al. (2005), *Earnings* is defined as net income before extraordinary items [IB] for firm *i* in year *t*. Total current accruals for firm *i* in year *t* is defined as $TCA_{i,t} = \Delta CA_{i,t} - \Delta CL_{i,t} - \Delta Cash_{i,t} + \Delta STDEBT_{i,t}$, where $\Delta CA_{i,t}$ is change in current assets, $\Delta CL_{i,t}$ is change in current liabilities, $\Delta Cash_{i,t}$ is change in cash, and $\Delta STDEBT_{i,t}$ is change in debt in current liabilities for firm *i* between year *t* - 1 and *t* (respectively). Cash flow from operations $(CFO_{i,t})$ is defined as difference between firm *i*'s earnings and total accruals $(TA_{i,t})$ in year *t*. Total accruals for firm *i* in year *t* is calculated as $TA_{i,t} = TCA_{i,t} - DEPN_{i,t}$, where $DEPN_{i,t}$ is firm *i*'s depreciation and amortization expense in year *t*. I calculate total accruals using the balance sheet (indirect) approach rather than the statement of cash flows (direct) approach because statement of cash flows data is not available prior to 1988. However, while estimating total accruals I control for mergers/acquisitions and divestitures as suggested by Hribar and Collins (2002).

I use data of U.S. companies from the Compustat Annual Industrial files and calculate earnings (cash flow) volatility measures and control variables, and from the Compustat Industrial Segment files to calculate *excess* earnings (cash flow) volatility and coinsurance measures for the period from 1979 to 2011.[114] For this investigation, I apply exactly the same requirements to the data as described in Section 3.4.2 to maintain consistency in the data. My final sample comprises 64,766 firm-year observations, of which 40,017 (24,749) observations are from focused (diversified) firms. Because I do not need to apply the restrictive data requirements of calculating earnings attributes, this sample is considerably larger than the sample I use for my investigation in Chapter 3.

4.2.3 Results and Discussion

Table 22 provides descriptive statistics on all *actual* and *excess* volatility measures, coinsurance measures and control variables for diversified and focused firms. In Panel A of Table 22, both mean and median differences between diversified and focused firms for all *actual* volatility measures (i.e., the volatility of earnings and its cash flow and accrual components) are negative and significant. Correspondingly, the *excess* volatility measures are also negative and significant. This finding provides initial support that diversification decreases the volatility of earnings and its components, even when comparing earnings (cash flow) volatility to the earnings (cash flow) volatility that its business units would have if operated as stand-alone firms. Note that the effect of diversification on earnings volatility is slightly higher than on cash flow volatility. The reason is that earnings volatility also incorporates the effect on accruals volatility and on the matching (i.e., correlation) between cash flows and accruals (see Section 4.3.2 for more details).

As described in Section 3.5.1, the coinsurance measures for focused firms equal one by construction because focused firms cannot realize coinsurance benefits. The mean (median) earnings and cash flow correlations for diversified firms are 0.6758 and 0.6699 (0.6858 and 0.6781) and thus slightly above the values from Chapter 3. This difference can be explained by the larger sample size. However, these cross-segment correlation values indicate a strong and consistent coinsurance effect within diversified firms. In addition, consistent with Chapter 3, I find that diversified firms are larger in size, have less growth opportunities, are more profitable, engage in more mergers, and are less likely to report losses than focused firms.

[114] The Compustat database is provided by Wharton Research Data Services (WRDS).

In Panel B (Panel C) of Table 22, I show the correlation between *actual* (*excess*) earnings volatility measures. As expected, all measures are positively correlated except for the correlation of cash flows and accruals and accruals volatility, which are slightly negatively correlated.

Table 22: Descriptive Statistics

Panel A: Main variables

	Diversified firms			Focused firms			Difference	
	Mean	SD	Med.	Mean	SD	Med.	Mean	Med.
Volatility measures								
EAR_vola	0.0334	0.0297	0.0243	0.0539	0.0574	0.0320	-0.0205***	-0-0077***
CF_vola	0.0604	0.0380	0.0510	0.0771	0.0594	0.0594	-0.0167***	-0.0084***
AC_vola	0.0543	0.0359	0.0457	0.0663	0.0502	0.0517	-0.0120***	-0.0060***
Corr_CF_AC	-0.7877	0.2656	-0.9023	-0.6820	0.4046	-0.8701	-0.1058***	-0.0322***
Excess volatility measures								
EX_EAR_vola	-0.0083	0.0324	-0.0089	0.0093	0.0405	0.0000	-0.0176***	-0.0089***
EX_CF_vola	-0.0070	0.0400	-0.0112	0.0096	0.0448	0.0000	-0.0165***	-0.0112***
EX_AC_vola	-0.0066	0.0362	-0.0101	0.0071	0.0360	0.0000	-0.0136***	-0.0101***
EX_Corr_CF_AC	-0.0134	0.2957	-0.0363	0.0905	0.3140	0.0000	-0.1046***	-0.0363***
Coinsurance measures								
EAR_correlations	0.6758	0.2596	0.6858	1.0000	0.0000	1.0000	-0.3242***	-0.3142***
CF_correlations	0.6699	0.2637	0.6781	1.0000	0.0000	1.0000	-0.3301***	-0.3219***
Control variables								
LogAsset	6.0771	2.1737	6.1396	5.5606	1.8590	5.3558	0.5165***	0.7838***
SalesGrowth	1.0975	0.2457	1.0718	1.1238	0.3769	1.0747	-0.0263***	-0.0029***
ROA	0.0361	0.0867	0.0448	0.0232	0.1908	0.0433	0.0129***	0.0015***
NegEarn	0.1640	0.3703	0.0000	0.2134	0.4097	0.0000	-0.0494***	0.0000***
Opcycle	4.7427	0.5764	4,7896	4.6415	0.7463	4.7205	0.1012***	0.0691***
Mergers	0.1655	0.3716	0.0000	0.1109	0.3140	0.0000	0.0546***	0.0000***
R&D	0.0176	0.0351	0.0000	0.0346	0.0772	0.0000	-0.0170***	0.0000***
Abs(Acc)	0.0594	0.0482	0.0477	0.0727	0.0666	0.0547	-0.0133***	0.0070***
Sales_vola	0.1430	0.0993	0.1179	0.1735	0.1403	0.1325	-0.0305***	-0.0146***
Corr_Rev_Exp	0.9411	0.1263	0.9885	0.8984	0.1892	0.9827	0.0427***	0.0058***
Observations	24,749			40,017				

Panel B: Pearson correlation coefficients for earnings volatility components

Variable	*EAR_vola*	*CF_vola*	*AC_vola*	*Corr_CF_AC*
EAR_vola	1.0000			
CF_vola	0.7144 (.0000)	1.0000		
AC_vola	0.4887 (.0000)	0.7701 (.0000)	1.0000	
Corr_CF_AC	0.6119 (.0000)	0.1302 (.0000)	-0.0584 (.0000)	1.0000

Table 22 (continued)

Panel C: Pearson correlation coefficients for excess earnings volatility components

Variable	*EX_EAR_vola*	*EX_CF_vola*	*EX_AC_vola*	*EX_Corr_CF_AC*
EX_EAR_vola	1.0000			
EX_CF_vola	0.6491	1.0000		
	(.0000)			
EX_AC_vola	0.4442	0.7265	1.0000	
	(.0000)	(.0000)		
EX_Corr_CF_AC	0.5134	0.0232	-0.1120	1.0000
	(.0000)	(.0000)	(.0000)	

This table reports summary statistics for all variables used in this preliminary analysis. The sample includes 64,766 observations between 1979 and 2011. For variable descriptions, see Table 21. Significance levels are stated for the difference between diversified and focused firms. The mean difference is based on a t-test and the median difference is based on a Wilcoxon Rank-Sum test. Asterisks indicate significance at the 1% (***), 5% (**), or 10% (*) level (respectively).

Table 23 presents the mean values of *EX_EAR_vola* (*EX_CF_vola*) sorted into coinsurance quintiles in Panel A (Panel B). Diversified firms are divided into quintiles based on their cross-segment earnings (cash flow) correlations, where the lowest correlation quintile contains diversified firms with the highest coinsurance effect and vice versa. For comparison only, I also report the results for focused firms. I find a monotonic increase in both *EX_EAR_vola* and *EX_CF_vola* from the lowest earnings (cash flow) correlation quintile (Q1) with the highest coinsurance effect to the highest earnings (cash flow) correlation quintile (Q5) with the lowest coinsurance effect. The mean differences between Q1 and Q5 are -0.0245 (-0.0246) and -0.0227 (-0.0216) and statistically significant. These results show that diversified firms realize coinsurance benefits which incrementally improve the extent of their earnings (cash flow) volatility. Thus, consistent with my hypothesis 4, diversified firms with less correlated business activities and thus greater coinsurance potential have lower earnings (cash flow) volatility. In unreported tests, I also compare the relation between both *actual* operating volatility measures and cross-segment correlations for diversified and focused firms. My inferences remain unchanged for such *naive* comparison.

Table 23: *Excess* Operating Volatility Measures and Cross-segment Correlations

Panel A: Excess earnings volatility

	Firms sorted by					
	EAR_correlations			***CF_correlations***		
	Sort Variable	*EX_EAR_ vola*	Obs.	Sort Variable	*EX_EAR_ vola*	Obs.
Diversified firms						
Q1 (Lowest)	0.4227	-0.0209	4,951	0.4147	-0.0208	4,951
Q2	0.5690	-0.0119	4,949	0.5600	-0.0120	4,949
Q3	0.6788	-0.0078	4,951	0.6727	-0.0072	4,951
Q4	0.7899	-0.0044	4,949	0.7850	-0.0052	4,949
Q5 (Highest)	0.9188	0.0036	4,949	0.9174	0.0038	4,949
Focused firms	1.0000	0.0093	40,017	1.0000	0.0093	40,017
Q1 – Q5		-0.0245***			-0.0246***	
Q1 – Focused		-0.0302***			-0.0301***	

Panel B: Excess cash flow volatility

	Firms sorted by					
	EAR_correlations			***CF_correlations***		
	Sort Variable	*EX_CF_ vola*	Obs.	Sort Variable	*EX_CF_ vola*	Obs.
Diversified firms						
Q1 (Lowest)	0.4227	-0.0187	4,951	0.4147	-0.0177	4,951
Q2	0.5690	-0.0099	4,949	0.5600	-0.0107	4,949
Q3	0.6788	-0.0073	4,951	0.6727	-0.0064	4,951
Q4	0.7899	-0.0031	4,949	0.7850	-0.0040	4,949
Q5 (Highest)	0.9188	0.0040	4,949	0.9174	0.0039	4,949
Focused firms	1.0000	0.0096	40,017	1.0000	0.0096	40,017
Q1 – Q5		-0.0227***			-0.0216***	
Q1 – Focused		-0.0283***			-0.0273***	

This table presents *excess* operating (i.e., *excess* earnings and *excess* cash flow) volatility sorts based on cross-segment earnings (cash flow) correlations. Diversified firms are sorted into quintiles based on their cross-segment earnings (cash flow) correlations. For variable descriptions, see Table 21. The significance of mean values is based on a t-test. Asterisks indicate significance at the 1% (***), 5% (**), or 10% (*) level (respectively).

In Table 24, I examine the impact of diversification and coinsurance measures on operating (i.e., earnings and cash flow) volatility for my sample of diversified and focused firms. I control for previously identified determinants of earnings (cash flow) volatility and use year and industry fixed effects and robust standard errors clustered by firm in parentheses. Industry dummies are specified for each Fama and French (1997) 48 industry groups.

I find a significant negative relation between my diversification indicator, which takes the value of 1 for diversified firms (i.e., firms that operate in at least two different four-digit SIC codes) and 0 otherwise, and earnings (cash flow) volatility. The coefficient estimates on diversification with *EX_EAR_vola* and *EX_CF_vola* as dependent variables are -0.0064 and

-0.0059 and all significant at the 1% level.[115] Therefore, I find that diversified firms have on average lower earnings (cash flow) volatility than focused firms. Concerning a potential coinsurance effect, I document a positive relation between cross-segment earnings (cash flow) correlations and earnings (cash flow) volatility. The coefficient estimates on cross-segment earnings correlations with earnings (cash flow) volatility as dependent variables is 0.0088 (0.0110) and significant. Accordingly, the coefficient estimates on cross-segment cash flow correlations is 0.0086 (0.0103) and significant. Thus, lower cross-segment correlations (i.e., more coinsurance benefits) are associated with lower earnings (cash flow) volatility.[116]

Overall, after controlling for previously identified determinants of earnings (cash flow) volatility, I find that corporate diversification and especially coinsurance lead to lower earnings (cash flow) volatility, consistent with my hypothesis 4. In addition, I repeat my investigation with *actual* earnings (cash flow) volatility measures and draw the same (unreported) conclusions. Therefore, I confirm that coinsurance benefits reduce a diversified firm's operating volatility.

Table 24: Regressions of *Excess* Operating Volatility on Diversification Measures

$$EX\_vola_{i,t} = \alpha_0 + \boldsymbol{\alpha_1 Div\_Measures_{i,t}} + \alpha_2 LogAsset_{i,t} + \alpha_3 SalesGrowth_{i,t} + \alpha_4 ROA_{i,t} + \alpha_5 NegEarn_{i,t} + \alpha_6 Opcycle_{i,t} + \alpha_7 Mergers_{i,t} + \alpha_8 R\&D_{i,t} + \alpha_9 Abs(Acc)_{i,t} + \alpha_{10} Sales\_vola_{i,t} + \alpha_{11} Corr\_Rev\_Exp_{i,t} + \sum INDUSTRY_t + \sum YEAR + \varepsilon_{i,t}$$

		***Excess* earnings volatility**			***Excess* cash flow volatility**		
	Pred.	**(1)**	**(2)**	**(3)**	**(4)**	**(5)**	**(6)**
Div_Dummy	-	-0.0064***			-0.0059***		
		(0.0004)			(0.0006)		
EAR_correlations	+		0.0088***			0.0110***	
			(0.0008)			(0.0012)	
CF_correlations	+			0.0086***			0.0103***
				(0.0008)			(0.0011)
LogAsset	-	-0.0024***	-0.0024***	-0.0024***	-0.0035***	-0.0035***	-0.0035***
		(0.0001)	(0.0001)	(0.0001)	(0.0002)	(0.0002)	(0.0002)
SalesGrowth	+	0.0035***	0.0036***	0.0036***	0.0075***	0.0075***	0.0075***
		(0.0006)	(0.0006)	(0.0006)	(0.0007)	(0.0007)	(0.0007)
ROA	-	-0.0154***	-0.0153***	-0.0153***	-0.0087***	-0.0087***	-0.0087***
		(0.0056)	(0.0055)	(0.0055)	(0.0027)	(0.0026)	(0.0026)
NegEarn	+	0.0120***	0.0119***	0.0119***	0.0038***	0.0037***	0.0037***
		(0.0010)	(0.0010)	(0.0010)	(0.0007)	(0.0007)	(0.0007)
Opcycle	+	-0.0003	-0.0004	-0.0004	0.0025***	0.0024***	0.0024***
		(0.0005)	(0.0005)	(0.0005)	(0.0006)	(0.0006)	(0.0006)
Mergers	+/-	-0.0021***	-0.0024***	-0.0024***	0.0006	0.0005	0.0004
		(0.0004)	(0.0004)	(0.0004)	(0.0005)	(0.0005)	(0.0005)

[115] Variance inflation factors (VIF) are all below common cut-off values.

[116] I also use leverage as an additional control variable, which does not change my inferences (unreported).

Table 24 (continued)

	Pred.	(1)	(2)	(3)	(4)	(5)	(6)
R&D	+	0.0075	0.0114*	0.0114*	0.0120*	0.0144**	0.0145**
		(0.0060)	(0.0060)	(0.0060)	(0.0068)	(0.0067)	(0.0067)
Abs(Acc)	+	0.0451***	0.0464***	0.0465***	0.1190***	0.1198***	0.1199***
		(0.0032)	(0.0032)	(0.0032)	(0.0039)	(0.0039)	(0.0039)
Sales_vola	+	0.1159***	0.1174***	0.1175***	0.1168***	0.1186***	0.1187***
		(0.0025)	(0.0025)	(0.0025)	(0.0027)	(0.0027)	(0.0027)
Corr_Rev_Exp	-	-0.1014***	-0.1024***	-0.1024***	-0.0677***	-0.0684***	-0.0684***
		(0.0018)	(0.0018)	(0.0018)	(0.0019)	(0.0019)	(0.0019)
Constant	+	0.0910***	0.0828***	0.0830***	0.0454***	0.0348***	0.0353***
		(0.0082)	(0.0084)	(0.0084)	(0.0098)	(0.0100)	(0.0100)
Industry dummies		Yes	Yes	Yes	Yes	Yes	Yes
Year dummies		Yes	Yes	Yes	Yes	Yes	Yes
Observations		64,766	64,766	64,766	64,766	64,766	64,766
R-squared		0.4267	0.4235	0.4234	0.2937	0.2928	0.2926

This table presents regressions of *excess* earnings and *excess* cash flow volatility on diversification measures (i.e., diversification indicator and cross-segment earnings and cash flow correlations) for a sample of diversified and focused firms. The diversification indicator *Div_Dummy* takes the value of 1 for diversified firms (i.e., firms that operate in at least two different four-digit SIC codes) and 0 otherwise. The predicted sign for *Div_Dummy* is negative because diversified firms are expected to have lower *excess* volatility of earnings and cash flows. The regressions are estimated over a time period of 1979 to 2011. Industry dummies are specified for each Fama and French's (1997) 48 industry groups. For variable descriptions, see Table 21. Robust standard errors clustered by firm are in parentheses. Asterisks indicate significance at the 1% (***), 5% (**), or 10% (*) level (respectively).

4.3 Literature Review and Hypotheses Development

4.3.1 Literature Review

Most studies in the financial economics literature find that, on average, diversified firms are valued at a diversification discount compared to industry-matched portfolios of focused firms.[117] As stated in Section 2.2.2 and Section 3.3.1, the explanations range from agency problems (Jensen 1986; Denis et al. 1997) or inefficient internal capital markets (Scharfstein and Stein 2000; Rajan et al. 2000), through self-selection and the endogeneity of the diversification decision (Campa and Kedia 2002; Graham et al. 2002; Maksimovic and Philips 2002) up to data and measurement problems (Villalonga 2004). However, the cross-sectional variation in firm valuation (or performance) is also determined by other factors like firm size, profitability, growth opportunities, leverage, or systematic market risk.[118] One such firm-specific factor has been identified as accounting information quality (risk).[119]

117 For example, see Lang and Stulz (1994), Berger and Ofek (1995), Comment and Jarrel (1995), Servaes (1996), Lins and Servaes (1999), Rajan et al. (2000), Lammont and Polk (2002), among others.

118 In my empirical analysis, I control for those factors that might explain variation in firm valuation (see Section 4.4.1 for more background information).

119 See Section 3.2.4 for an explanation about the association between accounting information quality (risk) and capital market consequences.

Because earnings quality is frequently used as a measure of accounting information risk (e.g., Francis et al. 2004, 2005; Hou 2015), higher earnings quality implies less accounting information risk and thus is positively related to firm valuation (Lambert et al. 2007; Hope and Thomas 2008). Moreover, recent studies have demonstrated a positive association between accounting information risk and idiosyncratic volatility (e.g., Rajgopal and Venkatachalam 2011; Chen et al. 2012). In this context, Rountree et al. (2008) focus on earnings and cash flow volatility as measures of idiosyncratic risk (i.e., firm-specific or operating volatility) and find a negative relation between idiosyncratic risk and firm value. Consequently, less idiosyncratic risk (volatility) implies less accounting information risk and higher firm valuation.[120]

While corporate diversification improves a firm's earnings quality (see Chapter 3) and reduces its operating volatility (see Section 4.2) through coinsurance benefits, the question arises whether the impact of diversification on a firm's valuation depends on its earnings quality (operating volatility). This is an important question because the accounting implications of corporate diversification may also have an economic relevance and thus may add a new perspective to the diversification discount puzzle (see Section 2.3). The rest of this chapter covers such an economic implication for firm excess value. In order to provide a better overview, I illustrate the respective relationships covered in this thesis in Figure 6.

Figure 6: Overview of Conceptual Relations

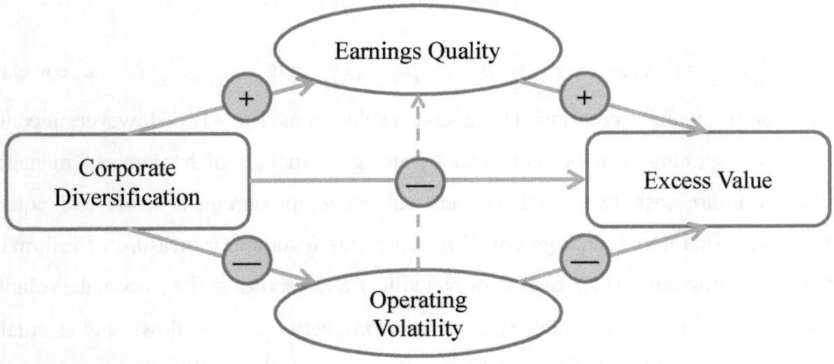

Source: Own illustration.

---

[120] Other capital market implications of less (lower) idiosyncratic risk (volatility) are, for example, a lower default probability (Lewellen 1971), lower capital-raising costs (Minton and Schrand 1999), lower stock return volatility (Wei and Zhang 2006), higher accuracy of accounting information (Dechow and Dichev 2002; Weiss 2010), more predictable earnings and less biased analysts forecasts (Dichev and Tang 2009), lower cost of capital (Francis et al. 2004, 2005), higher credit ratings (Hann et al. 2007), and lower credit risk (Correia et al. 2015).

4.3.2 Hypotheses Development

I argue that the positive (negative) relation between corporate diversification and earnings quality (operating volatility) has an impact on firm value because both earnings quality and operating volatility are associated to accounting information quality (risk), which has been identified as a firm-specific factor reducing agency costs (e.g., through improved monitoring) and thus affecting firm valuation. This is especially relevant for diversified firms which are exposed to higher agency costs than focused firms and thus are valued at a diversification discount. Note that I first examine the role of operating (i.e., earnings and its components) volatility in diversified firms' valuation because earnings and cash flow volatility also influence earnings quality (Dechow and Dichev 2002; Francis et al. 2005) and thus represents a preparatory analysis for the role of earnings quality in diversified firms' excess value.

Regarding operating volatility, coinsurance among a diversified firm's business units (i.e., on the segment-level) reduces the volatility of its business operations (i.e., on the firm-level) because of the aggregate nature of reported earnings and its components (cash flows and accruals). In this context, note that earnings volatility contains not only information about the variance of cash flows and the variance of accruals but also about the covariance between cash flows and accruals:

$$Ear_{i,t} = CF_{i,t} + Acc_{i,t}$$
$$\sigma^2_{Ear\,i,t} = \sigma^2_{CF_{i,t}} + \sigma^2_{Acc\,i,t} + 2\sigma_{CF_{i,t},Acc\,i,t}, \quad (15)$$

where $\sigma^2_{CF_{i,t},Acc\,i,t}$ is equal to $\sigma_{CF_{i,t}} \cdot \sigma_{Acc\,i,t} \cdot \rho_{CF_{i,t},Acc\,i,t}$ and $\rho_{CF_{i,t},Acc\,i,t}$ is the correlation between cash flows and accruals which can take a value from -1 to +1.[121] However, in contrast to cash flows, earnings can be smoothed by using accruals, which represent managerial estimates of future cash flows and thus are subject to measurement errors and potential manipulations. Therefore, earnings volatility represents a summary measure of information about a firm's operating (i.e., cash flow volatility) and reporting (i.e., accruals volatility) activities as well as the matching (i.e., correlation) between cash flows and accruals.[122] Moreover, earnings and cash flow volatility reflect the stability of firm's reported financial statements and thus have recently been used as measures of accounting information risk

[121] Because the fundamental role of accruals is to allocate cash flows to reporting periods in which they are recognized, cash flows and accruals are negatively correlated. Thus, a better matching between cash flows and accruals corresponds to a more negative correlation (covariance).

[122] The correlation term captures the linear dependency between cash flows and accruals and thus represents a measure for the extent to which contemporary cash flows and accruals are matched.

(Rountree et al. 2008).[123] Because the coinsurance effect of corporate diversification leads to a lower cash flow and accruals volatility, a better matching between cash flows and accruals due to less accrual estimation errors and overall less volatile earnings (see results in Section 3.5 and Section 4.2), I argue that diversified firms likely incur less accounting information risk compared with focused firms. For example, Subramanyam (1996) finds that a smooth earnings stream is more informative and useful to investors. Moreover, additional mandatory disclosures (e.g., SFAS 131) or anticipated synergies from internal transfers of resources (e.g., lower deadweight costs or less accrual estimation errors) should further reduce investors' information risk about diversified firms' performance (i.e., agency costs). As a result, the effect of earnings volatility (accounting information risk) on firm value should differ between diversified and focused firms. Accordingly, I expect that diversified firms benefit from substantial lower earnings volatility (less accounting information risk) by higher firm valuation. In other words, I expect a less strong association between earnings volatility and firm value for diversified firms. Thus, my first hypothesis is:

Hypothesis 5: Compared with focused firms, diversified firms' volatility of earnings is less strongly associated with firm value.

Regarding earnings quality, coinsurance among a diversified firm's business units leads to higher earnings quality because of less volatile operations and less estimation errors in the accrual process (see results in Chapter 3). Therefore, I argue that diversified firms exhibit less accounting information risk compared to focused firms. Note that earnings quality is - in the financial economics literature - used as a standard proxy for accounting information risk because high-quality earnings reduce the uncertainty about firms' financial performance (i.e., agency costs). For example, high-quality earnings decrease investors' concerns that management is opportunistically making accounting decisions which affect the required rate of return and, in turn, the firm valuation. Consequently, I expect that diversified firms have a lower discount in firm value because of higher earnings quality (less accounting information risk). In other words, I expect a more positive relation between earnings quality and firm value for diversified firms. Thus, my second hypothesis is:

Hypothesis 6: Compared with focused firms, diversified firms' earnings quality is more positively associated with firm value.

[123] In my empirical analysis, I control for idiosyncratic return volatility which proxies for non-systematic risk components to rule out the possibility that earnings volatility incorporates some kind of business (operating) risk.

However, the cross-sectional association between accounting information risk and capital market consequences has been challenged by more recent studies which find that idiosyncratic risk is diversified away (e.g., Hughes et al. 2007; Core et al. 2008; McInnis 2010). In such case, my hypothesis 5 and hypothesis 6 may not hold.

4.4 Research Design and Data

4.4.1 Methodology

Excess Value

In my empirical analysis, I examine the implication for the *Excess Value* of corporate diversification, a widely used measure developed by Berger and Ofek (1995) that represents the value of a diversified firm relative to its stand-alone peers. Following Berger and Ofek (1995), I compute excess values (hereafter, *EX_value*) as the natural logarithm of the ratio between a firm's actual value and its imputed value at the end of the year *t*:

$$EX\_value_{i,t} = \ln(actual\ value_{i,t}/imputed\ value_{i,t}). \quad (16)$$

A positive (negative) excess value indicates that a diversified firm is valued more (less) than a comparable portfolio of focused firms. A firm's actual value is defined as market value of common equity plus book value of debt. A firm's imputed value is the sum of its segments' imputed values, which are obtained by multiplying the segment's sales (or segment's assets) by the median multiple of the actual value- to-sales (assets) ratio of focused firms in the same industry and year:

$$imputed\ value_{i,t} = \sum_{i=1}^{n} acc\_item_{i,t} \times \left(Ind_{i,t} \left(\frac{actual\ value}{acc\_item} \right)_k \right), \quad (17)$$

where $EX\_value_{i,t}$ is firm *i*'s excess value, $acc\_item_{i,t}$ is segment *i*'s value of an accounting item (i.e., total sales or total assets) and $Ind_{i,t}\left(\frac{actual\ value}{acc\_item}\right)_k$ is the multiple of actual value to an accounting item (sales or assets) for the median focused firm in segment *i*'s industry.[124]

[124] Berger and Ofek (1995) note that the validity of their industry multiplier approach depends on the assumption that management discretion in terms of the ability to allocate sales (assets) between segments plays only a

The industry median multiples are based on the narrowest SIC grouping that includes at least five focused firms with at least $20 million of sales. In addition, I require that the sum of segment sales must be within 1% of total sales to ensure completely allocated sales among reported segments and that all firms operating in the financial service industry (SIC codes between 6000 and 6999) are eliminated from the sample. Note that the imputed value of a firm estimates the firm's value as if all of its business units were operated as typical focused firms in their respective industry. Therefore, I focus on whether accounting implications of corporate diversification have an effect on the diversification discount by examining excess values of diversified and focused firms.

Diversification Measures

I follow previous literature (e.g., Berger and Ofek 1995; Denis et al. 2002; Hann et al. 2013; Franco et al. 2016) and compute three diversification measures. First, the standard measure of diversification is an indicator variable which takes the value of 1 for firms with at least two segments operating in distinct four-digit SIC codes, and 0 otherwise. Second, I use the number of unique four-digit SIC business segments reported by the firm in a given year. Third, I calculate a sales-based Herfindahl Index as 1 minus the sum of the squares of each reported segment's sales divided by the firm's total sales in a given year. I check the results for the firm's number of segments and the Herfindahl Index to mitigate concerns that the diversification indicator captures some unobservable firm characteristics. Consistently, higher values of all three measures indicate higher industrial diversification and vice versa. In addition, I use the same volatility measures and earnings attributes (i.e., measures of earnings quality) as explained in Section 3.4.1.

Control Variables

In addition to the diversification measures, volatility measures and earnings attributes that are the focus of my analysis, I include control variables following Dechow and Dichev (2002), Dichev and Tang (2009), Rountree et al. (2008) and Demirkan et al. (2012) in all of my models as explained in Table 25. Specifically, I include several firm-specific characteristics to ensure that my results are not contaminated by previously identified factors explaining variation in firm valuation (e.g., firm size, profitability, and growth opportunities). I also control for the CAPM-Beta (*Beta*) as measure for systematic market risk and for idiosyncratic

minor role. Givoly et al. (1999) show some evidence that sales as top-line item of the income statement represents the "true" fundamental performance and is not as vulnerable to measurement errors as, for example, segment earnings.

return volatility (*RMSE*) as proxy for non-systematic risk components at the firm level. Finally, I control for the impact of the information environment by using the number of analysts (*Follow*) following the firm. All variables are winsorized at the 1st and 99th percentiles.

Table 25: Variable Descriptions

Variable name	*Description*
Excess Value	
$EXVAL\_SALES_{i,t}$	Firm *i*'s *excess* value (measured by total sales) is defined as the natural logarithm of the ratio of a firm's actual value to its imputed value in year *t*: see Equations (16) and (17). A positive *excess* value indicates that diversification enhances the value of segments beyond that of their stand-alone peers.
$EXVAL\_ASSET_{i,t}$	Firm *i*'s *excess* value (measured by total assets) is defined as the natural logarithm of the ratio of a firm's actual value to its imputed value in year *t*: see Equations (16) and (17). A positive *excess* value indicates that diversification enhances the value of segments beyond that of their stand-alone peers.
Diversification measures	
$Div\_Dummy_{i,t}$	The diversification indicator takes the value of 1 for diversified firms (i.e., firms that operate in at least two different four-digit SIC codes) and 0 otherwise.
$Seg\_Count_{i,t}$	Indicates the number of unique four-digit SIC business segments reported by firm *i* in year *t*.
$Herfindahl_{i,t}$	A sales-based Herfindahl Index computed as 1 minus the sum of the squares of each reported segment's sales divided by the firm *i*'s total sales in year *t*. Indices closer to 1 indicate higher industrial diversification (i.e., higher dispersion of the firm *i*'s sales).
Volatility measures	
$EAR\_vola_{i,t}$	Earnings volatility is the standard deviation of firm *i*'s earnings scaled by average total assets calculated over a 5-year window (*t* - 4 to *t*) following Dichev and Tang (2009).
$CF\_vola_{i,t}$	Cash flow volatility is the standard deviation of firm *i*'s cash flow from operations scaled by average total assets calculated over a 5-year window (*t* - 4 to *t*) following Dichev and Tang (2009).
$AC\_vola_{i,t}$	Accruals volatility is the standard deviation of firm *i*'s *total* accruals scaled by average total assets calculated over a 5-year window (*t* - 4 to *t*).
$Corr\_CF\_AC_{i,t}$	Correlation between cash flow from operations and *total* accruals is calculated pairwise for firm *i* over a 5-year window (*t* - 4 to *t*).
Earnings attributes	
$PRED_{i,t}$	The (inverse) measure for predictability is the standard deviation of firm *i*'s residuals estimated over a 5-year window (*t* - 4 to *t*) from commonly used autoregressive regressions: see Equation (5).
$ACQ1_{i,t}$	The first (inverse) measure for accruals quality is the standard deviation of firm *i*'s residuals estimated over a 5-year window (*t* - 4 to *t*) by the cross-sectional Dechow and Dichev (2002) model and modified with the fundamental variables from the Jones (1991) model following McNichols (2002) and Francis et al. (2005): see Equation (6).
$ACQ2_{i,t}$	The second (inverse) measure for accruals quality is the absolute value of the cross-sectional Jones (1991) model performance-matched abnormal accruals for firm *i* in year *t* following Kothari et al. (2005): see Equation (7).

Table 25 (continued)

Variable name	*Description*
Control variables	
$LogAsset_{i,t}$	Natural logarithm of firm *i*'s total asset (AT) in year *t*.
$Capex_{i,t}$	Firm *i*'s ratio of capital expenditures (CAPX) to sales (SALE) in year *t*.
$Ebit_{i,t}$	Firm *i*'s ratio of earnings before interest and tax (IB) to sales (SALE) in year *t*.
$SalesGrowth_{i,t}$	Firm *i*'s change in total sales (SALE) between year *t* - 1 and *t*.
$R\&D_{i,t}$	Firm *i*'s ratio of research and development expenses (XRD) to sales (SALE) in year *t*.
$ADV_{i,t}$	Firm *i*'s ratio of advertising expenses (XAD) to sales (SALE) in year *t*.
$ROA_{i,t}$	Firm *i*'s ratio of earnings to its average total assets (return on assets) in year *t*.
$Leverage_{i,t}$	Firm *i*'s ratio of total debt to its average total assets in year *t*.
$Mergers_{i,t}$	Indicator that equals 1 if firm *i* had a merger in year *t* and 0 otherwise.
$Beta_{i,t}$	The CAPM *Beta* is the slope coefficient estimate obtained by regressing a firm *i*'s monthly returns on the New York Stock Exchange (NYSE) equally weighted index from year *t*-6 to *t*-2. Higher CAPM *Beta* indicates higher systematic market risk for firm *i*.
$RMSE_{i,t}$	Firm *i*'s idiosyncratic return volatility measured by the Root-Mean-Squared-Error from the CAPM *Beta* -regressions.
$Follow_{i,t}$	The average monthly number of analysts following firm *i* in year *t*.

This table presents the description of all variables used in my main analysis. All variables are defined as listed and consistently computed as in previous sections (see Section 3.4.1 and Section 4.2.2).

4.4.2 Data Sample

I obtain my data from the intersection of the Compustat Annual Industrial, Compustat Industrial Segment, CRSP and I/B/E/S databases.[125] I use the Compustat files to calculate my excess value measures, diversification measures, volatility measures and earnings attributes. I use data from CRSP to calculate my systematic and idiosyncratic risk measures and data from I/B/E/S to compute my measure for firms' information environment. My final sample is composed of all observations for which I have available data on the excess value measures, all diversification and volatility measures, all earnings attributes and all control variables listed above. The final sample consists of 28,769 firm-year observations, of which 18,768 (10,001) observations pertain to focused (diversified) firms covering the period from 1979 to 2011. Because I use all described variables in my analysis, this sample is smaller than the sample I use for my investigations in Chapter 3.

125 All databases are provided by Wharton Research Data Services (WRDS). The Center for Research in Security Prices (CRSP) is a provider of U.S. stock market data. The Institutional Brokers' Estimate System (I/B/E/S) gathers and compiles different estimates made by stock analysts on future financial items (e.g., earnings) for U.S. publicly-traded companies.

4.5 Empirical Results

4.5.1 Descriptive Statistics

Table 26 presents descriptive statistics for the main variables (excess values, diversification measures, earnings volatility and components, earnings attributes, and control variables) for diversified and focused firms. Panel A of Table 26 reports negative differences in mean and median excess values between diversified and focused firms which indicates that, in a univariate setting, diversification reduces firm value. Following Berger and Ofek (1995), I also show excess values of focused firms to confirm that these values are well-behaved (i.e., constructed with median values of around zero). In terms of the diversification measures, the average diversified firm reports 2.7 distinct industrial segments and has a sales-based Herfindahl Index of 0.42. In addition, earnings and its components (cash flows and accruals) of diversified firms are less volatile compared to focused firms, and the contemporaneous correlation ("matching") between cash flows and accruals is stronger (more negative) for diversified firms. Moreover, diversified firms exhibit lower values for all earnings attributes which indicate higher quality compared to focused firms. Among my control variables, I find that diversified firms are larger in size, have lower growth opportunities, are higher leveraged, have more mergers, incur lower systematic and idiosyncratic risks, and have a better information environment.

Panel B of Table 26 shows the correlation between excess values (sales and assets), earnings volatility, and my measures of risk. On a univariate basis, the excess values are highly correlated and produce similar results. Earnings volatility is negatively correlated with both measures of firm value, confirming the previously explained negative association. In addition, excess values are positively correlated with both systematic and idiosyncratic risk. This is not surprising given that larger firms generally have less volatile equity returns and lower firm values. Finally, earnings volatility and idiosyncratic risk have a strong positive correlation which underlines their firm-specific nature, and both risk measures are positively correlated with each other. Overall, these statistics and correlations are consistent with results from prior research.[126]

[126] I compute variance inflation factors at the end of each analysis which indicate that multicollinearity is not a concern in the analysis.

Table 26: Descriptive Statistics

Panel A: Main variables

	Diversified firms			Focused firms			Difference	
	Mean	SD	Med.	Mean	SD	Med.	Mean	Med.
Valuation measures								
EXVAL_SALES	-0.0884	0.5793	-0.0971	-0.0041	0.5804	0.0000	-0.0843***	-0.0971***
EXVAL_ASSET	-0.0901	0.4834	-0.1453	-0.0039	0.5109	0.0000	-0.0862***	-0.1453***
Diversification measures								
Seg_Count	2.7031	0.9732	2.0000	1.000	0.000	1.0000	1.7031***	1.0000***
Herfindahl	0.4212	0.1863	0.4457	0.000	0.000	0.000	-0.5788***	-0.5543***
Volatility measures								
EAR_vola	0.0329	0.0293	0.0243	0.0614	0.0607	0.0385	-0.0285***	-0.0142***
CF_vola	0.0613	0.0379	0.0522	0.0839	0.0563	0.0614	-0.0226***	-0.0092***
AC_vola	0.0562	0.0363	0.0478	0.0702	0.0503	0.0561	-0.0140***	-0.0083***
Corr_CF_AC	-0.7969	0.2613	-0.9089	-0.6418	0.4257	-0.8383	-0.1551***	-0.0706***
Earnings attributes								
PRED	0.0336	0.0337	0.0240	0.0671	0.0777	0.0398	-0.0335***	-0.0158***
ACQ1	0.0361	0.0341	0.0276	0.0586	0.0570	0.0407	-0.0225***	-0.0131***
ACQ2	0.0571	0.0611	0.0383	0.0908	0.1141	0.0527	-0.0337***	-0.0114***
Control variables								
LogAsset	6.6633	1.6398	6.6449	6.0018	1.6477	5.8149	0.6615***	0.8300***
Capex	0.0694	0.0901	0.0437	0.0919	0.1866	0.0436	-0.0225***	-0.0001
Ebit	0.0923	0.1000	0.0863	0.0702	0.2661	0.0808	0.0221***	0.0055***
SalesGrowth	1.0945	0.2106	1.0755	1.1301	0.3588	1.0862	-0.0356***	-0.0107***
R&D	0.0175	0.0308	0.0032	0.0460	0.0916	0.0000	-0.0285***	0.0032***
ADV	0.0107	0.0238	0.0000	0.0115	0.0254	0.0000	-0.0008***	0.0000***
ROA	0.0488	0.0670	0.0527	0.0339	0.1591	0.0512	0.0149***	0.0015*
Leverage	0.2703	0.1806	0.2567	0.2559	0.2526	0.2105	0.0144***	0.0462***
Mergers	0.1985	0.3989	0.0000	0.1432	0.3503	0.0000	0.0553***	0.0000***
Beta	0.7725	1.1737	0.6449	0.9793	1.6742	0.7297	-0.2068***	-0.0848***
RMSE	0.3488	0.2766	0.2735	0.4970	0.4330	0.3654	-0.1482***	-0.0919***
Follow	8.6684	7.6050	6.1818	7.6060	7.1135	5.0000	1.0624***	1.1818***
Observations	10,001			18,768				

Panel B: Pearson correlation coefficients for excess values and risk proxies

Variable	*EXVAL_SALES*	*EXVAL_ASSET*	*EAR_vola*	*Beta*	*RMSE*
EXVAL_SALES	1.0000				
EXVAL_ASSET	0.7379 (.0000)	1.0000			
EAR_vola	-0.0241 (.0000)	-0.0198 (.0008)	1.0000		
Beta	0.0118 (.0461)	0.0047 (0.4231)	0.1823 (.0000)	1.0000	
RMSE	0.0311 (.0000)	0.0447 (0.0000)	0.3485 (0.0000)	0.3531 (0.0000)	1.0000

This table reports descriptive statistics for all main variables used in my analysis. The sample includes 28,769 observations between 1979 and 2011. For variable descriptions, see Table 25. Significance levels are stated for the difference between diversified and focused firms. The mean difference is based on a t-test and the median difference is based on a Wilcoxon Rank-Sum test. Asterisks indicate significance at the 1% (***), 5% (**), or 10% (*) level (respectively).

4.5.2 Results of Diversification on the Excess Value

I start my investigation by examining the effect of corporate diversification on firm excess value. Therefore, I replicate the standard regression of Berger and Ofek (1995) using firm excess value as dependent variable, a diversification indicator as independent variable and controlling for size (i.e., log of total assets), profitability (i.e., ebit-to-sales ratio) and growth options (i.e., capex-to-sales ratio). Panel A of Table 27 reports a diversification discount between 0.12 and 0.14, which is rather close to results obtained by Berger and Ofek (1995). These results are also robust to other diversification measures: number of segments and Herfindahl Index. The main implication of these results is that I document an average diversification discount in my sample, confirming previous findings about agency and behavioral problems of diversified firms.

Next, I run the same regressions using all of my control variables explained above.[127] Panel B of Table 27 shows that the diversification discount estimate drops by nearly 30% to values between 0.08 and 0.11, depending on the specification. In addition, the explanatory power is noticeably higher (adjusted R^2 of 16.63% compared to 4.03%) after controlling for other effects explaining variation in firm value (e.g., information environment). Overall, these results are robust to different diversification measures and provide evidence that diversified firms are indeed valued less than comparable portfolios of focused firms.

Table 27: Regressions of *Excess* Value on Diversification Measures

Panel A: Controls of Berger and Ofek (1995)

$$Excess\_Value_{i,t} = \alpha_0 + \boldsymbol{\alpha_1 Div\_Measures_{i,t}} + \alpha_2 LogAsset_{i,t} + \alpha_3 Capex_{i,t} + \alpha_4 Ebit_{i,t} + \varepsilon_{i,t}$$

		Excess Value (Sales)			*Excess* Value (Asset)		
	Pred.	(1)	(2)	(3)	(4)	(5)	(6)
Div_Dummy	-	-0.1228***			-0.1488***		
		(0.0068)			(0.0060)		
Seg_Count	-		-0.0656***			-0.0735***	
			(0.0028)			(0.0025)	
Herfindahl	-			-0.2791***			-0.3121***
				(0.0130)			(0.0113)
LogAsset	-	0.0423***	0.0452***	0.0433***	0.0065***	0.0092***	0.0070***
		(0.0021)	(0.0021)	(0.0021)	(0.0020)	(0.0020)	(0.0020)
Capex	+	0.3712***	0.3656***	0.3628***	0.0078	0.0044	0.0014
		(0.0217)	(0.0215)	(0.0214)	(0.0180)	(0.0179)	(0.0180)
Ebit	+	0.0934***	0.0890***	0.0900***	0.2239***	0.2187***	0.2198***
		(0.0331)	(0.0327)	(0.0328)	(0.0420)	(0.0414)	(0.0416)
Constant	?	-0.2328***	-0.1860***	-0.5171***	0.0183	0.0705***	-0.2999***
		(0.0128)	(0.0130)	(0.0182)	(0.0117)	(0.0118)	(0.0163)
Observations		28,769	28,769	28,769	28,769	28,769	28,769
R-squared		0.0403	0.0446	0.0434	0.0307	0.0349	0.0328

[127] All models include year and industry fixed effects, and standard errors that are clustered by firm and robust to heteroscedasticity and autocorrelation (Petersen 2009).

Table 27 (continued)

Panel B: All control variables

$$Excess\_Value_{i,t} = \alpha_0 + \boldsymbol{\alpha_1 Div\_Measures_{i,t}} + \alpha_2 LogAsset_{i,t} + \alpha_3 Capex_{i,t} + \alpha_4 Ebit_{i,t} + \alpha_5 SalesGrowth_{i,t} + \alpha_6 R\&D_{i,t} + \alpha_7 ADV_{i,t} + \alpha_8 ROA_{i,t} + \alpha_9 Leverage_{i,t} + \alpha_{10} Mergers_{i,t} + \alpha_{11} Beta_{i,t} + \alpha_{12} RMSE_{i,t} + \alpha_{13} Follow_{i,t} + \sum INDUSTRY_t + \sum YEAR + \varepsilon_{i,t}$$

		***Excess* Value (Sales)**			***Excess* Value (Asset)**		
	Pred.	**(1)**	**(2)**	**(3)**	**(4)**	**(5)**	**(6)**
Div_Dummy	-	-0.0883***			-0.1121***		
		(0.0151)			(0.0125)		
Seg_Count	-		-0.0537***			-0.0559***	
			(0.0065)			(0.0056)	
Herfindahl	-			-0.2309***			-0.2380***
				(0.0305)			(0.0260)
LogAsset	-	-0.0230***	-0.0174**	-0.0190***	-0.0766***	-0.0724***	-0.0741***
		(0.0070)	(0.0070)	(0.0070)	(0.0061)	(0.0062)	(0.0062)
Capex	+	0.5461***	0.5404***	0.5424***	0.0641**	0.0627**	0.0652**
		(0.0427)	(0.0422)	(0.0424)	(0.0299)	(0.0299)	(0.0299)
Ebit	+	0.1221**	0.1161**	0.1172**	0.0960*	0.0930*	0.0943*
		(0.0592)	(0.0581)	(0.0584)	(0.0548)	(0.0542)	(0.0545)
SalesGrowth	+	0.1296***	0.1302***	0.1289***	0.1622***	0.1632***	0.1619***
		(0.0196)	(0.0195)	(0.0195)	(0.0204)	(0.0204)	(0.0204)
R&D	+	1.6629***	1.6574***	1.6465***	0.5971***	0.6150***	0.6049***
		(0.1356)	(0.1352)	(0.1355)	(0.1224)	(0.1223)	(0.1225)
ADV	+	0.4930	0.5189	0.5255	0.5563*	0.5858*	0.5924*
		(0.3464)	(0.3471)	(0.3451)	(0.3307)	(0.3328)	(0.3310)
ROA	+	0.7346***	0.7314***	0.7320***	0.8320***	0.8285***	0.8292***
		(0.2520)	(0.2504)	(0.2509)	(0.2830)	(0.2814)	(0.2820)
Leverage	+	0.2361***	0.2304***	0.2333***	0.0906**	0.0851**	0.0881**
		(0.0407)	(0.0406)	(0.0406)	(0.0415)	(0.0415)	(0.0415)
Mergers	+/-	0.0565***	0.0582***	0.0587***	-0.0225***	-0.0220**	-0.0216**
		(0.0104)	(0.0104)	(0.0104)	(0.0087)	(0.0086)	(0.0086)
Beta	+	0.0055	0.0058*	0.0055	0.0008	0.0011	0.0008
		(0.0034)	(0.0034)	(0.0034)	(0.0029)	(0.0029)	(0.0029)
RMSE	+	0.0252	0.0248	0.0238	0.0083	0.0094	0.0084
		(0.0155)	(0.0154)	(0.0154)	(0.0128)	(0.0128)	(0.0128)
Follow	+	0.0187***	0.0184***	0.0184***	0.0231***	0.0229***	0.0229***
		(0.0015)	(0.0015)	(0.0015)	(0.0013)	(0.0013)	(0.0013)
Constant	?	-0.4034**	-0.3565**	-0.6377***	0.2453*	0.2954**	0.0051
		(0.1505)	(0.1513)	(0.1548)	(0.1284)	(0.1284)	(0.1315)
Industry dummies		Yes	Yes	Yes	Yes	Yes	Yes
Year dummies		Yes	Yes	Yes	Yes	Yes	Yes
Observations		28,769	28,769	28,769	28,769	28,769	28,769
R-squared		0.1663	0.1699	0.1693	0.1824	0.1843	0.1833

This table presents regressions of firm *excess* value on different diversification measures. *Div_Dummy* is an indicator which takes the value of 1 for diversified firms (i.e., firms that operate in at least two different four-digit SIC codes) and 0 otherwise. The predicted sign for *Div_Dummy* is negative because diversified firms are expected to have a lower *excess* value compared to focused firms. The regressions are estimated over a time period of 1979 to 2011. Industry dummies are specified for each Fama and French's (1997) 48 industry groups. For variable descriptions, see Table 25. Robust standard errors clustered by firm are in parentheses. Asterisks indicate significance at the 1% (***), 5% (**), or 10% (*) level (respectively).

4.5.3 Results of Diversification and Earnings Volatility on the Excess Value

After confirming that diversified firms are, on average, valued at a discount relative to their stand-alone peers, I first examine the valuation implications of earnings volatility (and its components). Prior research finds a strong negative relation between earnings (cash flow) volatility and firm value, suggesting that investors value smooth financial performance. In Table 28, I provide coefficient estimates from the regression of firm excess value on earnings volatility and on the separate components of earnings volatility. In the first column, the results illustrate that firm value has a strong negative relation to earnings volatility. The point estimate indicates an expected 2.87% change in firm value for a change in earnings volatility quintiles. To gauge the economic magnitude of the result, consider a firm in my sample that moves from the highest earnings volatility quintile to the lowest quintile. This large decrease in earnings volatility would be associated, *ceteris paribus*, with an 11.48% increase in firm value. In column 2 of Table 28, I report results for each of the separate components of earnings volatility. The results indicate that all earnings components are negatively valued. Interestingly, the volatility of the accrual component has the highest effect on firm value. This indicates that earnings smoothing via accruals appears to add value beyond the cash flow component of earnings. This is also consistent with the negative coefficient estimate of the correlation between cash flows and accruals, indicating that a better "matching" (i.e., lower correlation) between cash flows and accruals is more valued. These results are confirmed in columns 3–4 of Table 28 when using excess values computed with assets instead of sales. Overall, my findings confirm the negative relation between earnings volatility and firm value which indicates that investors prefer smooth financial performance in making capital allocation decisions. This result helps to understand the value of firms' internal risk compensation or risk-management activities in general (Rountree et al. 2008).

Table 28: Regressions of *Excess* Value on Earnings Volatility

$$Excess\_Value_{i,t} = \alpha_0 + \boldsymbol{\alpha_1 Vola\_Measures_{i,t}} + \alpha_2 LogAsset_{i,t} + \alpha_3 Capex_{i,t} + \alpha_4 Ebit_{i,t} + \alpha_5 SalesGrowth_{i,t} + \alpha_6 R\&D_{i,t} + \alpha_7 ADV_{i,t} + \alpha_8 ROA_{i,t} + \alpha_9 Leverage_{i,t} + \alpha_{10} Mergers_{i,t} + \alpha_{11} Beta_{i,t} + \alpha_{12} RMSE_{i,t} + \alpha_{13} Follow_{i,t} + \sum INDUSTRY_t + \sum YEAR + \varepsilon_{i,t}$$

		***Excess* Value (Sales)**		***Excess* Value (Asset)**	
	Pred.	**(1)**	**(2)**	**(3)**	**(4)**
EAR_vola	-	-0.0287***		-0.0191***	
		(0.0060)		(0.0056)	
CF_vola	-		-0.0101*		-0.0080
			(0.0057)		(0.0051)
AC_vola	-		-0.0325***		-0.0113**
			(0.0058)		(0.0050)
Corr_CF_AC	-		-0.0131***		-0.0061
			(0.0048)		(0.0045)
LogAsset	-	-0.0363***	-0.0415***	-0.0896***	-0.0906***
		(0.0068)	(0.0069)	(0.0060)	(0.0060)
Capex	+	0.5608***	0.5456***	0.0863***	0.0817***
		(0.0428)	(0.0420)	(0.0301)	(0.0301)
Ebit	+	0.1376**	0.1309**	0.1148**	0.1117**
		(0.0598)	(0.0585)	(0.0561)	(0.0560)
SalesGrowth	+	0.1305***	0.1377***	0.1639***	0.1674***
		(0.0194)	(0.0195)	(0.0203)	(0.0206)
R&D	+	1.8534***	1.8053***	0.7863***	0.7526***
		(0.1294)	(0.1279)	(0.1160)	(0.1159)
ADV	+	0.5590	0.5965*	0.6066*	0.6136*
		(0.3519)	(0.3482)	(0.3402)	(0.3389)
ROA	+	0.7001***	0.6960***	0.8087***	0.8129***
		(0.2440)	(0.2438)	(0.2797)	(0.2823)
Leverage	+	0.2485***	0.2524***	0.1001**	0.1003**
		(0.0387)	(0.0385)	(0.0398)	(0.0398)
Mergers	+/-	0.0449***	0.0478***	-0.0337***	-0.0312***
		(0.0105)	(0.0105)	(0.0089)	(0.0089)
Beta	+	0.0058*	0.0061*	0.0008	0.0009
		(0.0034)	(0.0034)	(0.0029)	(0.0029)
RMSE	+	0.0499***	0.0563***	0.0286*	0.0280**
		(0.0159)	(0.0159)	(0.0133)	(0.0133)
Follow	+	0.0195***	0.0194***	0.0239***	0.0238***
		(0.0015)	(0.0015)	(0.0013)	(0.0013)
Constant	?	-0.3047**	-0.2023	0.3143**	0.3413***
		(0.1542)	(0.1577)	(0.1268)	(0.1294)
Industry dummies		Yes	Yes	Yes	Yes
Year dummies		Yes	Yes	Yes	Yes
Observations		28,769	28,769	28,769	28,769
R-squared		0.1652	0.1684	0.1747	0.1745

This table presents regressions of *excess* value on earnings volatility (ranked in quintiles) and on the separate components (each ranked in quintiles) for a sample of diversified and focused firms. The regressions are estimated over a time period of 1979 to 2011. Industry dummies are specified for each Fama and French's (1997) 48 industry groups. For variable descriptions, see Table 25. Robust standard errors clustered by firm are in parentheses. Asterisks indicate significance at the 1% (***), 5% (**), or 10% (*) level (respectively).

My empirical tests indicate that diversified firms have distinct lower earnings volatility (see Section 4.2.3) but trade at a discount compared to focused firms (see Section 4.5.2), while earnings volatility and firm value are negatively associated (see results in this section). Consequently, I explore the association between earnings volatility and diversification discount by examining whether diversified firms benefit from lower earnings volatility by higher firm value. I present my regression model and my results in Table 29. My test variable is the interaction between *Div_Dummy* and *Vola_Measures* which captures the marginal difference in firm value between diversified and focused firms for a given level of earnings volatility (or one of its components). Based on my hypothesis 5, I expect the coefficient α_{12} to be positive. In addition, I expect *Div_Dummy* and *Vola_Measures* to be negatively associated with firm value.

I document a positive and significant interrelationship between both diversification and earnings volatility. The coefficient estimate on *Interaction* with *Excess_Value* computed with sales (assets) as dependent variable is 0.0254 (0.0375) and significant. This indicates that for the same level of earnings volatility, the firm excess value of diversified firms is higher compared with focused firms. In other words, the effect of earnings volatility (accounting information risk) on firm value is less strong for diversified firms.[128] This result is consistent with hypothesis 5. Moreover, I find negative and significant coefficient estimates on *Div_Dummy* and on *Vola_Measures*, consistent with my previous results. In terms of the earnings volatility components in column 2 and 4 of Table 29, diversified firms benefit in value through the cash flow component and correlation ("matching") component, while the effect of the accrual component is inconsistent.[129] Thus, investors differentiate between earnings volatility components especially with regard to the matching between cash flows and accruals. Overall, I find that diversified firms benefit from a lower volatility of earnings (and its components) by higher firm valuation. However, the discount in diversified firms' value still remains valid.

---

[128] I perform a Wald test to test the significance of the group of explanatory variables *Vola_Measures* and *Interaction* in my statistical model. While the Waldt test is significant for the model with *Excess_Value* computed with sales, the test is not significant for the *Excess_Value* computed with assets. Thus, the overall effect of earnings volatility on firm excess value is not positive for diversified firms.

[129] The negative interaction term of accruals volatility, shown in column 2 of Table 29, suggests that for the same level of accrual volatility, diversified firms exhibit a lower firm excess value than focused firms. This can be explained by investors anticipating that lower accrual volatility in diversified firms is a result of more intentional agency behavior (i.e., more accounting information risk) and thus demand a higher compensation.

Table 29: Regressions of *Excess* Value on Diversification and Earnings Volatility

$$Excess\_Value_{i,t} = \alpha_0 + \alpha_1 Div\_Dummy_{i,t} + \alpha_2 Vola\_Measures_{i,t} + \boldsymbol{\alpha_{12} Interaction} + \delta_1 LogAsset_{i,t} + \delta_2 Capex_{i,t} + \delta_3 Ebit_{i,t} + \delta_4 SalesGrowth_{i,t} + \delta_5 R\&D_{i,t} + \delta_6 ADV_{i,t} + \delta_7 ROA_{i,t} + \delta_8 Leverage_{i,t} + \delta_9 Mergers_{i,t} + \delta_{10} Beta_{i,t} + \delta_{11} RMSE_{i,t} + \delta_{12} Follow_{i,t} + \sum INDUSTRY_t + \sum YEAR + \varepsilon_{i,t}$$

		Excess Value (Sales)		*Excess* Value (Asset)	
	Pred.	**(1)**	**(2)**	**(3)**	**(4)**
Div_Dummy	-	-0.1657***	-0.1521***	-0.2209***	-0.2654***
		(0.0290)	(0.0415)	(0.0236)	(0.0353)
EAR_vola	-	-0.0401***		-0.0352***	
		(0.0070)		(0.0065)	
EAR_Interaction	+	0.0254***		0.0375***	
		(0.0086)		(0.0074)	
CF_vola	-		-0.0165**		-0.0141**
			(0.0068)		(0.0060)
CF_Interaction	+		0.0206*		0.0133
			(0.0110)		(0.0097)
AC_vola	-		-0.0283***		-0.0172***
			(0.0067)		(0.0056)
AC_Interaction	+		-0.0187*		0.0161*
			(0.0111)		(0.0096)
Corr_CF_AC	-		-0.0218***		-0.0160***
			(0.0058)		(0.0052)
Corr_Interaction	+		0.0190**		0.0231***
			(0.0077)		(0.0066)
LogAsset	-	-0.0296***	-0.0350***	-0.0814***	-0.0824***
		(0.0069)	(0.0069)	(0.0060)	(0.0060)
Capex	+	0.5393***	0.5261***	0.0602**	0.0542*
		(0.0424)	(0.0417)	(0.0299)	(0.0300)
Ebit	+	0.1229**	0.1175**	0.0967*	0.0938*
		(0.0575)	(0.0566)	(0.0537)	(0.0563)
SalesGrowth	+	0.1291***	0.1357***	0.1623***	0.1666***
		(0.0191)	(0.0193)	(0.0199)	(0.0203)
R&D	+	1.7771***	1.7314***	0.6990***	0.6604***
		(0.1290)	(0.1280)	(0.1144)	(0.1144)
ADV	+	0.5726*	0.5994*	0.6281*	0.6381*
		(0.3422)	(0.3391)	(0.3280)	(0.3272)
ROA	+	0.6926***	0.6898***	0.7983***	0.8013***
		(0.2412)	(0.2417)	(0.2759)	(0.2787)
Leverage	+	0.2473***	0.2522***	0.0985**	0.0980**
		(0.0384)	(0.0382)	(0.0393)	(0.0393)
Mergers	+/-	0.0509***	0.0539***	-0.0262***	-0.0239***
		(0.0104)	(0.0104)	(0.0088)	(0.0088)
Beta	+	0.0061*	0.0064*	0.0012	0.0012
		(0.0034)	(0.0034)	(0.0029)	(0.0029)
RMSE	+	0.0466***	0.0514***	0.0252*	0.0243*
		(0.0158)	(0.0159)	(0.0134)	(0.0135)
Follow	+	0.0191***	0.0190***	0.0234***	0.0234***
		(0.0015)	(0.0015)	(0.0013)	(0.0013)
Constant	?	-0.2742*	-0.1667	0.3583***	0.3991***
		(0.1552)	(0.1591)	(0.1320)	(0.1341)

Table 29 (continued)

	Pred.	(1)	(2)	(3)	(4)
Industry dummies		Yes	Yes	Yes	Yes
Year dummies		Yes	Yes	Yes	Yes
Observations		28,769	28,769	28,769	28,769
R-squared		0.1713	0.1745	0.1875	0.1865

This table presents regressions of *excess* value on diversification indicator (takes the value of 1 for diversified firms and 0 otherwise), earnings volatility (ranked in quintiles), and an *Interaction* with the diversification indicator and earnings volatility ($\alpha_{12} Div\_Dummy_{i,t} * EAR\_vola_{i,t}$) for a sample of diversified and focused firms. The regressions are estimated over a time period of 1979 to 2011. Industry dummies are specified for each Fama and French's (1997) 48 industry groups. For variable descriptions, see Table 25. Robust standard errors clustered by firm are in parentheses. Asterisks indicate significance at the 1% (***), 5% (**), or 10% (*) level (respectively).

4.5.4 Results of Diversification and Earnings Quality on the Excess Value

In this section, I examine the valuation implications of earnings quality. Prior research finds a positive relation between earnings quality and firm value, suggesting that investors value less accounting information risk. Panel A of Table 30 reports coefficient estimates from the regression of firm excess value on earnings attributes (i.e., *PRED*, *ACQ1* and *ACQ2* respectively). Note that the earnings attributes are all inversely related to earnings quality such that lower values indicate high-quality earnings and vice versa.[130] I find that all three earnings attributes are negatively associated with firm excess value when measured with sales, indicating that high-quality earnings lead to higher firm value. However, while the negative association between *PRED* and firm value remains unchanged when excess value is computed with assets, the coefficient estimates on both accruals quality measures turn positive but insignificant. This result rather supports the view that firm-specific information risk is diversified away and thus not priced in the capital market. Because of these inconclusive results regarding both measures of accruals quality, I follow Francis et al. (2005) and disentangle the accruals quality measures into an innate and a discretionary component (see Equation 11 in Section 3.6.3). Panel B of Table 30 provides coefficient estimates from the regression of firm excess value on the innate and discretionary accrual attributes (i.e., *IACQ1 and DACQ1* as well as *IACQ2* and *DACQ2* respectively). The results show that the innate components of accrual attributes are negatively and significantly related to firm value, indicating that higher innate accruals quality leads to higher firm value. However, the results of the discretionary components of accruals quality remain ambiguous. Francis et al. (2005) find that the innate component of accruals quality has larger capital market consequences than

[130] Due to the ordinal scale of the earnings quality measurement, it is only possible to make a statement with regard to the magnitude of attributes (i.e., rank-ordered) but not about distances between attributes (i.e., no measurement of differences).

the discretionary component, which consists of three components: signaling, opportunism and noise.[131] Therefore, I conclude that high-quality accruals are positively valued which is explained by firm fundamentals (i.e., the innate component) and not opposed by managerial discretion (i.e., the discretionary component). Overall, I confirm the positive association between earnings quality and firm value which indicates that investors prefer and value less accounting information risk.

Table 30: Regressions of *Excess* Value on Earnings Attributes

Panel A: Earnings attributes

$$Excess\_Value_{i,t} = \alpha_0 + \boldsymbol{\alpha_1 EAR\_Attributes_{i,t}} + \alpha_2 LogAsset_{i,t} + \alpha_3 Capex_{i,t} + \alpha_4 Ebit_{i,t} + \alpha_5 SalesGrowth_{i,t} + \alpha_6 R\&D_{i,t} + \alpha_7 ADV_{i,t} + \alpha_8 ROA_{i,t} + \alpha_9 Leverage_{i,t} + \alpha_{10} Mergers_{i,t} + \alpha_{11} Beta_{i,t} + \alpha_{12} RMSE_{i,t} + \alpha_{13} Follow_{i,t} + \sum INDUSTRY_t + \sum YEAR + \varepsilon_{i,t}$$

		***Excess* Value (Sales)**			***Excess* Value (Asset)**		
	Pred.	**(1)**	**(2)**	**(3)**	**(4)**	**(5)**	**(6)**
PRED	-	-0.0269***			-0.0203***		
		(0.0069)			(0.0061)		
ACQ1	-		-0.0231***			0.0017	
			(0.0049)			(0.0043)	
ACQ2	-			-0.0051*			0.0024
				(0.0027)			(0.0024)
LogAsset	-	-0.0368***	-0.0343***	-0.0303***	-0.0906***	-0.0850***	-0.0850***
		(0.0069)	(0.0068)	(0.0069)	(0.0061)	(0.0061)	(0.0061)
Capex	+	0.5641***	0.5614***	0.5657***	0.0882***	0.0906***	0.0908***
		(0.0427)	(0.0424)	(0.0430)	(0.0302)	(0.0301)	(0.0302)
Ebit	+	0.1409**	0.1376**	0.1355**	0.1174**	0.1136**	0.1139**
		(0.0607)	(0.0605)	(0.0608)	(0.0567)	(0.0567)	(0.0566)
SalesGrowth	+	0.1323***	0.1338***	0.1324***	0.1652***	0.1644***	0.1641***
		(0.0197)	(0.0198)	(0.0199)	(0.0205)	(0.0208)	(0.0208)
R&D	+	1.8567***	1.7784***	1.7704***	0.7966***	0.7273***	0.7262***
		(0.1311)	(0.1343)	(0.1350)	(0.1171)	(0.1229)	(0.1230)
ADV	+	0.5639	0.5391	0.5119	0.6153*	0.5671*	0.5656*
		(0.3507)	(0.3534)	(0.3538)	(0.3398)	(0.3404)	(0.3403)
ROA	+	0.7109***	0.7206***	0.7316***	0.8139***	0.8322***	0.8324***
		(0.2465)	(0.2488)	(0.2520)	(0.2799)	(0.2847)	(0.2841)
Leverage	+	0.2473***	0.2431***	0.2387***	0.1000**	0.0929**	0.0930**
		(0.0392)	(0.0401)	(0.0407)	(0.0401)	(0.0414)	(0.0417)
Mergers	+/-	0.0473***	0.0498***	0.0506***	-0.0324***	-0.0297***	-0.0297***
		(0.0105)	(0.0105)	(0.0105)	(0.0088)	(0.0088)	(0.0088)
Beta	+	0.0057*	0.0055	0.0053	0.0008	0.0005	0.0005
		(0.0034)	(0.0034)	(0.0034)	(0.0029)	(0.0029)	(0.0029)
RMSE	+	0.0511***	0.0417**	0.0323**	0.0312**	0.0159	0.0164
		(0.0160)	(0.0156)	(0.0155)	(0.0134)	(0.0130)	(0.0127)
Follow	+	0.0194***	0.0192***	0.0191***	0.0238***	0.0236***	0.0236***
		(0.0015)	(0.0015)	(0.0015)	(0.0013)	(0.0013)	(0.0013)
Constant	?	-0.3108**	-0.3432**	-0.3815**	0.3179**	0.2482**	0.2443*
		(0.1551)	(0.1515)	(0.1519)	(0.1262)	(0.1251)	(0.1251)

131 The signaling component of discretionary accruals leads to higher earnings quality which is contradicted by the opportunism and noise components (Guay et al. 1996).

Table 30 (continued)

	Pred.	(1)	(2)	(3)	(4)	(5)	(6)
Industry dummies		Yes	Yes	Yes	Yes	Yes	Yes
Year dummies		Yes	Yes	Yes	Yes	Yes	Yes
Observations		28,769	28,769	28,769	28,769	28,769	28,769
R-squared		0.1643	0.1639	0.1619	0.1746	0.1727	0.1728

Panel B: Innate and discretionary components of accruals quality

		Excess Value (Sales)		*Excess* Value (Asset)	
	Pred.	(1)	(2)	(3)	(4)
IACQ1	-	-0.0403***		-0.0182***	
		(0.0058)		(0.0048)	
DACQ1	-	-0.0041		0.0061*	
		(0.0039)		(0.0033)	
IACQ2	-		-0.0203***		-0.0256***
			(0.0057)		(0.0047)
DACQ2	-		-0.0052		0.0019
			(0.0036)		(0.0032)
LogAsset	-	-0.0491***	-0.0342***	-0.0915***	-0.0819***
		(0.0072)	(0.0071)	(0.0063)	(0.0062)
Capex	+	0.6422***	0.6549***	0.0991***	0.1036***
		(0.0582)	(0.0593)	(0.0381)	(0.0381)
Ebit	+	0.2632***	0.2705***	0.1811***	0.1887***
		(0.0729)	(0.0742)	(0.0649)	(0.0648)
SalesGrowth	+	0.1221***	0.1213***	0.1461***	0.1443***
		(0.0174)	(0.0175)	(0.0184)	(0.0183)
R&D	+	2.0840***	2.0410***	1.0575***	1.0769***
		(0.1361)	(0.1379)	(0.1160)	(0.1167)
ADV	+	0.7901**	0.7893**	0.7652**	0.8277**
		(0.3577)	(0.3575)	(0.3412)	(0.3407)
ROA	+	0.9838***	0.9952***	1.1884***	1.1509***
		(0.0799)	(0.0811)	(0.0933)	(0.0924)
Leverage	+	0.3200***	0.3144***	0.1500***	0.1548***
		(0.0301)	(0.0303)	(0.0278)	(0.0277)
Mergers	+/-	0.0367***	0.0417***	-0.0353***	-0.0368***
		(0.0107)	(0.0107)	(0.0090)	(0.0090)
Beta	+	0.0067*	0.0066*	0.0022	0.0025
		(0.0036)	(0.0036)	(0.0031)	(0.0031)
RMSE	+	0.0503***	0.0348**	0.0243*	0.0282**
		(0.0165)	(0.0165)	(0.0135)	(0.0134)
Follow	+	0.0182***	0.0182***	0.0217***	0.0218***
		(0.0015)	(0.0015)	(0.0013)	(0.0013)
Constant	?	-0.2183	-0.3632**	0.3015**	0.2496**
		(0.1504)	(0.1574)	(0.1237)	(0.1172)
Industry dummies		Yes	Yes	Yes	Yes
Year dummies		Yes	Yes	Yes	Yes
Observations		26,148	26,148	26,148	26,148
R-squared		0.1826	0.1782	0.1982	0.2002

This table presents regressions of *excess* value on earnings attributes (i.e., *PRED*, *ACQ1* and *ACQ2* respectively) for a sample of diversified and focused firms. The regressions are estimated over a time period of 1979 to 2011. Industry dummies are specified for each Fama and French's (1997) 48 industry groups. For variable descriptions, see Table 25. Robust standard errors clustered by firm are in parentheses. Asterisks indicate significance at the 1% (***), 5% (**), or 10% (*) level (respectively).

Because my findings suggest that diversified firms have higher earnings quality (see Chapter 3) and that earnings quality is positively related to firm value (see results in this section), I expect that diversified firms may benefit from higher earnings quality by higher firm valuation. My prediction is also in line with the fact that earnings (cash flow) volatility is negatively related to earnings quality (Dechow and Dichev 2002), and that diversified firms benefit in value from lower earnings (cash flow) volatility (see Section 4.5.3). This may also be true for higher earnings quality. Accordingly, I now investigate the association between earnings quality and diversification discount. The regression model and results are reported in Panel A of Table 31. My test variable is the interaction between *Div_Dummy* and *EAR_Attributes*. Its coefficient α_{12} captures the marginal difference in firm value between diversified and focused firms for a given level of earnings quality. Based on my hypothesis 6, I expect this coefficient to be positive. In addition, based on my prior results, I expect *Div_Dummy* and *EAR_Attributes* to be negatively associated with firm value.

I find a positive and significant coefficient estimate for the interaction between *Div_Dummy* and *PRED*, which is not surprising because earnings volatility and earnings predictability are closely related (see results in Section 4.5.3).[132] This result shows that for the same level of earnings predictability, the excess value of diversified firms is higher compared with focused firms. However, while the interaction term also reports a positive interrelationship between diversification and both measures of accruals quality, this relation is only significant when excess value is computed with assets.[133] Therefore, I disentangle accruals quality into its innate and discretionary components to examine whether investors differentiate between underlying sources that drive earnings (accrual) quality. I report regression results of excess value on the innate and discretionary accrual components (i.e., *IACQ1 and DACQ1* as well as *IACQ2* and *DACQ2* respectively) in Panel B of Table 31. The coefficient estimate on *Interaction* with *Excess_Value* computed with assets remains positive and significant for both measures of innate accruals quality, indicating that firm fundamentals explain higher firm valuation. Thus, I presume that the innate accruals quality captures elements of the firms' business environment other than that captured in my controls. For example, innate accruals might be correlated with investors' beliefs on firm's growth opportunities or risk compensation capacities. Overall, consistent with hypothesis 6, I find that diversified firms

---

132 See Dichev and Tang (2009).

133 I perform a Wald test to test the significance of the group of explanatory variables *EAR_Attributes* and *Interaction* in my statistical model. The Wald test is not significant for the model with *Excess_Value* computed with assets. Thus, the overall effect of earnings quality on firm value does not become negative for diversified firms.

have a relatively lower discount in firm value due to higher earnings quality (less accounting information risk). Nevertheless, the documented diversification discount is not eliminated by less accounting information risk of diversified firms.

Table 31: Regressions of *Excess* Value on Diversification and Earnings Attributes

Panel A: Earnings Attributes

$$
\begin{aligned}
Excess\_Value_{i,t} = {} & \alpha_0 + \alpha_1 Div\_Dummy_{i,t} + \alpha_2 EAR\_Attributes_{i,t} + \boldsymbol{\alpha_{12} Interaction} + \delta_1 LogAsset_{i,t} \\
& + \delta_2 Capex_{i,t} + \delta_3 Ebit_{i,t} + \delta_4 SalesGrowth_{i,t} + \delta_5 R\&D_{i,t} + \delta_6 ADV_{i,t} + \delta_7 ROA_{i,t} \\
& + \delta_8 Leverage_{i,t} + \delta_9 Mergers_{i,t} + \delta_{10} Beta_{i,t} + \delta_{11} RMSE_{i,t} + \delta_{12} Follow_{i,t} \\
& + \sum INDUSTRY_t + \sum YEAR + \varepsilon_{i,t}
\end{aligned}
$$

		***Excess* Value (Sales)**			***Excess* Value (Asset)**		
	Pred.	**(1)**	**(2)**	**(3)**	**(4)**	**(5)**	**(6)**
Div_Dummy	-	-0.1898***	-0.1166***	-0.1079***	-0.2499***	-0.2065***	-0.1477***
		(0.0320)	(0.0270)	(0.0210)	(0.0257)	(0.0227)	(0.0174)
PRED	-	-0.0435***			-0.0428***		
		(0.0081)			(0.0070)		
PRED_Interaction	+	0.0333***			0.0474***		
		(0.0099)			(0.0083)		
ACQ1	-		-0.0307***			-0.0154***	
			(0.0058)			(0.0051)	
ACQ1_Interaction	+		0.0065			0.0336***	
			(0.0083)			(0.0072)	
ACQ2	-			-0.0098***			-0.0050*
				(0.0033)			(0.0029)
ACQ2_Interaction	+			0.0061			0.0124***
				(0.0056)			(0.0047)
LogAsset	-	-0.0303***	-0.0276***	-0.0237***	-0.0826***	-0.0772***	-0.0769***
		(0.0069)	(0.0069)	(0.0070)	(0.0060)	(0.0061)	(0.0061)
Capex	+	0.5429***	0.5374***	0.5437***	0.0628**	0.0639**	0.0635**
		(0.0421)	(0.0420)	(0.0427)	(0.0300)	(0.0299)	(0.0300)
Ebit	+	0.1273**	0.1227**	0.1208**	0.1010*	0.0976*	0.0955*
		(0.0583)	(0.0584)	(0.0589)	(0.0543)	(0.0546)	(0.0547)
SalesGrowth	+	0.1313***	0.1324***	0.1311***	0.1642***	0.1636***	0.1626***
		(0.0194)	(0.0196)	(0.0197)	(0.0201)	(0.0205)	(0.0205)
R&D	+	1.7976***	1.6717***	1.6689***	0.7320***	0.6294***	0.6022***
		(0.1310)	(0.1343)	(0.1350)	(0.1157)	(0.1216)	(0.1220)
ADV	+	0.5899*	0.5382	0.5103	0.6520**	0.5764*	0.5674*
		(0.3391)	(0.3450)	(0.3461)	(0.3259)	(0.3297)	(0.3308)
ROA	+	0.7019***	0.7169***	0.7304***	0.8019***	0.8233***	0.8306***
		(0.2429)	(0.2473)	(0.2512)	(0.2754)	(0.2816)	(0.2831)
Leverage	+	0.2465***	0.2416***	0.2367***	0.0991**	0.0903**	0.0904**
		(0.0388)	(0.0400)	(0.0405)	(0.0395)	(0.0410)	(0.0415)
Mergers	+/-	0.0536***	0.0560***	0.0565***	-0.0246***	-0.0225***	-0.0223**
		(0.0104)	(0.0104)	(0.0104)	(0.0087)	(0.0087)	(0.0087)
Beta	+	0.0061*	0.0059*	0.0055	0.0013	0.0009	0.0008
		(0.0034)	(0.0034)	(0.0034)	(0.0029)	(0.0029)	(0.0029)
RMSE	+	0.0507***	0.0372**	0.0260*	0.0313**	0.0131	0.0086
		(0.0160)	(0.0156)	(0.0155)	(0.0135)	(0.0130)	(0.0128)
Follow	+	0.0191***	0.0189***	0.0188***	0.0235***	0.0232***	0.0232***
		(0.0015)	(0.0015)	(0.0015)	(0.0013)	(0.0013)	(0.0013)
Constant	?	-0.2652*	-0.3312**	-0.3718**	0.3804***	0.2831**	0.2615**
		(0.1595)	(0.1513)	(0.1519)	(0.1275)	(0.1292)	(0.1294)

Table 31 (continued)

	Pred.	(1)	(2)	(3)	(4)	(5)	(6)
Industry dummies		Yes	Yes	Yes	Yes	Yes	Yes
Year dummies		Yes	Yes	Yes	Yes	Yes	Yes
Observations		28,769	28,769	28,769	28,769	28,769	28,769
R-squared		0.1713	0.1695	0.1667	0.1892	0.1843	0.1827

Panel B: Innate and discretionary components of accruals quality

		***Excess* Value (Sales)**		***Excess* Value (Asset)**	
	Pred.	**(1)**	**(2)**	**(3)**	**(4)**
Div_Dummy		-0.1014**	-0.0915*	-0.2276***	-0.1790***
		(0.0410)	(0.0492)	(0.0344)	(0.0411)
IACQ1	-	-0.0536***		-0.0430***	
		(0.0068)		(0.0054)	
IACQ1_Interaction	+	0.0095		0.0383***	
		(0.0093)		(0.0079)	
DACQ1	-	-0.0028		0.0046	
		(0.0044)		(0.0038)	
DACQ1_Interaction	+	-0.0104		0.0002	
		(0.0084)		(0.0070)	
IACQ2	-		-0.0283***		-0.0381***
			(0.0069)		(0.0055)
IACQ2_Interaction	+		0.0115		0.0221**
			(0.0104)		(0.0088)
DACQ2	-		-0.0023		0.0027
			(0.0041)		(0.0037)
DACQ2_Interaction	+		-0.0097		-0.0006
			(0.0083)		(0.0070)
LogAsset	-	-0.0438***	-0.0271***	-0.0853***	-0.0725***
		(0.0072)	(0.0072)	(0.0062)	(0.0062)
Capex	+	0.6073***	0.6311***	0.0583	0.0715*
		(0.0572)	(0.0585)	(0.0370)	(0.0374)
Ebit	+	0.2304***	0.2473***	0.1418**	0.1572**
		(0.0702)	(0.0721)	(0.0614)	(0.0621)
SalesGrowth	+	0.1199***	0.1193***	0.1446***	0.1417***
		(0.0172)	(0.0173)	(0.0181)	(0.0180)
R&D	+	1.9615***	1.9457***	0.9409***	0.9503***
		(0.1364)	(0.1381)	(0.1152)	(0.1161)
ADV	+	0.7936**	0.7841**	0.7877**	0.8245**
		(0.3488)	(0.3490)	(0.3302)	(0.3293)
ROA	+	0.9777***	0.9870***	1.1748***	1.1403***
		(0.0787)	(0.0802)	(0.0921)	(0.0914)
Leverage	+	0.3202***	0.3148***	0.1489***	0.1551***
		(0.0299)	(0.0301)	(0.0275)	(0.0274)
Mergers	+/-	0.0428***	0.0475***	-0.0281***	-0.0291***
		(0.0106)	(0.0107)	(0.0090)	(0.0089)
Beta	+	0.0071**	0.0070*	0.0028	0.0030
		(0.0036)	(0.0036)	(0.0031)	(0.0031)
RMSE	+	0.0482***	0.0310*	0.0024*	0.0231*
		(0.0164)	(0.0165)	(0.0135)	(0.0134)
Follow	+	0.0179***	0.0179***	0.0214***	0.0214***
		(0.0015)	(0.0015)	(0.0013)	(0.0013)
Constant	?	-0.1722	-0.3549**	0.3960***	0.2751**
		(0.1493)	(0.1587)	(0.1339)	(0.1211)

Table 31 (continued)

	Pred.	(1)	(2)	(3)	(4)
Industry dummies		Yes	Yes	Yes	Yes
Year dummies		Yes	Yes	Yes	Yes
Observations		26,148	26,148	26,148	26,148
R-squared		0.1896	0.1836	0.2122	0.2123

This table presents regressions of *excess* value on diversification indicator (takes the value of 1 for diversified firms and 0 otherwise), earnings attributes (i.e., *PRED*, *ACQ1* and *ACQ2* respectively), and an *Interaction* with the diversification indicator and earnings attributes ($\alpha_{12} Div\_Dummy_{i,t} * EAR\_Attributes_{i,t}$) for a sample of diversified and focused firms. The regressions are estimated over a time period of 1979 to 2011. Industry dummies are specified for each Fama and French's (1997) 48 industry groups. For variable descriptions, see Table 25. Robust standard errors clustered by firm are in parentheses. Asterisks indicate significance at the 1% (***), 5% (**), or 10% (*) level (respectively).

4.6 Sensitivity Analyses

4.6.1 Endogeneity Concerns

To test the robustness of my results regarding the association between earnings volatility (earnings quality) and diversification discount, I first run firm-fixed effects regressions to check the cause of changes in excess value within a firm.[134] Table 32 reports results from this modification of my main regression analysis for earnings volatility (earnings quality) in Panel A (Panel B). Regarding earnings volatility, the coefficient estimates on *Interaction* with *Excess_Value* computed with sales as dependent variable turn negative but insignificant. However, the coefficient estimate on *Interaction* with *Excess_Value* computed with assets remains positive and significant for earnings volatility and for its correlation ("matching") component. Regarding earnings quality, the coefficient of the test variable *Interaction* remains positive and significant only for *PRED* and *ACQ1* when using *Excess_Value* computed with assets as dependent variable. Note that firm-fixed effects in these regressions provide only identification from firms that either become diversified or refocus during the sample period. Thus, unobserved heterogeneity at the firm level seems to explain a significant portion of the effect of earnings volatility (earnings quality) on the diversification discount, but not all of it.

[134] Fixed effects regressions control for all time-invariant differences across firms while considering only those characteristics that vary over time within each firm (i.e., unobserved heterogeneity).

Table 32: Regressions of *Excess* Value on Diversification Indicator: Controlling for Unobserved Heterogeneity

Panel A: Earnings volatility and components

$$Excess\_Value_{i,t} = \alpha_0 + \alpha_1 Div\_Dummy_{i,t} + \alpha_2 Vola\_Measures_{i,t} + \boldsymbol{\alpha_{12} Interaction} + \delta_1 LogAsset_{i,t} + \delta_2 Capex_{i,t} + \delta_3 Ebit_{i,t} + \delta_4 SalesGrowth_{i,t} + \delta_5 R\&D_{i,t} + \delta_6 ADV_{i,t} + \delta_7 ROA_{i,t} + \delta_8 Leverage_{i,t} + \delta_9 Mergers_{i,t} + \delta_{10} Beta_{i,t} + \delta_{11} RMSE_{i,t} + \delta_{12} Follow_{i,t} + \sum INDUSTRY_t + \sum YEAR + \varepsilon_{i,t}$$

		***Excess* Value (Sales)**		***Excess* Value (Asset)**	
	Pred.	**(1)**	**(2)**	**(3)**	**(4)**
Div_Dummy	-	-0.0457	0.1035	-0.1356***	-0.1603***
		(0.0289)	(0.0410)	(0.0230)	(0.0324)
EAR_vola	-	-0.0165***		-0.0196***	
		(0.0052)		(0.0047)	
EAR_Interaction	+	-0.0079		0.0142**	
		(0.0076)		(0.0065)	
CF_vola	-		0.0028		-0.0019
			(0.0053)		(0.0050)
CF_Interaction	+		-0.0118		-0.0003
			(0.0089)		(0.0082)
AC_vola	-		-0.0020		-0.0042
			(0.0055)		(0.0051)
AC_Interaction	+		-0.0125		0.0102
			(0.0089)		(0.0082)
Corr_CF_AC	-		-0.0115***		-0.0109***
			(0.0042)		(0.0038)
Corr_Interaction	+		-0.0024		0.0130**
			(0.0067)		(0.0057)
LogAsset	-	0.0226*	0.0246*	-0.1409***	-0.1384***
		(0.0135)	(0.0136)	(0.0124)	(0.0124)
Capex	+	0.3992***	0.3996***	0.0906***	0.0925***
		(0.0443)	(0.0446)	(0.0309)	(0.0310)
Ebit	+	0.0321	0.0334	0.0997**	0.1012**
		(0.0293)	(0.0296)	(0.0479)	(0.0482)
SalesGrowth	+	0.0571***	0.0572***	0.1247***	0.1252***
		(0.0141)	(0.0141)	(0.0155)	(0.0156)
R&D	+	1.0238***	1.0230***	0.0404	0.0405
		(0.1807)	(0.1817)	(0.1789)	(0.1800)
ADV	+	-0.1013	-0.1043	-0.4580	-0.4605
		(0.4052)	(0.4051)	(0.3589)	(0.3572)
ROA	+	0.4538***	0.4576***	0.4673***	0.4720***
		(0.1534)	(0.1552)	(0.1749)	(0.1772)
Leverage	+	0.2709***	0.2677***	0.1280***	0.1250***
		(0.0336)	(0.0336)	(0.0305)	(0.0307)
Mergers	+/-	0.0310***	0.0314***	-0.0182***	-0.0176***
		(0.0076)	(0.0076)	(0.0068)	(0.0068)
Beta	+	0.0034	0.0033	0.0035	0.0034
		(0.0028)	(0.0028)	(0.0027)	(0.0027)
RMSE	+	0.0616***	0.0597***	0.0470***	0.0447***
		(0.0140)	(0.0141)	(0.0129)	(0.0130)
Follow	+	0.0103***	0.0104***	0.0167***	0.0234***
		(0.0016)	(0.0016)	(0.0014)	(0.0013)

Table 32 (continued)

	Pred.	(1)	(2)	(3)	(4)
Constant	?	-0.2829***	-0.3048***	0.4952***	0.4776***
		(0.0708)	(0.0752)	(0.0655)	(0.0687)
Year dummies		Yes	Yes	Yes	Yes
Observations		28,769	28,769	28,769	28,769
R-squared		0.0841	0.0840	0.0992	0.0983

Panel B: Earnings attributes

$$Excess\_Value_{i,t} = \alpha_0 + \alpha_1 Div\_Dummy_{i,t} + \alpha_2 EAR\_Attributes_{i,t} + \boldsymbol{\alpha_{12} Interaction} + \delta_1 LogAsset_{i,t} + \delta_2 Capex_{i,t} + \delta_3 Ebit_{i,t} + \delta_4 SalesGrowth_{i,t} + \delta_5 R\&D_{i,t} + \delta_6 ADV_{i,t} + \delta_7 ROA_{i,t} + \delta_8 Leverage_{i,t} + \delta_9 Mergers_{i,t} + \delta_{10} Beta_{i,t} + \delta_{11} RMSE_{i,t} + \delta_{12} Follow_{i,t} + \sum INDUSTRY_t + \sum YEAR + \varepsilon_{i,t}$$

		***Excess* Value (Sales)**			***Excess* Value (Asset)**		
	Pred.	**(1)**	**(2)**	**(3)**	**(4)**	**(5)**	**(6)**
Div_Dummy	-	-0.0473	-0.0297	-0.0575***	-0.1678***	-0.1429***	-0.1046***
		(0.0353)	(0.0279)	(0.0217)	(0.0276)	(0.0230)	(0.0174)
PRED	-	-0.0134*			-0.0266***		
		(0.0079)			(0.0065)		
PRED_Interaction	+	-0.0078			0.0255***		
		(0.0103)			(0.0086)		
ACQ1	-		-0.0016			-0.0022	
			(0.0047)			(0.0042)	
ACQ1_Interaction	+		-0.0133*			0.0180***	
			(0.0077)			(0.0065)	
ACQ2	-			0.0007			0.0007
				(0.0023)			(0.0021)
ACQ2_Interaction	+			-0.0025			0.0039
				(0.0041			(0.0035)
LogAsset	-	0.0223	0.0260*	0.0275**	-0.1423***	-0.1357***	-0.1366***
		(0.0137)	(0.0135)	(0.0135)	(0.0125)	(0.0123)	(0.0123)
Capex	+	0.4014***	0.4035***	0.4037***	0.0919***	0.0949***	0.0954***
		(0.0444)	(0.0443)	(0.0444)	(0.0312)	(0.0308)	(0.0308)
Ebit	+	0.0347	0.0348	0.0342	0.1024**	0.1017**	0.1019**
		(0.0298)	(0.0299)	(0.0298)	(0.0483)	(0.0484)	(0.0484)
SalesGrowth	+	0.0581***	0.0586***	0.0586***	0.1255***	0.1255***	0.1253***
		(0.0142)	(0.0143)	(0.0143)	(0.0157)	(0.0158)	(0.0158)
R&D	+	1.0244***	1.0184***	1.0213***	0.0515	0.0355	0.0312
		(0.1823)	(0.1833)	(0.1839)	(0.1798)	(0.1813)	(0.1813)
ADV	+	-0.1173	-0.1216	-0.1143	-0.4897	-0.4607	-0.4580
		(0.4075)	(0.4073)	(0.4095)	(0.3606)	(0.3565)	(0.3571)
ROA	+	0.4606***	0.4654***	0.4661***	0.4711***	0.4774***	0.4781***
		(0.1559)	(0.1574)	(0.1576)	(0.1761)	(0.1781)	(0.1784)
Leverage	+	0.2691***	0.2661***	0.2645***	0.1277***	0.1226***	0.1235***
		(0.0338)	(0.0340)	(0.0340)	(0.0308)	(0.0311)	(0.0311)
Mergers	+/-	0.0325***	0.0328***	0.0327***	-0.0174**	-0.0170**	-0.0169**
		(0.0076)	(0.0076)	(0.0076)	(0.0068)	(0.0068)	(0.0068)
Beta	+	0.0034	0.0033	0.0032	0.0034	0.0033	0.0034
		(0.0028)	(0.0028)	(0.0028)	(0.0027)	(0.0027)	(0.0027)
RMSE	+	0.0608***	0.0568***	0.0566***	0.0478***	0.0430***	0.0427***
		(0.0139)	(0.0140)	(0.0140)	(0.0129)	(0.0129)	(0.0128)
Follow	+	0.0102***	0.0105***	0.0105***	0.0165***	0.0169***	0.0169***
		(0.0016)	(0.0016)	(0.0016)	(0.0014)	(0.0014)	(0.0014)

Table 32 (continued)

	Pred.	(1)	(2)	(3)	(4)	(5)	(6)
Constant	?	-0.2930***	-0.3400***	-0.3479***	0.5225***	0.4284***	0.4188***
		(0.0748)	(0.0689)	(0.0676)	(0.0680)	(0.0636)	(0.0622)
Year dummies		Yes	Yes	Yes	Yes	Yes	Yes
Observations		28,769	28,769	28,769	28,769	28,769	28,769
R-squared		0.0828	0.0824	0.0819	0.0995	0.0982	0.0976

This table presents firm-fixed effects regressions of *excess* value on diversification indicator (takes the value of 1 for diversified firms and 0 otherwise), earnings volatility (earnings attributes), and an interaction with the diversification indicator and earnings volatility (earnings attributes) for a sample of diversified and focused firms to control for unobserved firm characteristics. The regressions are estimated over a time period of 1979 to 2011. For variable descriptions, see Table 25. Robust standard errors clustered by firm are in parentheses. Asterisks indicate significance at the 1% (***), 5% (**), or 10% (*) level (respectively).

In order to account for the selection of firms into the diversified status, I now examine the association between earnings volatility (earnings quality) and firm excess value using the Heckman (1979) two-step procedure. As explained in Section 3.6.2, I estimate the inverse Mills ratio from a first-stage probit model (with and without instruments) and report the second-stage regressions including the inverse Mills ratio to correct for potential self-selection bias.[135] Panel A of Table 33 shows regression results regarding earnings volatility, whereas Panel B (Panel C) shows results without instruments (with instruments) regarding earnings quality. The obtained results are comparable to the main regression results and confirm that lower earnings volatility (higher earnings quality) reduce the discount in diversified firms' value. Overall, I conclude that my main results are robust to self-selection models that account for the fact that the diversified status is not pursued randomly.

Table 33: Regressions of *Excess* Value on Diversification Indicator: Controlling for Self-selection Effects

Panel A: Heckman's second stage regression – earnings volatility

		Excess Value (Sales)		*Excess* Value (Asset)	
	Pred.	(1)	(2)	(3)	(4)
Div_Dummy	-	-0.1767***	-0.1979***	-0.2350***	-0.2401***
		(0.0011)	(0.0296)	(0.0242)	(0.0241)
EAR_vola	-	-0.0391***	-0.0407***	-0.0199***	-0.0235***
		(0.0066)	(0.0070)	(0.0058)	(0.0065)
EAR_Interaction	+	0.0298***	0.0293***	0.0393***	0.0381***
		(0.0089)	(0.0089)	(0.0076)	(0.0076)
LogAsset	-	0.0498	-0.0312***	0.0789**	-0.0561***
		(0.0315)	(0.0066)	(0.0315)	(0.0057)
Capex	+	-0.1126***	0.4719***	-0.9369***	0.0488
		(0.2371)	(0.0431)	(0.2363)	(0.0332)

135 A positive (negative) coefficient of the inverse Mills ratio indicates that the firm characteristics, that cause firms to self-select into the diversified status, positively (negatively) correlate with firm excess value.

Table 33 (continued)

	Pred.	(1)	(2)	(3)	(4)
Ebit	+	-0.1290***	0.0954**	-0.2982***	0.0726
		(0.0811)	(0.0469)	(0.0740)	(0.0488)
SalesGrowth	+	-0.0009***	0.1340***	-0.0679	0.1637***
		(0.0493)	(0.0188)	(0.0479)	(0.0197)
R&D	+	-0.7417***	1.8344***	-3.4672***	0.8559***
		(1.0439)	(0.1518)	(1.0487)	(0.1284)
ADV	+	0.2207***	1.1199***	-0.6260	0.9054***
		(0.4693)	(0.3256)	(0.4502)	(0.3157)
ROA	+	0.9472***	0.6227***	1.3247***	0.7665***
		(0.1718)	(0.2348)	(0.1769)	(0.2713)
Leverage	+	0.2330***	0.2170***	0.0738**	0.0452
		(0.0348)	(0.0381)	(0.0344)	(0.0397)
Mergers	+/-	0.1515*	0.0189	0.1847***	-0.0382***
		(0.0527)	(0.0120)	(0.0521)	(0.0098)
Beta	+	0.0125***	0.0024	0.0137***	-0.0031
		(0.0052)	(0.0035)	(0.0048)	(0.0029)
RMSE	+	-0.1719	0.1018***	-0.3922***	0.0740***
		(0.1083)	(0.0180)	(0.1078)	(0.0146)
Follow	+	0.0113***	0.0155***	0.0103***	0.0174***
		(0.0020)	(0.0014)	(0.0018)	(0.0012)
Inverse Mills ratio	+	0.5576***	-0.1788***	1.1300***	-0.0960***
		(0.2835)	(0.0315)	(0.2871)	(0.0257)
Constant	?	-0.8674***	0.0610	-1.3527***	0.1672***
		(0.3427)	(0.0602)	(0.3432)	(0.0520)
Instruments		No	Yes	No	Yes
Observations		28,769	28,769	28,769	28,769
R-squared		0.1285	0.1337	0.1423	0.1406

Panel B: Heckman's second stage regression – earnings attributes with No Instrument

		***Excess* Value (Sales)**			***Excess* Value (Asset)**		
	Pred.	**(1)**	**(2)**	**(3)**	**(4)**	**(5)**	**(6)**
Div_Dummy	-	-0.1996***	-0.1218***	-0.1129***	-0.2611***	-0.2196***	-0.1553***
		(0.0325)	(0.0273)	(0.0212)	(0.0264)	(0.0229)	(0.0176)
PRED	-	-0.0413***			-0.0215***		
		(0.0074)			(0.0060)		
PRED_Interaction	+	0.0374***			0.0499***		
		(0.0102)			(0.0086)		
ACQ1	-		-0.0310***			-0.0040	
			(0.0056)			(0.0046)	
ACQ1_Interaction	+		0.0079			0.0358***	
			(0.0087)			(0.0074)	
ACQ2	-			-0.0116***			-0.0018
				(0.0034)			(0.0029)
ACQ2_Interaction	+	-		0.0078	-		0.0107**
				(0.0058)			(0.0049)
LogAsset	-	0.0460	0.0576*	0.0709**	0.0800**	0.0881***	0.0830**
		(0.0317)	(0.0332)	(0.0337)	(0.0317)	(0.0332)	(0.0336)
Capex	+	-0.0750	-0.1727	-0.2553	-0.9398***	-0.9939***	-0.9643***
		(0.2381)	(0.2489)	(0.2530)	(0.2371)	(0.2483)	(0.2508)
Ebit	+	-0.1112	-0.1460*	-0.1826**	-0.2975***	-0.3197***	-0.3091***
		(0.0607)	(0.0836)	(0.0849)	(0.0741)	(0.0770)	(0.0777)

Table 33 (continued)

	Pred.	(1)	(2)	(3)	(4)	(5)	(6)
SalesGrowth	+	0.0086	-0.0065	-0.0298	-0.0686	-0.0823*	-0.0746
		(0.0494)	(0.0511)	(0.0517)	(0.0480)	(0.0498)	(0.0503)
R&D	+	-0.5770	-0.9811	-1.4555	-3.4743***	-3.7878***	-3.6509***
		(1.0527)	(1.0999)	(1.1197)	(1.0553)	(1.1058)	(1.1204)
ADV	+	0.2572	0.1366	0.0115	-0.6305	-0.7377	-0.6851
		(0.4699)	(0.4828)	(0.4884)	(0.4517)	(0.4657)	(0.4687)
ROA	+	0.9371***	0.9960***	1.0607***	1.3315***	1.3716***	1.3542***
		(0.1724)	(0.1696)	(0.1694)	(0.1764)	(0.1714)	(0.1695)
Leverage	+	0.2289***	0.2249***	0.2352***	0.0730**	0.0769**	0.0751**
		(0.0352)	(0.0356)	(0.0355)	(0.0346)	(0.0348)	(0.0345)
Mergers	+/-	0.1477***	0.1674***	0.1841***	0.1870***	0.1968***	0.1901***
		(0.0531)	(0.0554)	(0.0562)	(0.0525)	(0.0550)	(0.0554)
Beta	+	0.0120**	0.0129**	0.0142***	0.0139***	0.0145***	0.0139***
		(0.0053)	(0.0054)	(0.0054)	(0.0048)	(0.0049)	(0.0050)
RMSE	+	-0.1532	-0.1961*	-0.2574**	-0.3948***	-0.4307***	-0.4119***
		(0.1092)	(0.1143)	(0.1165)	(0.1085)	(0.1141)	(0.1158)
Follow	+	0.0114***	0.0107***	0.0105***	0.0103***	0.0101***	0.0102***
		(0.0020)	(0.0020)	(0.0021)	(0.0018)	(0.0019)	(0.0019)
Inverse Mills ratio	+	0.5193*	0.6099**	0.7185**	1.1363***	1.1999***	1.1590***
		(0.2852)	(0.2972)	(0.3021)	(0.2872)	(0.2998)	(0.3029)
Constant	?	-0.8181**	-0.9631***	-1.1566***	-1.3584***	-1.4899***	-1.4427***
		(0.3473)	(0.3629)	(0.3686)	(0.3474)	(0.3641)	(0.3692)
Instruments		No	No	No	No	No	No
Observations		28,769	28,769	28,769	28,769	28,769	28,769
R-squared		0.1285	0.1275	0.1239	0.1435	0.1419	0.1396

Panel C: Heckman's second stage regression – earnings attributes with With Instruments

		***Excess* Value (Sales)**			***Excess* Value (Asset)**		
	Pred.	**(1)**	**(2)**	**(3)**	**(4)**	**(5)**	**(6)**
Div_Dummy	-	-0.2235***	-0.1503***	-0.1367***	-0.2693***	-0.2321***	-0.1632***
		(0.0328)	(0.0276)	(0.0216)	(0.0264)	(0.0228)	(0.0179)
PRED	-	-0.0429***			-0.0261***		
		(0.0078)			(0.0067)		
PRED_Interaction	+	0.0379***			0.0494***		
		(0.0101)			(0.0086)		
ACQ1	-		-0.0310***			-0.0057	
			(0.0058)			(0.0049)	
ACQ1_Interaction	+		0.0110			0.0371***	
			(0.0086)			(0.0073)	
ACQ2	-			-0.0121***			-0.0026
				(0.0035)			(0.0030)
ACQ2_Interaction	+	-		0.0087	-		0.0108**
				(0.0058)			(0.0048)
LogAsset	-	-0.0305***	-0.0277***	-0.0275***	-0.0558***	-0.0549***	-0.0547***
		(0.0066)	(0.0066)	(0.0066)	(0.0057)	(0.0057)	(0.0057)
Capex	+	0.4770***	0.4473***	0.4589***	0.0525	0.0531	0.0442
		(0.0426)	(0.0433)	(0.0442)	(0.0331)	(0.0337)	(0.0335)
Ebit	+	0.1011**	0.0913*	0.0904*	0.0762	0.0747	0.0703
		(0.0478)	(0.0477)	(0.0483)	(0.0494)	(0.0492)	(0.0492)
SalesGrowth	+	0.1358***	0.1369***	0.1361***	0.1646***	0.1644***	0.1629***
		(0.0190)	(0.0193)	(0.0195)	(0.0199)	(0.0202)	(0.0202)

Table 33 (continued)

	Pred.	(1)	(2)	(3)	(4)	(5)	(6)
R&D	+	1.8566***	1.7408***	1.6821***	0.8799***	0.7993***	0.7626***
		(0.1528)	(0.1579)	(0.1599)	(0.1292)	(0.1354)	(0.1377)
ADV	+	1.1051***	1.0926***	1.1158***	0.9071***	0.8920***	0.8855***
		(0.3230)	(0.3265)	(0.3295)	(0.3136)	(0.3171)	(0.3184)
ROA	+	0.6320***	0.6335***	0.6638***	0.7702***	0.7820***	0.7870***
		(0.2365)	(0.2409)	(0.2458)	(0.2712)	(0.2742)	(0.2737)
Leverage	+	0.2137***	0.2079***	0.2153***	0.0437	0.0459	0.0456
		(0.0385)	(0.0395)	(0.0396)	(0.0400)	(0.0409)	(0.0405)
Mergers	+/-	0.0227*	0.0270**	0.0224*	-0.0367***	-0.0397***	-0.0378***
		(0.0120)	(0.0120)	(0.0119)	(0.0098)	(0.0098)	(0.0098)
Beta	+	0.0025	0.0021	0.0019	-0.0030	-0.0034	-0.0034
		(0.0035)	(0.0035)	(0.0035)	(0.0029)	(0.0029)	(0.0029)
RMSE	+	0.1051***	0.0925***	0.0764***	0.0754***	0.0628***	0.0627***
		(0.0181)	(0.0178)	(0.0179)	(0.0147)	(0.0144)	(0.0142)
Follow	+	0.0153***	0.0151***	0.0156***	0.0173***	0.0176***	0.0174***
		(0.0014)	(0.0014)	(0.0014)	(0.0012)	(0.0012)	(0.0012)
Inverse Mills ratio	+	-0.1764***	-0.1697***	-0.1791***	-0.0964***	-0.1040***	-0.0967***
		(0.0315)	(0.0316)	(0.0316)	(0.0257)	(0.0259)	(0.0258)
Constant	?	0.0596	0.0095	-0.0367	0.1731***	0.1179**	0.1027**
		(0.0609)	(0.0587)	(0.0578)	(0.0518)	(0.0495)	(0.0496)
Instruments		Yes	Yes	Yes	Yes	Yes	Yes
Observations		28,769	28,769	28,769	28,769	28,769	28,769
R-squared		0.1337	0.1319	0.1286	0.1419	0.1400	0.1377

This table presents second-stage *excess* value regressions that control for the inverse Mills ratio (i.e., the correction for self-selection) from first-stage probit models for earnings volatility in Panel A and earnings attributes in Panel B (Panel C). Under "No Instruments", the inverse Mills ratio is from a first-stage probit model with all of the control variables in the second stage. Under "With Instruments", the first-stage probit model additionally includes *PNDIV* and *PSDIV* following Campa and Kedia (2002). *PNDIV* is the fraction of all firms in the industry which are diversified, and *PSDIV* is the fraction of sales in the industry accounted for by diversified firms. The regressions are estimated over a time period of 1979 to 2011. For variable descriptions, see Table 25. Robust standard errors clustered by firm are in parentheses. Asterisks indicate significance at the 1% (***), 5% (**), or 10% (*) level (respectively).

4.6.2 Alternative Specifications

In this section, I check the robustness of my main results by modifying the composition of control variables. First, I repeat my main analysis regarding the association between earnings volatility and diversification discount and follow Rountree et al. (2008) in their choice of control variables (all explained in Table 25). Rountree el al. (2008) provide empirical evidence that investors value smooth financial performance, measured by less earnings (cash flow) volatility, and suggest that risk management activities generally serve to add value. I report the results of this modification of my analysis in Table 34. The coefficient estimates of the main variables are slightly less significant but qualitatively similar. Thus, my inferences remain unchanged such that diversified firms benefit from less earnings volatility and in particular less correlation (i.e., better "matching") between cash flows and accruals by higher firm value.

Table 34: Alternative Controls for Value Implications of Earnings Volatility

$$Excess\_Value_{i,t} = \alpha_0 + \alpha_1 Div\_Dummy_{i,t} + \alpha_2 Vola\_Measures_{i,t} + \boldsymbol{\alpha_{12} Interaction} + \delta_1 Beta_{i,t} + \delta_2 RMSE_{i,t} + \delta_3 LogAsset_{i,t} + \delta_4 ROA_{i,t} + \delta_5 SalesGrowth_{i,t} + \delta_6 Capex_{i,t} + \delta_7 Leverage_{i,t} + \delta_8 R\&D_{i,t} + \delta_9 ADV_{i,t} + \sum INDUSTRY_t + \sum YEAR + \varepsilon_{i,t}$$

		Excess Value (Sales)		*Excess* Value (Asset)	
	Pred.	**(1)**	**(2)**	**(3)**	**(4)**
Div_Dummy	-	-0.1598***	-0.1327***	-0.2132***	-0.2584***
		(0.0263)	(0.0374)	(0.0212)	(0.0311)
EAR_vola	-	-0.0243***		-0.0243***	
		(0.0063)		(0.0059)	
EAR_Interaction	+	0.0190**		0.0432***	
		(0.0079)		(0.0067)	
CF_vola	-		-0.0063		-0.0104*
			(0.0063)		(0.0056)
CF_Interaction	+		0.0095		0.0162*
			(0.0104)		(0.0090)
AC_vola	-		-0.0260***		-0.0161***
			(0.0064)		(0.0056)
AC_Interaction	+		-0.0170		0.0199**
			(0.0106)		(0.0092)
Corr_CF_AC	-		-0.0087*		-0.0019
			(0.0050)		(0.0046)
Corr_Interaction	+		0.0172**		0.0222***
			(0.0069)		(0.0058)
Beta	+	0.0033	0.0036	0.0003	0.0002
		(0.0030)	(0.0030)	(0.0027)	(0.0027)
RMSE	+	0.0596***	0.0637***	0.0526***	0.0517***
		(0.0139)	(0.0139)	(0.0123)	(0.0122)
LogAsset	-	0.0534***	0.0477***	0.0182***	0.0168***
		(0.0045)	(0.0046)	(0.0040)	(0.0040)
ROA	+	0.7179***	0.7162***	0.8716***	0.8770***
		(0.1606)	(0.1612)	(0.1971)	(0.1994)
SalesGrowth	+	0.1185***	0.1241***	0.1411***	0.1453***
		(0.0146)	(0.0148)	(0.0160)	(0.0163)
Capex	+	0.5799***	0.5662***	0.1007***	0.0921***
		(0.0411)	(0.0403)	(0.0289)	(0.0288)
Leverage	+	0.1970***	0.2038***	0.0715*	0.0717*
		(0.0336)	(0.0336)	(0.0366)	(0.0369)
R&D	+	1.9308***	1.8838***	1.0487***	0.9969***
		(0.1119)	(0.1114)	(0.1059)	(0.1064)
ADV	+	0.7925***	0.8096**	1.0338***	1.0454***
		(0.3206)	(0.3188)	(0.3170)	(0.3160)
Constant	?	-0.5856**	-0.5154***	-0.1558	-0.1426
		(0.1341)	(0.1398)	(0.1400)	(0.1447)
Industry dummies		Yes	Yes	Yes	Yes
Year dummies		Yes	Yes	Yes	Yes
Observations		39,574	39,574	39,574	39,574
R-squared		0.1466	0.1501	0.1138	0.1141

This table presents the same regressions as in my main analysis (see Table 29) except for the composition of the control variables that follow Rountree et al. (2008). The sample consists of 25,972 (13,602) focused (diversified) firms. The regressions are estimated over a time period of 1979 to 2011. Industry dummies are specified for each Fama and French's (1997) 48 industry groups. For variable descriptions, see Table 25. Robust standard errors clustered by firm are in parentheses. Asterisks indicate significance at the 1% (***), 5% (**), or 10% (*) level (respectively).

To validate the association between earnings quality and diversification discount, I follow Demirkan et al. (2012) and use *LogAsset*, *Ebit* and *Capex* as controls for size, profitability, and capital expenditures as in Berger and Ofek (1995) and augment the regression model by other control variables for firms' information environment as in Bens and Monahan (2004). Table 35 presents results of this modification. I find that the interaction between *Div_Dummy* and *EAR_Attributes* are all positive and significant when excess value is computed with assets. This result indicates that diversified firms benefit in value from higher earnings quality. Overall, this modification supports the main conclusions drawn from my original analysis.

Table 35: Alternative Controls for Value Implications of Earnings Quality

$$Excess\_Value_{i,t} = \alpha_0 + \alpha_1 Div\_Dummy_{i,t} + \alpha_2 EAR\_Attributes_{i,t} + \boldsymbol{\alpha_{12} Interaction} + \delta_1 LogAsset_{i,t} + \delta_2 Ebit_{i,t} + \delta_3 Capex_{i,t} + \delta_4 Leverage_{i,t} + \delta_5 SalesGrowth_{i,t} + \delta_6 MAR_{i,t} + \delta_7 StdROE_{i,t} + \delta_8 Corr_{i,t} + \delta_9 Surprise_{i,t} + \delta_{10} Follow_{i,t} + \delta_{11} Error_{i,t} + \delta_{12} Disperse_{i,t} + \delta_{13} StdRevise_{i,t} + \sum INDUSTRY_t + \sum YEAR + \varepsilon_{i,t}$$

		***Excess* Value (Sales)**			***Excess* Value (Asset)**		
	Pred.	**(1)**	**(2)**	**(3)**	**(4)**	**(5)**	**(6)**
Div_Dummy	-	-0.1689***	-0.1077***	-0.1321***	-0.2498***	-0.2175***	-0.1821***
		(0.0330)	(0.0283)	(0.0221)	(0.0264)	(0.0232)	(0.0182)
PRED	-	-0.0147*			-0.0318***		
		(0.0080)			(0.0063)		
PRED_Interaction	+	0.0167			0.0406***		
		(0.0106)			(0.0087)		
ACQ1	-		-0.232***			-0.0122**	
			(0.0059)			(0.0048)	
ACQ1_Interaction	+		-0.0092			0.0299***	
			(0.0091)			(0.0075)	
ACQ2	-			-0.0083**			-0.0081***
				(0.0034)			(0.0028)
ACQ2_Interaction	+			0.0028			0.0156***
				(0.0059)			(0.0049)
LogAsset	-	-0.0543***	-0.0559***	-0.0521***	-0.1006***	-0.0955***	-0.0952***
		(0.0074)	(0.0072)	(0.0072)	(0.0063)	(0.0063)	(0.0063)
Ebit	+	0.0785*	0.0815*	0.0812*	0.1733***	0.1812***	0.1819***
		(0.0473)	(0.0472)	(0.0477)	(0.0465)	(0.0473)	(0.0477)
Capex	+	0.5069***	0.4995***	0.5036***	0.0708**	0.0686**	0.0664**
		(0.0436)	(0.0434)	(0.0438)	(0.0311)	(0.0313)	(0.0314)
Leverage	+	0.2195***	0.2208***	0.2172***	0.0518***	0.0455*	0.0459*
		(0.0293)	(0.0291)	(0.0292)	(0.0270)	(0.0270)	(0.0270)
SalesGrowth	+	0.1546***	0.1550***	0.1544***	0.1433***	0.1419***	0.1408***
		(0.0160)	(0.0160)	(0.0160)	(0.0155)	(0.0156)	(0.0156)
MAR	+	0.1913***	0.1916***	0.1917***	0.2223***	0.2226***	0.2227***
		(0.0078)	(0.0078)	(0.0078)	(0.0070)	(0.0070)	(0.0070)
StdROE	-	-0.0535***	-0.0536***	-0.0578***	-0.0386***	-0.0468***	-0.0484***
		(0.0103)	(0.0102)	(0.0101)	(0.0093)	(0.0093)	(0.0092)
Corr	-	-0.0861***	-0.0863***	-0.0891***	-0.0671***	-0.0728***	-0.0737***
		(0.0136)	(0.0136)	(0.0137)	(0.0107)	(0.0108)	(0.0108)

Table 35 (continued)

	Pred.	(1)	(2)	(3)	(4)	(5)	(6)
Surprise	-	-0.0000***	-0.0000***	-0.0000***	-0.0000	-0.0000*	-0.0000*
		(0.0000)	(0.0000)	(0.0000)	(0.0000)	(0.0000)	(0.0000)
Follow	+	0.0221***	0.0220***	0.0219***	0.0249**	0.0245***	0.0244***
		(0.0014)	(0.0014)	(0.0011)	(0.0013)	(0.0013)	(0.0013)
Error	+	0.0001	-0.0003	0.0006	-0.0031	-0.0033	-0.0035
		(0.0047)	(0.0047)	(0.0049)	(0.0047)	(0.0047)	(0.0047)
Disperse	+	-0.0760***	-0.0783***	-0.0798***	-0.1097***	-0.1159***	-0.1177***
		(0.0296)	(0.0297)	(0.0297)	(0.0249)	(0.0249)	(0.0250)
StdRevise	-	0.0118	0.0119	0.0114	0.0153	0.0148	0.0142
		(0.0207)	(0.0206)	(0.0208)	(0.0176)	(0.0179)	(0.0179)
Constant	?	-0.2458	-0.2426	-0.2688	0.4307***	0.3578**	0.3514**
		(0.1697)	(0.1638)	(0.1655)	(0.1397)	(0.1415)	(0.1419)
Industry dummies		Yes	Yes	Yes	Yes	Yes	Yes
Year dummies		Yes	Yes	Yes	Yes	Yes	Yes
Observations		25,096	25,096	25,096	25,096	25,096	25,096
R-squared		0.1510	0.1530	0.1507	0.2158	0.2132	0.2122

This table presents the same regressions as in my main analysis (see Table 31) except for the composition of the control variables that follow Demirkan et al. (2012): *MAR* is one plus the market-adjusted stock return for year *t*, *StdROE* is historical standard deviation of return on equity computed over the preceding 10 years, *Corr* is correlation between annual stock returns and earnings per share (EPS) computed over the preceding 10 years, *Surprise* is the absolute value of the difference between current year EPS and previous year EPS (deflated by stock price at the beginning of the year), *Error* is the negative of the absolute value of I/B/E/S consensus analyst forecast error divided by stock price at the beginning of year *t*, *Disperse* is the average monthly standard deviation of analysts' forecasts divided by the stock price at the beginning of year *t*, and *StdRevise* is the standard deviation of changes over the fiscal year in the median analysts' forecast from the preceding month divided by stock price at the beginning of year *t*. All other variables are explained in Table 25. The sample consists of 16,245 (8,851) focused (diversified) firms. The regressions are estimated over a time period of 1979 to 2011. Industry dummies are specified for each Fama and French's (1997) 48 industry groups. Robust standard errors clustered by firm are in parentheses. Asterisks indicate significance at the 1% (***), 5% (**), or 10% (*) level (respectively).

4.6.3 Alternative Estimation Techniques

As explained in Section 2.1.1, new disclosure requirements about firms' segments (SFAS 131) issued in 1997 represent a structural break in time which may have changed the properties of firm excess value. Therefore, I test whether the valuation of firms which prior to this accounting event declared to be focused (i.e., "hidden diversified firms") has an impact on the diversification discount. While firm-fixed effects regressions in Section 4.6.1 should control, to some extent, for such change over time, I now run annual Fama-MacBeth (1973) regressions to account for time effects in the panel data. Thus, I control for cross-sectional dependencies of observations over time or any other distortions caused by time-period clustering. Panel A of Table 36 reports the mean of the annual coefficient estimates from the regression of firm excess value on a diversification indicator. The results indicate that the diversification discount is slightly smaller between 0.01 and 0.02 in the Fama-MacBeth

(1973) specification compared to the results in my main analysis (see Section 4.5.2).[136] Accordingly, the Fama-MacBeth (1973) regressions indicate similar results on firm excess value and lead to identical conclusions.

To investigate the potential impact of a structural break around the introduction of SFAS 131, I use an indicator variable *SFAS 131* (which takes the value of 1 when SFAS 131 is applied and 0 otherwise) and interact this indicator with all explanatory variables in the regression model shown in Panel B of Table 36. For example, while the coefficient estimate on *Div_Dummy* indicates the effect of corporate diversification on firm value until SFAS 131 became effective in 1997, the sum of the coefficient estimates of *Div_Dummy* and *Div_Dummy_Interaction* represents the valuation implication of diversification since 1997. I find that the diversification discount has, in some cases significantly, decreased since the introduction of SFAS 131. However, my results suggest that diversified firms still trade at a discount compared to industry-matched portfolios of focused firms. This is in line with Berger and Hann (2003) who find that the new segment reporting under SFAS 131 affected diversified firms' valuation through an improved information and monitoring environment. Overall, these additional investigations performed as robustness tests confirm my analytical approach and the conclusions drawn from my original analysis.

Table 36: Control for Accounting Event

Panel A: Fama-MacBeth (1973) regressions

$$\begin{aligned} Excess\_Value_{i,t} = {} & \alpha_0 + \boldsymbol{\alpha_1 Div\_Dummy_{i,t}} + \delta_1 LogAsset_{i,t} + \delta_2 Capex_{i,t} + \delta_3 Ebit_{i,t} \\ & + \delta_4 SalesGrowth_{i,t} + \delta_5 R\&D_{i,t} + \delta_6 ADV_{i,t} + \delta_7 ROA_{i,t} + \delta_8 Leverage_{i,t} \\ & + \delta_9 Mergers_{i,t} + \delta_{10} Beta_{i,t} + \delta_{11} RMSE_{i,t} + \delta_{12} Follow_{i,t} + \varepsilon_{i,t} \end{aligned}$$

		***Excess* Value (Sales)**		***Excess* Value (Asset)**	
	Pred.	**(1)**	**(2)**	**(3)**	**(4)**
Div_Dummy	-	-0.1129***	-0.0695***	-0.1328***	-0.0935***
		(0.0099)	(0.0128)	(0.0094)	(0.0115)
LogAsset	-	-0.0292***	-0.0254***	-0.0072	-0.0767***
		(0.0058)	(0.0059)	(0.0124)	(0.0048)
Capex	+	0.3693***	0.3597***	-0.1678***	-0.1578**
		(0.0432)	(0.0415)	(0.0616)	(0.0678)
Ebit	+	0.9260***	0.5380***	1.0516***	0.4454***
		(0.1569)	(0.1104)	(0.0223)	(0.1071)
SalesGrowth	+		0.0786***		0.1071***
			(0.0236)		(0.0312)
R&D	+		0.6025***		-0.2203
			(0.1628)		(0.1700)

136 The inferences drawn from using other diversification measures (i.e., *Seg_Count* and *Herfindahl*) are qualitatively similar (unreported).

Table 36 (continued)

	Pred.	(1)	(2)	(3)	(4)
ADV	+		0.3884		-0.4080
			(0.5102)		(1.1995)
ROA	+		1.1149***		1.3168***
			(0.1038)		(0.1285)
Leverage	+		0.2764***		0.1604***
			(0.0206)		(0.0271)
Mergers	+/-		0.0381**		-0.0260***
			(0.0142)		(0.0074)
Beta	+		0.0001		-0.0021
			(0.0047)		(0.0041)
RMSE	+		0.0180		0.0070
			(0.0140)		(0.0180)
Follow	+		0.0167***		0.0217***
			(0.0012)		(0.0010)
Constant	?	-0.2321***	-0.2575***	0.0315	0.1183**
		(0.0302)	(0.0489)	(0.0223)	(0.0563)
Observations		28,769	28,769	28,769	28,769
R-squared		0.0997	0.1972	0.1043	0.2460

Panel B:Control for SFAS 131 event

$$Excess\_Value_{i,t} = \alpha_0 + \alpha_1 Div\_Dummy_{i,t} + \alpha_2 SFAS131 + \boldsymbol{\alpha_{12} Interaction} + \delta_1 \sum(Controls_{i,t}) + \gamma_1 \sum(Controls_{i,t} \times SFAS131) + \sum INDUSTRY_t + \sum YEAR + \varepsilon_{i,t}$$

		***Excess* Value (Sales)**		***Excess* Value (Asset)**	
	Pred.	**(1)**	**(2)**	**(3)**	**(4)**
Div_Dummy	-	-0.1321***	-0.1163***	-0.1521***	-0.1391***
		(0.0084)	(0.0086)	(0.0072)	(0.0072)
SFAS131	-	-0.1724***	0.0415	-0.0681***	0.2223***
		(0.0265)	(0.0938)	(0.0242)	(0.0836)
Div_Dummy_Interaction	+	0.0373***	0.0936***	0.0391***	0.0897***
		(0.0142)	(0.0140)	(0.0124)	(0.0121)
LogAsset	-	0.0138***	-0.0411***	-0.0204***	-0.0866***
		(0.0031)	(0.0046)	(0.0028)	(0.0040)
LogAsset_Interaction	+	0.0464***	0.0305***	0.0355***	0.0164***
		(0.0045)	(0.0064)	(0.0041)	(0.0058)
Capex	+	0.5026***	0.7455***	-0.0435	0.1316***
		(0.0521)	(0.0564)	(0.0446)	(0.0387)
Capex_Interaction	-	-0.2705***	-0.3514***	0.0001	-0.1506***
		(0.0570)	(0.0602)	(0.0491)	(0.0428)
Ebit	+	1.1693***	0.9364***	1.2609***	0.7115***
		(0.1474)	(0.1503)	(0.1373)	(0.1308)
Ebit_Interaction	-	-1.2454***	-0.9235***	-1.1747***	-0.6872***
		(0.1487)	(0.1526)	(0.1406)	(0.1346)
SalesGrowth	+		0.1225***		0.1579***
			(0.0220)		(0.0199)
SalesGrowth_Interaction	-		-0.0120		-0.0186
			(0.0291)		(0.0279)
R&D	+		1.8658***		0.5802***
			(0.1433)		(0.1304)
R&D_Interaction	-		-0.2736*		-0.0165
			(0.1533)		(0.1441)

Table 36 (continued)

	Pred.	(1)	(2)	(3)	(4)
ADV	+		0.6624***		0.5422***
			(0.1754)		(0.1589)
ADV_Interaction	-		-0.4421*		0.0219
			(0.2665)		(0.2615)
ROA	+		0.9470***		1.2381***
			(0.1446)		(0.1695)
ROA_Interaction	-		-0.3993		-0.6325**
			(0.2673)		(0.3030)
Leverage	+		0.2882***		0.1488***
			(0.0263)		(0.0254)
Leverage_Interaction	-		-0.0748*		-0.0708*
			(0.0400)		(0.0415)
Mergers	+/-		0.0561***		-0.0082
			(0.0108)		(0.0089)
Mergers_Interaction	+/-		-0.0043		-0.0350**
			(0.0165)		(0.0139)
Beta	+		0.0105***		0.0004
			(0.0034)		(0.0029)
Beta_Interaction	-		-0.0065		0.0024
			(0.0046)		(0.0040)
RMSE	+		0.0467***		0.0289**
			(0.0152)		(0.0128)
RMSE_Interaction	-		-0.0369*		-0.0377**
			(0.0196)		(0.0171)
Follow	+		0.0155***		0.0187***
			(0.0009)		(0.0008)
Follow_Interaction	+		0.0080***		0.0106***
			(0.0014)		(0.0012)
Constant	?	-0.1653***	-0.3444***	0.0641***	0.2702***
		(0.0155)	(0.1080)	(0.0137)	(0.0817)
Industry dummies		No	Yes	No	Yes
Year dummies		No	Yes	No	Yes
Observations		28,769	28,769	28,769	28,769
R-squared		0.0694	0.1933	0.0656	0.2125

This table presents the same regressions as in my main analysis (see Table 27) with a Fama-MacBeth (1973) specification in Panel A and an interaction approach to control for the SFAS 131 adoption in 1997 in Panel B. The regressions are estimated over a time period of 1979 to 2011 for a sample of diversified and focused firms. Industry dummies are specified for each Fama and French's (1997) 48 industry groups. For variable descriptions, see Table 25. Robust standard errors clustered by firm are in parentheses. Asterisks indicate significance at the 1% (***), 5% (**), or 10% (*) level (respectively).

4.7 Conclusion

The vast majority of results in the financial economics literature find that diversified firms are related to more agency costs and thus are, on average, undervalued relative to their stand-alone peers. However, Stein (2003) finds significant variation across diversified firms in the premiums and discounts at which they trade, whereas the sources of this variation have yet received much less attention. In this chapter, I examine whether accounting information quality (risk) can explain cross-sectional variation in the value of corporate diversification. I argue that accounting information of high-quality (low-risk) reduces the discount of diversified firms through lowering agency costs. My empirical results confirm the presumed positive (negative) association between accounting information quality (risk) and firm value. I find that diversified firms benefit from less accounting information risk (i.e., higher earnings quality or lower operating volatility) by higher firm valuation. Moreover, I find that investors assess the value of accounting information on an aggregated earnings level and pay particular attention to the components of earnings quality (earnings volatility) that are related to firm fundamentals (matching between cash flows and accruals). Overall, the documented discount of diversified firms is, however, not eliminated by less accounting information risk.

This finding contributes to the debate on the valuation effects of corporate diversification by revealing a new dimension on how coinsurance can affect firm valuation, namely, accounting information quality (risk). Accordingly, I advance the limited literature examining variation in the value of corporate diversification and thereby advance our understanding of determinants affecting the diversification discount or firm valuation in general. This is of special interest to investors for their capital allocation decisions.

5 Concluding Remarks

5.1 Summary and Implications of Main Findings

Throughout this thesis, I examine the two related research questions of *whether coinsurance matters for a firm's earnings quality* and *whether earnings quality can explain cross-sectional variation in the value of corporate diversification.* I demonstrate the benefits of coinsurance for a firm's earnings quality and how these benefits translate into a reduction of the diversification discount. Furthermore, I explore the potential sources of the coinsurance effect on earnings quality and whether investors assess the value of accounting information on an aggregated earnings level or if they differentiate between underlying sources that drive earnings quality (volatility).

In Chapter 2, I present the basics of the diversification strategy underlying a firm's organizational form and its empirical measurement. In addition, I provide a structured review of relevant research on corporate diversification in the financial economics literature and the application of its potential benefits and costs in the accounting literature. The following empirical investigations in Chapter 3 and Chapter 4 are based on these insights.

In Chapter 3, I contribute to the accounting literature by advancing our understanding of determinants of earnings quality. I identify coinsurance among a firm's business units as a new earnings quality determinant and provide empirical evidence suggesting that coinsurance is positively associated with earnings quality. Prior accounting research studies have found that the complex nature of diversified firms' business activities and resulting agency problems reduce the quality of accounting information. For example, managers may estimate accruals with more unintentional (e.g., through a higher level of complexity in estimating accruals) or even more intentional (e.g., actively pursuing private benefits) estimation errors. However, I show that less than perfectly correlated estimation errors among a firm's segment-level accruals cancel out and result in overall less estimation errors in firm-level accruals. Accordingly, I find higher earnings quality for diversified firms with less correlated segment earnings, consistent with a coinsurance effect. In particular, I find that diversified firms exhibit more predictable earnings, superior mapping of accruals to cash flows, and a lower absolute value of abnormal accruals. Furthermore, I find that the positive association between coinsurance and earnings quality increases with higher levels of operating volatility. This supports the important role of the coinsurance effect for firms that operate in volatile and uncertain environments.

In Chapter 4, I contribute to the financial economics literature by demonstrating that earnings quality can explain differences in firms' market valuation. Commonly, the literature finds an average discount in diversified firms' value relative to comparable portfolios of focused firms. However, the variation across diversified firms in the premiums and discounts at which they trade remains quite significant (Stein 2003). Therefore, I examine the valuation implications of differences in firm's earnings quality (operating volatility) for diversified and focused firms. I find that for a given level of earnings quality (operating volatility), diversified firms have a higher excess value than their focused counterparts. This evidence suggests that diversified firms with higher earnings quality (lower operating volatility) incur less accounting information risk and thus exhibit a lower diversification discount. Therefore, I reveal that accounting information of high-quality (low-risk) helps diversified firms to diminish more severe agency problems associated with corporate diversification. Moreover, I reveal that investors assess the value of accounting information on an aggregated earnings level and pay particular attention to sources related to firm fundamental characteristics.

Overall, my doctoral thesis reconciles the wide range of research on corporate diversification in a structured review and advances our understanding of coinsurance as a determinant of earnings quality as well as its implication for firms' market valuation. Although the financial economics literature arrives at contradictory conclusions regarding the value of corporate diversification, it suggests that under certain circumstances, diversified firms outperform their focused peers. Kuppuswamy and Villalonga (2010) show that coinsurance can reduce financial constraints by providing diversified firms with easier access to credit markets to realize optimal amounts of funding capital. Besides this positive effect of coinsurance regarding the cash flow component of earnings, I reveal that coinsurance is a fundamental force that shapes the level of a diversified firm's accruals. Because information on such firm fundamentals drives the expectation of market participants, this should provide valuable information to managers and investors. For example, assumptions about benefits of diversification (e.g., synergies or risk reduction) influence managerial choice of M&A activities and investors' choice on the optimal diversification strategy in portfolio analysis.

Moreover, my findings address recent calls to explore the drivers of cross-sectional variation in the diversification discount, rather than its average effect. Therefore, I add evidence related to the fundamental economic question of why so many firms remain diversified as diversification is often an *ex-ante* value-reducing and thus an inefficient strategy. My analyses explain in part the reluctance of diversified firms to adopt a more focused organizational form, especially when coinsurance benefits are of a certain value.

5.2 Limitations and Suggestions for Future Research

My empirical analyses offer a wide range of important insights, but they are inevitably subject to certain limitations. These limitations, however, provide the potential for future research.

The main limitation of my doctoral thesis is the measurement of earnings quality itself. Dechow et al. (2010) show that earnings quality is contextual, that is, different users of financial reporting have different objectives and the applied measures of earnings quality depend on these objectives. I consider three measures of earnings quality that capture the volatility of a firm's business operations and estimation errors in accruals: However, my results may not hold for market-based attributes such as value relevance or asymmetric timeliness. Moreover, one caveat of my analysis belongs to potential measurement errors in earnings quality. To the extent that the measures of earnings quality do not accurately reflect the underlying properties of reported earnings, my excess earnings quality will be contaminated and the obtained results in Chapter 3 will be misleading.

Another limitation is that the calculation of excess earnings quality in Chapter 3 is based on the implicit assumption that investors either cannot or do not fully diversify in their own portfolios (i.e., imperfect capital markets). If this assumption was not valid, my measurement of excess earnings quality would be flawed and my results could be questioned. In this regard, my robustness checks based on a naive comparison between diversified and focused firms using actual earnings quality in Section 3.6.4 confirm my main results and thus give me some confidence about my methodological approach.

Two other limitations apply to the data and sample selection process. First, I do not obtain the necessary data to calculate controls regarding agency problems (i.e., ownership data). Therefore, I cannot rule out the possibility that such controls would influence my results. However, Demirkan et al. (2012) find "qualitatively similar results" when executing their analysis without an agency control for institutional ownership. Second, the required long sample period for calculating measures of coinsurance and earnings quality offers some pitfalls. For example, because the introduction of SFAS 131 in 1997 represents a structural break in time, this event may have changed the properties of earnings quality. Moreover, potential benefits and costs of corporate diversification are conditional on certain environmental states, for example, the beneficial effect of coinsurance during the financial crisis between 2007 and 2009. These events may have driven my results, despite controlling for year fixed effects.

Besides the propositions for future research arising from the limitations of my empirical analyses, I suggest that the analysis of coinsurance and its benefits could be further enhanced by measuring the extent of internal transfers. Thereby, coinsurance would provide more insights about enabling internal activities with regard to managers' flexibility in resource allocations, rather than measuring rigid correlations among a firm's business units.

Furthermore, instead of focusing on the average diversification effect, it should be of interest to identify more firm, industry and macroeconomic factors explaining variation in the value of corporate diversification. For example, conditions of the institutional environment like frictions in the capital, labor or product market could constitute a promising area for further research.

Finally, in the wake of the global financial and economic crises in recent years, corporate diversification will continue to play a crucial role in the economy. While my research is based on the strategy of industrial diversification, large corporations are also globally diversified. Gaining a better understanding of diversification activities of those firms across countries with different regulatory requirements and institutional characteristics should lead to a fruitful path for future research.

Overall, although my doctoral thesis strongly contributes to our understanding of accounting and economic implications of corporate diversification, there is still considerable potential for further investigations to provide additional insights under which conditions corporate diversification is beneficial or unfavorable for market participants.

Appendix

Appendix A: Relevance of Corporate Diversification

Panel A: Degree of Diversification over the last 40 Years

No. of business units	1976	1985	1995	2005	2015
1 (focused firms)	906	4,226	6,495	2,486	1,788
More than 1 (diversified firms)	1,308	1,834	1,601	3,934	2,789
- 2	528	862	850	2,593	1,926
- 3	395	549	450	781	542
- 4	237	254	180	315	212
- 5	100	106	72	146	70
- More than 5	48	63	49	99	39

Panel B: Development of basic accounting items over the last 40 Years

Accounting items	1976	1985	1995	2005	2015
Total sales					
focused firms	106.263	250.759	433.572	257.742	439.390
diversified firms	408.559	437.658	644.188	2,288.739	3,692.212
Total assets					
focused firms	86.735	271.354	478.249	369.867	794.016
diversified firms	315.757	412.647	754.308	2,925.586	5,623.592
Earnings					
focused firms	3.870	12.065	19.850	12.715	8.004
diversified firms	19.398	15.563	28.809	141.801	170.609

This table presents the development of the number of business units (segments) in Panel A and mean values (in millions $) of basic accounting items (i.e., total sales, total assets, and earnings) in Panel B for diversified and focused firms over the last 40 years. The data was retrieved from Compustat Annual Industrial and Compustat Industrial Segment files on July 26, 2016. The sample consists of observations for the time period of 1976 to 2015 (data from the Compustat Industrial Segment database is only available since 1976).

References

Amihud, Y., and B. Lev. 1981. Risk Reduction as a Managerial Motive for Conglomerate Mergers. *The Bell Journal of Economics* 12 (2): 605–617.

Ansoff, H. I. 1957. Strategies for Diversification. *Harvard Business Review* 35 (5): 113–124.

Ansoff, H. I. 1965. *Corporate strategy: an analytic approach to business policy for growth and expansion*. New York, NY: McGraw-Hill/Irwin.

Ball, R., S. P. Kothari, and A. Robin. 2000. The effect of international institutional factors on properties of accounting earnings. *Journal of Accounting and Economics* 29: 1–51.

Ball, R., and L. Shivakumar. 2005. Earnings quality in UK private firms: comparative loss recognition timeliness. *Journal of Accounting and Economics* 39: 83–128.

Barth, M. E., Y. Konchitchki, and W. R. Landsman. 2013. Cost of capital and earnings transparency. *Journal of Accounting and Economics* 55 (2-3): 206–224.

Basu, S. 1997. The conservatism principle and the asymmetric timeliness of earnings. *Journal of Accounting and Economics* 24: 3 – 37.

Bens, D. A., P. G. Berger, and S. J. Monahan. 2011. Discretionary disclosure in financial reporting: An examination comparing internal firm data to externally reported segment data. *The Accounting Review* 86 (2): 417–449.

Bens, D. A., and S. J. Monahan. 2004. Disclosure quality and the excess value of diversification. *Journal of Accounting Research* 42 (4): 691–730.

Berger, P. G., and R. N. Hann. 2003. The impact of SFAS No. 131 on information and monitoring. *Journal of Accounting Research* 41 (2): 163–223.

Berger, P. G., and R. N. Hann. 2007. Segment profitability and the proprietary and agency costs of disclosure. *The Accounting Review* 82 (4): 869–906.

Berger, P. G., and E. Ofek. 1995. Diversification's effect on firm value. *Journal of Financial Economics* 37: 39–65.

Berger, P. G., and E. Ofek. 1996. Bustup Takeovers of Value-Destroying Diversified Firms. *Journal of Finance* 51 (4): 1175–1200.

Berger, P. G., and E. Ofek. 1999. Causes and Effects of Corporate Refocusing Programs. *Review of Financial Studies* 37 (2): 311–345.

Bhojraj, S., C. M. C. Lee, and D. K. Oler. 2003. What's My Line? A Comparison of Industry Classification Schemes for Capital Market Research. *Journal of Accounting Research* 41 (5): 745–774.

Campa, J. M., and S. Kedia. 2002. Explaining the diversification discount. *Journal of Finance* 57: 1731–1762.

Caskey, J., J. S. Hughes, and J. Liu. 2015. Strategic Informed Trades, Diversification and Expected Returns. *The Accounting Review* 90 (5): 1811–1837.

Chandler, A. D. 1962. *Strategy and Structure: Chapters in the History of the Industrial Enterprise*. Cambridge, MA: MIT Press.

Chandler, A. D. 1977. *The Visible Hand.* Cambridge, MA: Belknap Press.

Chen, C., A. G. Huang, and R. Jha. 2012. Idiosyncratic Return Volatility and the Information Quality Underlying Managerial Discretion. *Journal of Financial and Quantitative Analysis* 47 (4): 873–899.

Chin, C., Y. Chen, and T. Hsieh. 2009. International diversification, ownership structure, legal origin, and earnings management: evidence from Taiwan. *Journal of Accounting, Auditing & Finance* 24 (2): 233–262.

Collins, D. W., and S. P. Kothari. 1989. An Analysis of Intertemporal and Cross-sectional Determinants of Earnings Response Coefficients. *Journal of Accounting and Economics* 11: 143–181.

Comment, R., and G. A. Jarrell. 1995. Corporate focus and stock returns. *Journal of Financial Economics* 37 (1): 67–87.

Core, J. E., W. R. Guay, and R. Verdi. 2008. Is Accruals Quality A Priced Risk Factor? *Journal of Accounting and Economics* 46 (1): 2–22.

Correia, M., J. Kang, and S. Richardson. 2015. Does Fundamental Volatility Help Explain Credit Risk? Working Paper. London Business School.

Dechow, P. M. 1994. Accounting earnings and cash flows as measures of firm performance: The role of accounting accruals. *Journal of Accounting and Economics* 18: 3–42.

Dechow, P. M., and I. D. Dichev. 2002. The quality of accruals and earnings: the role of accrual estimation errors. *The Accounting Review* 77: 35–59.

Dechow, P. M., W. Ge, and C. Schrand. 2010. Understanding earnings quality: A review of the proxies, their determinants and their consequences. *Journal of Accounting and Economics* 50: 344–401.

Dechow, P. M., and C. M. Schrand. 2004. *Earnings Quality*. Charlottesville, VA: The Research Foundation of CFA Institute.

Dechow, P. M., and D. J. Skinner. 2000. Earnings Management: Reconciling the Views of Accounting Academics, Practitioners, and Regulators. *Accounting Horizon* 14 (2): 235–250.

Demirkan, S., S. Radhakrishnan, and O. Urcan. 2012. Discretionary accruals quality, cost of capital, and diversification. *Journal of Accounting, Auditing, and Finance* 27 (4): 496–525.

Denis, D. J., D. K. Denis, and A. Sarin. 1997. Agency problems, equity ownership, and corporate diversification. *Journal of Finance* 52 (1): 135–160.

Denis, D. J., D. K. Denis, and K. Yost. 2002. Global diversification, industrial diversification, and firm value. *Journal of Finance* 57: 1951–1979.

Dichev, I. D., J. R. Graham, C. R. Harvey, and S. Rajgopal. 2013. Earnings quality: Evidence from the field. *Journal of Accounting and Economics* 56: 1–33.

Dichev, I. D., and V. W. Tang. 2008. Matching and the changing properties of accounting earnings over the last 40 years. *The Accounting Review* 83 (6): 1425–1460.

Dichev, I. D., and V. W. Tang. 2009. Earnings volatility and earnings predictability. *Journal of Accounting and Economics* 47: 160–180.

Dimitrov, V., and S. Tice. 2006. Corporate Diversification and Credit Constraints: Real Effects across the Business Cycle. *Review of Financial Studies* 19 (4): 1465–1498.

Duchin, R. 2010. Cash holdings and corporate diversification. *Journal of Finance* 65: 955–992.

Duru, A., and D. M. Reeb. 2002. International Diversification and Analysts' Forecast Accuracy and Bias. *The Accounting Review* 77 (2): 415–433.

Easley, D., and M. O'Hara. 2004. Information and the cost of capital. *Journal of Finance* 59 (4): 1553–1583.

Fama, E. F., and K. R. French. 1992. The Cross-section of Expected Stock Returns. *Journal of Finance* 47 (2): 427–465.

Fama, E. F., and K. R. French. 1993. Common risk factors in the returns on stocks and bonds. *Journal of Financial Economics* 33: 3–56.

Fama, E. F., and K. R. French. 1997. Industry costs of equity. *Journal of Financial Economics* 43: 153–193.

Fama, E. F., and J. MacBeth. 1973. Risk, Return, and Equilibrium: Empirical Tests. *Journal of Political Economy* 3: 607–636.

Financial Accounting Standards Board (1978): Statement of Financial Accounting Concepts (SFAC) No. 1 – Objective of Financial Reporting by Business Enterprises, November 1978. Available at: http://www.fasb.org/st/index.shtml (last visit: June 22, 2016).

Financial Accounting Standards Board (1980): Statement of Financial Accounting Concepts (SFAC) No. 2 – Qualitative Characteristics of Accounting Information, May 1980. Available at: http://www.fasb.org/st/index.shtml (last visit: June 22, 2016).

Financial Accounting Standards Board (1997): Statement of Financial Accounting Standards (SFAS) No. 131 – Disclosure about Segments of an Enterprise and Related Information, June 1997. Available at: http://www.fasb.org/st/index.shtml (last visit: June 22, 2016).

Francis, J., R. LaFond, P. M. Olsson, and K. Schipper. 2004. Cost of equity and earnings attributes. *The Accounting Review* 79 (4): 967–1010.

Francis, J., R. LaFond, P. M. Olsson, and K. Schipper. 2005. The market pricing of accruals quality. *Journal of Accounting and Economics* 39: 295–327.

Francis, J., D. Nanda, and P. Olsson. 2008a. Voluntary Disclosure, Earnings Quality, and Cost of Capital. *Journal of Accounting Research* 46 (1): 53–99.

Francis, J., P. M. Olsson, and K. Schipper. 2008b. Earnings Quality. *Foundations and Trends in Accounting* 1 (4): 259–340.

Francis, J., and K. Schipper. 1999. Have Financial Statements Lost Their Relevance? *Journal of Accounting Research* 37 (2): 319–352.

Franco, F., O. Urcan, and F. P. Vasvari. 2016. Corporate diversification and the cost of debt: The role of segment disclosures. *The Accounting Review* 91 (4): 1139–1165.

Gertner, R. H., D. S. Scharfstein, and J. C. Stein. 1994. Internal versus external capital markets. *Quarterly Journal of Economics* 109: 1211–1230.

Givoly, D., C. K. Hayn, and J. D'Souza. 1999. Measurement Errors and Information Content of Segment Reporting. *Review of Accounting Studies* 4: 15–43.

Gomes, J., and D. Livdan. 2004. Optimal diversification: reconciling theory and evidence. *Journal of Finance* 59 (2): 507–535.

Graham, J. R., C. R. Harvey, and S. Rajgopal. 2005. The economic implications of corporate financial reporting. *Journal of Accounting and Economics* 40: 3–73.

Graham, J. R., M. L. Lemmon, and J. G. Wolf. 2002. Does corporate diversification destroy value? *Journal of Finance* 57: 695–720.

Guay, W. R., S. P. Kothari, and R. L. Watts. 1996. A market-based evaluation of discretionary accrual models. *Journal of Accounting Research* 34: 83–105.

Hann, R. N., F. Heflin, and K. R. Subramanyam. 2007. Fair-value pension accounting. *Journal of Accounting and Economics* 44 (3):328–358.

Hann, R. N., M. Ogneva, and O. Ozbas. 2013. Corporate diversification and the cost of capital. *Journal of Finance* 68 (5): 1961–1999.

Hausman, J. A. 1978. Specification tests in econometrics. *Econometrica* 46 (6): 1251-1271.

Healy, P. M., and J. M. Wahlen. 1999. A review of the earnings management literature and its implications for standard setting. *Accounting Horizons* 13 (4): 365–383.

Heckman, J. J. 1979. Sample selection bias as a specification error. *Econometrica* 47 (1): 153-161.

Homburg, C., J. Nasev, and D. Nussmann. 2016. Corporate Diversification and Earnings Quality. Working Paper. University of Cologne.

Hope, O.-K., and W. B. Thomas. 2008. Managerial Empire Building and Firm Disclosure. *Journal of Accounting Research* 46 (3): 591–626.

Hou, Y. 2015. The role of diversification in the pricing of accruals quality. *Review of Accounting Studies* 20: 1059–1092.

Hribar, P., and D. W. Collins. 2002. Errors in estimating accruals: implications for empirical research. *Journal of Accounting Research* 40 (1): 105–134.

Hughes, J. S., J. Liu, and J. Liu. 2007. Information Asymmetry, Diversification, and Cost of Capital. *The Accounting Review* 82 (3): 705–729.

Jensen, M. C. 1986. Agency costs of free cash flow, corporate finance, and takeovers. *American Economic Review* 76: 323–329.

Jensen, M. C., and W. H. Meckling. 1976. Theory of the Firm: Managerial Behavior, Agency Costs and Ownership Structure. *Journal of Financial Economics* 3: 305–360.

Jensen, M. C., and K. J. Murphy. 1990. Performance Pay and Top-Management Incentives. *Journal of Political Economy* 98 (2): 225–264.

Jones, J. J. 1991. Earnings management during import relief investigations. *Journal of Accounting Research* 29 (2): 193–228.

Kothari, S. P., A. J. Leone, and C. E. Wasley. 2005. Performance matched discretionary accrual measures. *Journal of Accounting and Economics* 39: 163–197.

Krishnaswami, S., and V. Subramaniam. 1999. Information asymmetry, valuation, and the corporate spin-off decision. *Journal of Financial Economics* 53: 73–112.

Kuppuswamy, V., and B. Villalonga. 2010. *Does Diversification Create Value in the Presence of External Financing Constraints? Evidence from the 2007–2009 Financial Crisis*. Working Paper. Harvard Business School.

Lambert, R. A. 2001. Contracting theory and accounting. *Journal of Accounting and Economics* 32: 3–87.

Lambert, R. A., C. Leuz, and R. Verrecchia. 2007. Accounting information, disclosure, and the cost of capital. *Journal of Accounting Research* 45 (2): 385–420.

Lammont, O., and C. Polk. 2002. Does diversification destroy value? Evidence from industry shocks. *Journal of Financial Economics* 63: 51–77.

Lang, L. H. P., and R. M. Stulz. 1994. Tobin's q, corporate diversification, and firm performance. *Journal of Political Economy* 102: 1248–1280.

Leland, H. E. 2007. Financial synergies and the optimal scope of the firm: implications for mergers, spinoffs, and structured finance. *Journal of Finance* 62 (2): 765–807.

Leuz, C., and R. E. Verrecchia. 2000. The Economic Consequences of Increased Disclosure. *Journal of Accounting Research* 38: 91–124.

Leuz, C., D. Nanda, and P. D. Wysocki. 2003. Earnings management and investor protection: an international comparison. *Journal of Financial Economics* 69: 505–527.

Lewellen, W. G. 1971. A pure financial rationale for the conglomerate merger. *Journal of Finance* 26: 527–537.

Lim, C. Y., T. Y. Thong, and D. K. Ding. 2008. Firm diversification and earnings management: evidence from seasoned equity offerings. *Review of Quantitative Finance and Accounting* 30 (1): 69–92.

Lins, K., and H. Servaes. 1999. International evidence on the value of corporate diversification. *Journal of Finance* 54 (6): 2215–2239.

Lipe, R. 1990. The relation between stock returns and accounting earnings given alternative information. *The Accounting Review* 65 (1): 49–71.

Maksimovic, V., and G. M. Phillips. 2002. Do Conglomerate Firms Allocate Resources Inefficiently Across Industries? Theory and Evidence. *Journal of Finance* 57 (2): 721–767.

Maksimovic, V., and G. M. Phillips. 2007. Conglomerate firms and internal capital markets. In *Handbook of Corporate Finance: Empirical Corporate Finance*, edited by B. E. Eckbo. Amsterdam, NL: Elsevier / North-Holland.

Mansi, S. A., and D. M. Reeb. 2002. Corporate Diversification: What Gets Discounted? *Journal of Finance* 57 (5): 2167–2183.

Markowitz, H. 1952. Portfolio Selection. *Journal of Finance* 7 (1): 77–91.

Martin, J. D., and A. Sayrak. 2003. Corporate diversification and shareholder value: A survey of recent literature. *Journal of Corporate Finance* 9: 37–57.

McInnis, J. 2010. Earnings Smoothness, Average Returns, and Implied Cost of Equity Capital. *The Accounting Review* 85: 315–341.

McNichols, M. F. 2002. Discussion of the quality of accruals and earnings: The role of accrual estimation errors. *The Accounting Review* 77: 61–69.

Minton, B.A., and C. Schrand. 1999. The Impact of Cash Flow Volatility on Discretionary Investment and the Cost of Debt and Equity Financing. *Journal of Financial Economics* 54 (3): 423–460.

Modigliani, F., and M. H. Miller. 1958. The cost of capital, corporation finance and the theory of investment. *The American Economic Review* 48 (3): 261-297.

Montgomery, C. A. 1994. Corporate Diversification. *Journal of Economic Perspectives* 8 (3): 163–178.

Myers, J. N., L. A. Myers, and D. J. Skinner. 2007. Earnings momentum and earnings management. *Journal of Accounting, Auditing, and Finance* 22: 249–284.

Palepu, K. G., and P. M. Healy. 2013. *Business Analysis and Valuation.* 5th edition. Mason, OH: South-Western Cengage Learning.

Penman, S. H. 2013. *Financial Statement Analysis and Security Valuation.* 5th edition. New York, NY: McGraw-Hill.

Penman, S. H., and X. Zhang. 2002. Accounting conservatism, the quality of earnings, and stock returns. *The Accounting Review* 77 (2): 237–264.

Petersen, M. A. 2009. Estimating standard errors in finance panel data sets: Comparing approaches. *Review of Financial Studies* 22: 435–480.

Pitts, R. A., and H. D. Hopkins. 1982. Firm Diversity: Conceptualization and Measurement. *Academy of Management Review* 7 (4): 620–629.

Rajan, R., H. Servaes, and L. Zingales. 2000. The cost of diversity: The diversification discount and inefficient investment. *Journal of Finance* 55 (1): 35–80.

Rajgopal, S., and M. Venkatachalam. 2011. Financial Reporting Quality and Idiosyncratic Return Volatility. *Journal of Accounting and Economics* 51 (1-2): 1–20.

Ramanujam, V., and P. Varadarajan. 1989. Research on Corporate Diversification: A Synthesis. *Strategic Management Journal* 10: 523–551.

Rodríguez-Pérez, G., and S. van Hemmen. 2010. Debt, diversification and earnings management. *Journal of Accounting and Public Policy* 29: 138–159.

Rountree, B., J. P. Weston, and G. Allayannis. 2008. Do investors value smooth performance? *Journal of Financial Economics* 90: 237–251.

Scharfstein, D. S., and J. C. Stein. 2000. The dark side of internal capital markets: Divisional rent-seeking and inefficient investment. *Journal of Finance* 55 (6): 2537–2564.

Schipper, K., and L. Vincent. 2003. Earnings Quality. *Accounting Horizons* (Supplement): 97–110.

Schoar, A. 2002. Effects of Corporate Diversification on Productivity. *Journal of Finance* 57 (6): 2379–2403.

Servaes, H. 1996. The value of diversification during the conglomerate merger wave. *Journal of Finance* 51 (4): 1201–1225.

Shin, H. H., and R. M. Stulz. 1996. An Analysis of Divisional Investment Policies. Working Paper 5639. National Bureau of Economic Research.

Shin, H. H., and R. M. Stulz. 2000. Shareholder Wealth and Firm Risk. Working Paper. Ohio State University.

Shleifer, A., and R. W. Vishny. 1989. Management Entrenchment. *Journal of Financial Economics* 25: 123–139.

Sloan, R. G. 1996. Do Stock Prices Fully Reflect Information in Accruals and Cash Flows About Future Earnings? *The Accounting Review* 71 (3): 289 – 315.

Stein, J. C. 1997. Internal capital markets and the competition for corporate resources. *Journal of Finance* 52 (1): 111–133.

Stein, J. C. 2003. Agency, information and corporate investment. In *Handbook of the Economics and Finance*, edited by G. M. Constantinides, M. Harris, and R. M. Stulz. Amsterdam, NL: Elsevier NH.

Stulz, R. M. 1990. Managerial discretion and optimal financing policies. *Journal of Financial Economics* 26: 3–27.

Subramanyam, K. R. 1996. The pricing of discretionary accruals. *Journal of Accounting and Economics* 22: 249–281.

Teece, D. J. 2010. Business models, business strategy and innovation. *Long Range Planning* 43: 172–194.

Thomas, S. 2002. Firm diversification and asymmetric information: evidence from analysts' forecasts and earnings announcements. *Journal of Financial Economics* 64: 373–396.

Tong, Z. 2012. Coinsurance effect and bank lines of credit. *Journal of Banking and Finance* 36: 1592–1603.

Villalonga, B. 2003. *Round Table Discussion: The Diversification Discount*. April 24, 2003, Case and Teaching Paper Series. Harvard Business School.

Villalonga, B. 2004. Diversification discount or premium? New evidence from the business information tracking series. *Journal of Finance* 59 (2): 479–506.

Watts, R. L. 2003. Conservatism in Accounting Part II: Evidence and Research Opportunities. *Accounting Horizons* 17 (4): 287 – 301.

Wei, S. X., and C. Zhang. 2006. Why Did Individual Stocks Become More Volatile? *The Journal of Business* 79 (1): 259–292.

Weiss, D. 2010. Cost Behavior and Analysts' Earnings Forecasts. *The Accounting Review* 85 (4): 1441–1471.

Whited, T. M. 2001. Is It Inefficient Investment that Causes the Diversification Discount? *Journal of Finance* 56 (5): 1667–1691.

Williamson, O. 1975. *Markets and Hierarchies: Analysis and Antitrust Implications*. New York, NY: The Free Press.

Yan, A., Z. Yang, and J. Jiao. 2010. Conglomerate investment under various capital market conditions. *Journal of Banking and Finance* 34: 103–115.

MIX
Papier aus verantwortungsvollen Quellen
Paper from responsible sources
FSC® C105338

If you have any concerns about our products,
you can contact us on
ProductSafety@springernature.com

In case Publisher is established outside the EU,
the EU authorized representative is:
Springer Nature Customer Service Center GmbH
Europaplatz 3, 69115 Heidelberg, Germany

Printed by Libri Plureos GmbH
in Hamburg, Germany